Temptations of Power

*Also by Robert J. Jackson*

CANADIAN GOVERNMENT IN TRANSITION (*co-author*)

COMPARATIVE GOVERNMENT: An Introduction to Political Science (*co-author*)

COMPARATIVE INTRODUCTION TO POLITICAL SCIENCE (*co-author*)

CONTEMPORARY GOVERNMENT AND POLITICS: Democracy and Authoritarianism (*co-author*)

CONTINUITY OF DISCORD: Crises and Responses in the Atlantic Community (*author and editor*)

EUROPE IN TRANSITION: The Management of Security after the Cold War (*author and co-editor*)

INTRODUCTION TO POLITICAL SCIENCE: Comparative and World Politics (*co-author*)

ISSUES IN COMPARATIVE POLITICS (*co-author*)

NATO LOOKS EAST (*author and co-editor*)

NORTH AMERICAN POLITICS (*co-author*)

POLITICS IN CANADA: Culture, Institutions, Behaviour and Public Policy (*co-author*)

STAND UP FOR CANADA (*co-author*)

THE CANADIAN LEGISLATIVE SYSTEM (*co-author*)

THE POLITICISATION OF BUSINESS IN WESTERN EUROPE (*author and co-editor*)

*Also by Philip Towle*

ARMS CONTROL AND EAST–WEST RELATIONS

DEMOCRACY AND PEACEMAKING: Negotiations and Debates

ENFORCED DISARMAMENT FROM THE NAPOLEONIC CAMPAIGNS TO THE GULF WAR

ESTIMATING FOREIGN MILITARY POWER (*editor*)

FROM ALLY TO ENEMY: Anglo–Japanese Military Relations 1905–45

JAPANESE PRISONERS OF WAR (*co-editor*)

PILOTS AND REBELS: The Use of Aircraft in Unconventional Warfare 1918–1988

# Temptations of Power

## The United States in Global Politics after 9/11

Robert J. Jackson
*Fletcher Jones Professor of Government and Director of International Relations*
*University of Redlands, California*

and

Philip Towle
*Reader in International Relations, Centre of International Studies*
*Cambridge University*

First published 2006 by
PALGRAVE MACMILLAN
Houndmills, Basingstoke, Hampshire RG21 6XS and
175 Fifth Avenue, New York, N.Y. 10010
Companies and representatives throughout the world

PALGRAVE MACMILLAN is the global academic imprint of the Palgrave Macmillan division of St. Martin's Press, LLC and of Palgrave Macmillan Ltd. Macmillan® is a registered trademark in the United States, United Kingdom and other countries. Palgrave is a registered trademark in the European Union and other countries.

ISBN-13: 978-1-4039-4676-8    hardback
ISBN-10: 1-4039-4676-0    hardback
ISBN-13: 978-1-4039-4677-5    paperback
ISBN-10: 1-4039-4677-9    paperback

This book is printed on paper suitable for recycling and made from fully managed and sustained forest sources.

A catalogue record for this book is available from the British Library.

Library of Congress Cataloging-in-Publication Data
Jackson, Robert J., 1936–
    Temptations of power: the United States in global politics after 9/11/
Robert J. Jackson and Philip Towle.
        p. cm.
    Includes bibliographical references and index.
    ISBN 1-4039-4676-0 — ISBN 1-4039-4677-9 (pbk.)
        1. United States—Foreign relations—2001–2. United States—Military policy. 3. Bush, George W. (George Walker), 1946–Political and social views. 4. Balance of power. 5. World politics—1989–6. International relations. 7. September 11 Terrorist Attacks, 2001—Influence. 8. War on Terrorism, 2001–9. Terrorism—Government policy—United States. 10. National Security—United States. I. Towle, Philip, 1945– II. Title.
E902.J32 2006
327.73009′0511—dc22                                              2006045717

10   9   8   7   6   5   4   3   2   1
15   14   13   12   11   10   09   08   07   06

Printed and bound in Great Britain by
Antony Rowe Ltd, Chippenham and Eastbourne

# Contents

*Acknowledgements*                                                          viii

*Introduction: Temptations of Power*                                          ix

1   **Grappling with the New World:**
    **Concepts and Realities**                                               1
    September 11 2001 and its aftermath                                      2
    Concepts and realities                                                  4
    Concepts in international relations                                      6
    Realities in international relations                                     9
    The security debate                                                    10
    Limited sovereignty                                                    12
    International intervention                                              13
    The old and new security dilemmas                                      14

2   **Ideologies, Ideas and Political Slogans in the**
    **Formation of George W. Bush's Foreign Policy**                       16
    A clash of civilizations                                               18
    America as empire                                                      22
    The neoconservatives                                                   28
    From commentators and analysts to George W. Bush                       36

3   **The United States, Europe and the World**                            44
    From victim to pariah                                                  44
    The temptation of Iraq                                                 45
    The anti-Iraq coalition, 2003                                          49
    Why Europeans often disagreed with the United States                   51
    The growth of US military power                                        53
    The end of the balance of power?                                       55
    The United States' unipolar moment                                     57

4   **New Challenges to US Hegemony: China and the**
    **Muslim World**                                                       64
    The challenge from China                                               65
    The Muslim challenge                                                   71

| | | |
|---|---|---|
| **5** | **Military Power and Democratic Transition** | **84** |
| | The uses and abuses of military power | 85 |
| | Military power and democracy | 89 |
| | Coalition-building or unilateral action? | 93 |
| | The importance of restraint | 96 |
| | | |
| **6** | **The Temptation of Preventive War** | **102** |
| | Modern precedents for pre-emptive and preventive wars | 105 |
| | Israel's preventive war precedents in the Middle East | 106 |
| | The United States creeps toward pre-emptive and preventive strategies | 108 |
| | The US decision to launch preventive war | 110 |
| | Fire discipline | 113 |
| | Precision attacks | 115 |
| | Preventive war and the 'axis of evil' | 117 |
| | Advantages and disadvantages of preventive war | 119 |
| | | |
| **7** | **Misunderstanding Terrorism: The Sword** | **123** |
| | The new face of conflict | 123 |
| | Terrorism as a concept | 126 |
| | New and old terrorism | 127 |
| | Al-Qaeda, affiliates, regional jihadists and copycats | 130 |
| | Anti-terrorist strategies | 134 |
| | Bush's moment: war without purpose | 136 |
| | | |
| **8** | **Homeland (In)Security: The Shield** | **139** |
| | Civil liberties | 143 |
| | The Patriot Act | 144 |
| | Enemy combatants | 147 |
| | Prison abuses | 151 |
| | Justice or security? | 152 |
| | The Department of Homeland Security | 154 |
| | Border controls | 155 |
| | The Intelligence agencies | 157 |
| | Nuclear terrorism | 159 |
| | Financial costs | 163 |
| | Homeland insecurities | 164 |
| | Security or insecurity? | 165 |

9   **Creating Quagmires: Winning the Wars,**
     **Losing the Peace**                                    **168**
     Context and war in Afghanistan                         169
     Context and war in Iraq                                171
     Justifications and denunciations of the wars           173
     Consequences of the wars                               176
     Afghanistan since the war                              177
     Iraq since the war                                     178
     Constitutional developments in Iraq                    181
     Staying power and counter-insurgency                   184
     Ending insurgencies                                    185
     Quagmires                                              188

10  **The Burden of Power**                                 **196**

*Bibliography*                                              204

*Index*                                                    213

# Acknowledgements

The authors wish to thank their respective institutions, the University of Cambridge and the University of Redlands, without whose support this collaborative effort would have been impossible. They would also like to thank the National Europe Centre of the Australian National University for providing them with Visiting Fellowships while they were working on this book. Canberra provided a calm but intellectually stimulating environment for surveying the international scene. Robert J. Jackson would also like to thank Clare Hall in Cambridge for making him a Life Member and the Cambridge Centre of International Studies for his Visiting Fellowships.

Most of all, we thank Veronica and Doreen for their patience and assistance through all the years.

The cooperative and shared rewriting of every chapter is always difficult when the authors are thousands of miles apart. Although the authors are jointly responsible for the entire book, the Introduction, Chapters 1, 2, 7, 8 and 9 were written for the most part by Robert J. Jackson, and Chapters 3, 4, 5, 6 and 10 chiefly by Philip Towle. Scott Schneider and Jessica Kump provided excellent research assistance. The authors would like to thank Wendy Cooke and Lynnae Pattison-Merget for their administrative and secretarial skills in helping to bring this book to fruition, and Keith Povey (with Mark Hendy) of Palgrave Macmillan for superb editorial assistance.

ROBERT J. JACKSON
PHILIP TOWLE

# Introduction:
# Temptations of Power

On September 11 2001 President George W. Bush came face to face with the *new* security dilemma posed by ubiquitous insecurity.

No longer could a president rely on thousands of miles of unguarded frontiers with peaceful neighbours and on the Pacific and Atlantic Oceans to separate Americans from possible enemies. Nor could he count on well-managed relations with a nuclear-equipped communist bloc to allow the United States to deflect and defuse crises. The ground rules for security had changed abruptly. Instead of a powerful communist state, the United States now had to confront a hidden enemy capable of launching surprise terrorist attacks on anyone or any target in the homeland. The United States could not respond in routine or standardized ways. It could not bring its massive military power to bear as it had done to deter the communist threat after the Second World War or to retaliate after the attack on Pearl Harbor in 1941. It was the first manifestation of the *new* security dilemma that will haunt all future presidents.

It is perhaps not surprising that George W. Bush did not recognize the implications of ubiquitous insecurity – violent threats coming from a number of places at the same time – and, therefore, responded inappropriately to the first major attack in this new era. An assault of such intensity and on such symbolic targets in the homeland was unanticipated. It was provoked by hatred of the United States and its policies in foreign lands and facilitated by the new global order of mass transportation systems, electronic communications and miniaturized explosive devices. The president lashed back at America's brazen enemies with the full support of US citizens. It was not just Bush's personality or arrogance, or his reliance on the ideas of neoconservatives that caused such an inappropriate reaction. It was the interaction between these factors combined with the extent of US military power and the novelty and threat to its national security. The nature of the threat to the homeland had evolved and become more unpredictable.

If the aftermath of 9/11 has taught the US anything, it is how *not* to respond to ubiquitous insecurity. This book shows how President Bush was tempted by the imbalance in power that followed the collapse of the Soviet Union. The United States was lured into its aggression by many circumstances – by the ease with which its forces had driven the Iraqis from Kuwait in 1991, then forced the Serbs to compromise over Bosnia–Herzegovina in 1994 and Kosovo in 1999; by the practice which has grown up in recent years of dragging foreign leaders, such as Noriega of Panama and Milosevic of Serbia, to stand trial before American or international courts for their corruption, incompetence and brutality; by the frequency of multinational and international intervention in the internal affairs of 'failed' states; and by the ability of the world's remaining superpower to dismiss or ignore international conventions produced after months or years of negotiation and compromise.

Many of these American actions may have been amply justified because of the violence and mass killings which occurred when 'failed states' (no effective government or rule of law) were unable to maintain order in their territories, or because of the inadequacy of the diplomatic process of compromise. But they all contributed to a belief, in Washington and elsewhere, that a superpower could impose its solutions at will and ignore the restraints and inhibitions that previously modified its conduct. Yet, today more than ever, subtle, multifaceted solutions are required on such occasions, not least because a far greater proportion of the population in every country is politically active and, if necessary, willing to sacrifice lives in the struggle to stop intervention by a foreign power. The Bush administration holds up democracy as the panacea for political problems, but democracy means involvement of the people, and foreigners may have ideas very different from those held by politicians in Washington.

Politics abhors imbalances of power, just as the natural world shuns vacuums, and it was inevitable that the United States would eventually encounter ever-increasing resistance to its superpower status and willingness to use force. This might have come from other major states, but in fact it came on 9/11 from Islamist terrorists and, after March 2003, from the Iraqi resistance against the US-led invasion. The administration played into the hands of its enemies by becoming involved in a war that minimized its advantages and maximized its deficiencies. It needs to recognize that the temptation to use military power has to be moderated by an understanding that it will eventually meet growing opposition. The whole basket of other US attributes – social, cultural, financial and diplomatic – should be used first and with much greater effort and subtlety than it was in the responses to 9/11. The United States does not always need to go to war to get its way. American armed forces lost the Vietnam War but the Vietnamese were later forced to beg to enter the world market, to persuade US veterans to return as tourists and US companies to invest there. Eighty years ago, after a tour round Asia, a US academic wrote of what he called 'the revolt of Asia' which led him to conclude that 'we are passing from the era of Empire by conquest into the era of Empire by attraction, service and business'.[1] His diagnosis has become increasingly valid as globalization has proceeded.

After 9/11 the administration naturally tried to insulate the homeland from its enemies. While the United States attacked other lands, it also began to curtail liberties at home in an effort to make the country secure from terrorists. In its insecurity, it was ready to give up what America prized most – the rights of free citizens, open borders and the civil treatment of its own people and foreigners. Repressive laws were enacted, civil liberties curtailed and prisons constructed with the promise that the 'war on terror' could be won once and for all – the laws could be repealed at a later date when the threats subsided.

But ubiquitous insecurity is permanent or at least very long-term. The threats which underly it come from the privatization of war, proliferation of more deadly weapons including weapons of mass destruction (WMD), failing and failed states, and the interaction between the West and the Islamic states. They need to be approached in the light of the new circumstance that states are no longer the only purveyors of international violence and that new, stateless actors can do great harm because they are hard to identify and have global reach. These are the key factors in the *new* security dilemma, and the stability of the world will depend upon how American governments confront this dilemma at the same time as they deal with more traditional threats from the rise of powerful states such as China, India and Brazil.

Our approach is neither anti-American nor based on a slavish adherence to a particular theoretical tradition. No single approach can do justice to the complex reality that comprises both a *new* and an *old* security dilemma. Like the realists, we believe states remain the main international actors and that the traditional military and security issues are still relevant. Yet, we also gain insights from the liberals' perspective about the *new* security dilemma with its roots among domestic political actors and feelings of injustice. The realist view leads to an understanding of the importance of power but also to an appreciation of the importance of prudence in its use, if it is not to meet increasingly violent resistance. This is an attribute of power that the Bush administration has often ignored. Moreover, as some liberals have pointed out, it has not sustained the institutions and rules which are the glue that binds the heterogeneous inter-state order.

Those who analyse US power divide not only between realists and liberals but also between the, not necessarily synonymous, pessimists and optimists. After the cold war, the optimists believed that America would become predominant or hegemonic, and the pessimists, including many realists, maintained that new conflicts or balances would emerge to diminish US power. The optimists asserted that Washington's predominance was desirable, that Washington's was a benevolent empire and that, accordingly, history, in terms of struggles between ideologies and religions, had ended. The pessimists argued, on the contrary, that its predominance was not assured and possibly not desirable. Some maintained that it would exhaust its finances and go into decline, that possibly a grouping made up of China, India, Russia and Europe would emerge to balance the United States or that clashes would occur between different 'civilizations' of which the United States and the European democracies were but one.

9/11 greatly sharpened the debate. While, intellectually, the optimists were now on the defensive, in practice they became the predominant influence behind the Bush administration. Bush accepted their ultra-optimistic view that, if history had not ended, it could be made to end as dictatorships were crushed in the Middle East and elsewhere, nuclear proliferation was ended by preventive wars and terrorists wiped from the face of the earth. The United States was a benevolent empire and those who opposed it were inherently evil. Some of the pessimists by contrast saw the Islamist attacks on the Twin Towers as proof of the growing conflict between the West and the Muslim world. They believed the United States would exhaust itself in futile guerrilla wars in Afghanistan, Iraq and elsewhere. Moreover, the pessimists believed that resistance would increase the more the United States asserted itself in these ways and wasted its finances.

The authors of this book accept many of the optimists' liberal ideals. We admit that, in theory, democracy is the best form of government developed so far, but argue that it is not suitable for all states and cannot normally be imposed from outside. We also agree with many realists and pessimists that the more the United States tries to impose democracy on other states and cultures, the more resistance it will eventually evoke. 'Democratization', in the wide sense of the politicization of the masses, has already occurred world-wide and, consequently imperialism, whether desirable or undesirable, is obsolete because today it always evokes ferocious terrorist and guerrilla resistance. Thus the United States would have been better advised to pay attention to the pessimists after 9/11, resist the temptation to use its immense military power and rely, as the liberal pessimists would argue, on 'soft' power or influence to move the world gradually towards democracy.

Governments are always tempted to think only in the short or, at best, the medium term. This is particularly the case when a state is enjoying the benefits of massive power, flexing its muscles and exerting its influence on the world stage. The United States is the only superpower, but its administrations need to contemplate the ways in which international institutions can be developed and strengthened. The current laws and institutions are very largely Western artifacts, shaped by Western ideals and Western understanding of the best ways to avoid conflict and enhance the freedom of small and weak states. By upholding them we have spread these ideas around the world. If we abandon or weaken our principles we are open to the reasonable charge of hypocrisy. If we imprison people without trial, if we extradite suspects to countries where torture is practised or if we launch preventive wars, we will be guilty of more than hypocrisy. We will be guilty of making the world a worse place to live in than the one we inherited. The next generation of superpowers will not be steeped in European culture and may be only too happy to ignore the laws, norms and customs the West has built up. Now, while the West is ascendant, is the moment to resist the temptations of power, build international institutions and prepare, as best we can, for the future.

In the following chapters we attempt to elucidate the errors in the way the United States has acted since the events of 9/11. Chapter 1, 'Grappling with the New World: Concepts and Realities', discusses the new threats to the international state system and how a new conceptual framework is needed to understand them. The idea of a *new* security dilemma to supplement the traditional concept of the 'security dilemma' as a framework for understanding international relations is considered. Chapter 2, 'Ideologies, Ideas and Slogans in the formation of George W. Bush's Foreign Policy', describes the intellectual environment around the Bush administration that influenced the decision to attack Iraq. It defines and outlines the ideas about the 'clash of civilizations' and 'empire' and shows how they were expounded by neoconservatives, and eventually helped to underpin the Bush foreign policy. In other words, we do not try to examine all the different ways of analysing Bush's foreign policy, only those which we believe influenced its major foreign policy decisions.

The next four chapters dissect the ideas and values of the Bush period. Chapter 3, 'The United States, Europe and the World', describes the wars in Afghanistan and Iraq and the way in which the post-9/11 consensus evaporated when the United States declared that it was faced with a trio of states that formed an 'axis of evil'. Chapter 4, 'New Challenges to US Hegemony: China and the Muslim World', outlines the evolution of US policy towards China and the similar effort it will need to make to conciliate the Muslim world. Chapter 5, 'Military Power and Democratic Transition', shows how the United States has exaggerated the importance of military power and also its ability to spread democracy. Chapter 6, 'The Temptation of

Preventive War', argues that the new US policy of preventive war is unnecessary to deal with current threats and dangerously undermines the rule of law and the international system.

The next three chapters show how the Bush strategy cannot be successful and will have to be changed radically or 'the war on terrorism' will be lost. Chapter 7, 'Misunderstanding Terrorism: The Sword', examines the motives and explanations for terrorists and terrorism, and shows how the American and British governments chose the wrong interpretation of terrorism and therefore made grave mistakes in their foreign policies. Chapter 8, 'Homeland (In)Security: The Shield', discusses the inadequate efforts by the US government to insulate the country from further terrorist attacks. It analyses the Patriot Act and other new devices in terms of human rights and economics and again finds the Bush strategy to be unsatisfactory. It also reveals the ineffective policies of the Bush administration for dealing with the threat of nuclear terrorism. Chapter 9, 'Creating Quagmires: Winning Wars and Losing the Peace', shows the difficulties of making beneficial regime changes in such countries as Iraq and Afghanistan and the bleak choices with which the US administration is now faced. US armies are overstretched in the former Yugoslavia, Afghanistan and Iraq, and the costs are exacerbating US budget and balance of payments deficits.

Chapter 10, 'The Burden of Power', concludes the book by summarizing the many ways the Bush administration succumbed to the temptations of power in the face of ubiquitous threats to its security. It suggests how the administration might instead have prepared for the future by developing international institutions while it still had the power to do so. Hubris is repaid by nemesis.

## Note

1   Upton Close, *The Revolt of Asia: The End of the White Man's World Dominance* (New York: Putnam's, 1927), pp. 320 and 325.

# 1
## Grappling with the New World: Concepts and Realities

This book demonstrates the inadequacy of the American response to the terrorist attacks on New York and Washington on September 11 2001. It contests the American argument that terrorism can be stopped by making preventive attacks on countries that harbour enemies or by occupying the lands of other people and shows how the Bush doctrine, with its ascendant principle of preventive war, is inherently faulty. The coercive action in Iraq, combined with the combative rhetoric towards the other 'axis of evil' countries, has done more harm than good. The consequences in terms of dead and wounded, economic burdens and reduced freedoms have been alarming, and there is no end in sight.

The symbol of US suffering at the hands of terrorists – the destruction of the Twin Towers and the massive damage to the Pentagon – has been overlaid with images of raw US power: bombs and missiles raining down on Afghanistan and Iraq. The humane and democratic mission of George Washington and Abraham Lincoln has been all but obliterated under the harsh military reality of precision-guided missiles and collateral damage.

After the terrible events of September 11, President George W. Bush launched the US campaign against terrorism by propagating lofty ideals backed up by military power. With pride and purpose laced liberally with moralizing self-righteousness, the United States increasingly acted like the hegemon it is. President Bush took a series of unilateral actions based on a doctrine of exceptionalism – remaking the world in America's own self-image. But this American and British foreign policy has faced increasing resistance and shown that even US power is finite.

Supporters of the Anglo-American cause have mocked Europeans as wimps and appeasers for not joining in the war on Iraq. But, because of their colonial histories, European governments and armed forces have more experience of many parts of the world than Americans do. Their forces are trained for peacekeeping and they have lived with terrorism for decades. They know that terrorists have to be countered by good intelligence and policing, and undermined by conciliating their supporters. They understand that democracies cannot destroy terrorists and corrosive ideas by raw power alone.

## September 11 2001 and its aftermath

Trying to eliminate Saddam ... would have incurred incalculable human and political costs ... We would have been forced, to occupy Baghdad and, in effect, rule Iraq ... there was no viable 'exit strategy' we could see, violating another of our principles. Furthermore, we had been self-consciously trying to set a pattern for handling aggression in the post-Cold-War world. Going in and occupying Iraq, thus unilaterally exceeding the United Nations' mandate, would have destroyed the precedent of international response to aggression that we hoped to establish. Had we gone the invasion route, the United States could conceivably still be an occupying power in a bitterly hostile land. (George H. W. Bush 1998)

Going into this period, I was praying for strength to do the Lord's will ... I'm surely not going to justify the war [in Iraq] based upon God. Understand that. Nevertheless, in my case, I pray to be as good a messenger of his will as possible. (George W. Bush 2003)

These contrasting quotations from the first President George Bush in 1998 and the second President George Bush in 2003 succinctly delineate the current policy differences over international relations that divide not only policymakers but also intellectuals, journalists and academics. How thoughtful people understand the present world and the dangers inherent in it is determined, to a large extent, by how they visualize the world – by their education and upbringing, their experiences and their sources of information. Obviously, not everything a father knows is learned by his child!

Equally, not everything a father thinks is without fault. But, after his experience in the US Navy during the Second World War and as ambassador at the United Nations and in China, director of the CIA and vice president, Bush the father had grasped the realities of international relations as well as the strengths and weaknesses of US power. His less-experienced son did not. But his son was impelled by the horrific violence of September 11 and the strength of conviction, based on his religion, to act on his impulses and intuitions. He would attack Baghdad even though his father had faltered.

Father Bush had stressed the need for multilateral support in international relations. He understood the delicate balance of forces that characterized the cold war period and the need for realistic assumptions about what America could do alone and what actions required international help if hostility to US policy was not to increase. But George Senior never had to confront the more confusing, more anarchic period after the fall of the Berlin Wall and the dismantling of communism in Europe. Son Bush had never really grasped the complexities of world power. But he felt he knew exactly how to overcome the problem of ubiquitous insecurity and confront the evils of terrorism on American soil – with an avenging sword abroad and a defensive shield at home, just like the Christian crusaders of earlier periods.

Perhaps in their combined approaches we can see what has happened to tear apart the institutions, practices and norms that provided world order and progress during much of the early post-Cold-War period. We can also see how the language, debates and even issues that characterize foreign policymaking have evolved beyond their characterizations by political leaders: neither cold war analogies nor religious crusades have much utility today.

To a large extent, the earlier arguments of Bush senior represent the same analysis of contemporary international politics as that of many Europeans. International law and collective decisionmaking in the United Nations are preferable to independent, ad-hoc decisionmaking by any one country, even if it is the United States of America. Bush junior represents the school of thought which argues that the exceptional virtue and righteousness of American culture and understanding of the world are self-evident. For him, concern for international law and arguments in favour of a balance of power are far outweighed by the nature of transnational ethnic and religious differences and violence. America must fend for itself.

But the difficulty for those who support present US policy is that there is growing anti-Americanism in many parts of the world, which may be increased by actively promoting US values.[1] Bush and supporters of an aggressive US foreign policy miss the point that many Muslims are upset with both American policies *and* culture. They despise Hollywood as much as they dislike US policies in supporting Israel, in attacking Iraq, in controlling oil in the Persian Gulf and in supporting pro-western governments in the Middle East. Bush senior understood this better than his son.

## Concepts and realities

America's global image is the worst it has been since the Vietnam War. It sacrificed its reputation, as well as many friendships, in a powerful show of retribution in Iraq that did nothing to decrease the threat of violence and terrorism to the homeland. To understand how this came about, with its disastrous consequences for American foreign policy, we need to go back over the conceptual arguments of the past decade and trace the combined wisdom and folly of leading statesmen over that time.

The standard concepts of international relations have become inadequate in the new world of global terrorism and US hegemonic power. To a large extent, the literature and language of international relations continue to be based on cold war analogies. While the world became more complex and diverse from the early 1990s onwards, specialists and diplomatic practitioners by and large still accepted the concepts and prejudices that had carried them through the post-Second-World-War period and the cold war, basically analysing the new world in terms of the *old* security dilemma. When the 9/11 disaster struck the United States, political leaders continued to use the language of retaliation which had strengthened deterrence during the cold war: 'An eye for an eye.' Revealingly, both Bush and his challenger said in the 2004 presidential election campaign that if elected they would 'hunt down' and 'kill' their adversaries, yet what is needed to defeat terrorists is the ability to infiltrate or eavesdrop on their organizations and to isolate them politically from their supporters.

In order to understand and explain the new world order there is a necessity to link it with novel concepts and theories and to revive some ideas which have fallen into abeyance. Our discussion of international relations therefore relies on a revised vocabulary that is more appropriate for contemporary circumstances. In particular, we develop the idea of a 'new' security dilemma to supplement and enhance the old framework for understanding international relations.

Four interwoven trends or strands in international relations characterize the new world order:

1. The rise of the US as a hegemon or empire and the growing opposition to this in the rest of the world, symbolized by the rise of powerful states such as China and the alienation of large parts of the Muslim community.
2. The rise of militant Islamist groups with virulent anti-Western, particularly anti-US, prejudices and actions. Resulting from and concomitant with this has been an increase in organizations intent on

using terrorism as a tool of international politics, thus producing ubiquitous insecurity.

3. A growth in the acceptance of the idea that foreign intervention in the affairs of weak countries is justifiable. Sovereignty has come to be seen as expendable following Western interventions in East Timor, Cambodia, Bosnia, Kosovo, Afghanistan, Iraq and large swathes of Africa.

4. The US claim that preventive war is legitimate to defend its territory and that terrorism can be defeated once and for all.

This new world order is messy, and particularly dangerous when the trends interact with each other. In the final analysis they all stem from the collapse of the Soviet Union, the resulting absence of a balance of power and the temptations for the United States to which this gives rise. The massive power and influence of the West today thus provokes terrorism, just as earlier colonialism gave rise to insurgency and peoples' wars. The simultaneous development of a new unipolar reality and the gradual acceptance of limited sovereignty are unprecedented and dangerous.

During the cold war the bipolar world was interpreted in terms of realism or liberalism, with Marxism, feminism, deconstruction and other assorted approaches thrown in to describe and explain specific features of international politics. However, such broad approaches cannot explain the complexity of the new post-cold war realities. The events of 9/11 shattered many of these arguments even further by revealing the world-wide hegemony of the USA and the Islamist threat to that dominance.

By the turn of the millennium the West had already encountered two novel security challenges: the development of nuclear weapons after the US Manhattan project and the evolution of peoples' wars throughout the Third World, particularly in Asia. In the first case, considerable numbers of America's cleverest diplomats and academics devoted most of their professional careers to reflecting on how to integrate nuclear weapons into foreign and security policy. Despite the constant anxieties of the cold war years, the strategy of nuclear deterrence, which they defined, enabled the West both to avoid another, far more disastrous, world war and to emerge victorious from the confrontation with the Soviet Union.

It was quite otherwise with peoples' wars, which proved a forerunner to today's terrorism. From the moment in 1946 when the French plunged into war with the Vietminh to the US flight from Saigon in 1975, Western armies generally emerged from wars in Asia frustrated and humiliated. In large part this was because, while Western analysts meditated long and hard about how the Soviets might react to Western nuclear threats, Western armed forces only intermittently grasped the ways in which guerrillas and terrorists think, and thus shunned the predominantly political methods which alone could defeat them.

From the time when the French General Leclerc sent his first aircraft and tanks out from Saigon to 'mop up' Vietminh guerrilla resistance to March 2003, when President Bush sent his advanced bombers and tanks to 'shock and awe' the Iraqis into submission, the mistake was the same—the exaggeration of the importance of military technology and the underestimation of the power of nationalism and local loyalties. Moreover, unless the West finally learns from its past mistakes, the outcome of the latest Western initiative will be much more serious. From 1954, when the French fled from Indochina, to 1973 when the Americans followed in their wake, the possibility of retreat from the sea of popular support in which the guerrillas were swimming was always open. But in the twenty-first century that sea laps all around the global village and particularly among the Muslim diasporas in the West. Just as there can be no victory through technology and military might, so there can be no retreat from the ubiquitous challenge posed by the new terrorist threat.

## Concepts in international relations

There are many reasons for challenging the intellectual community to confront the dilemmas that have arisen, especially since September 11 2001, over traditional concepts and organizing devices for understanding human affairs. At the end of the Second World War a combination of realism and liberalism became the conventional wisdom about the nature of international relations; and, while the United Nations incorporated idealistic beliefs about the sanctity of state sovereignty and collective security, realism was reflected in the veto power of the Big Five states which are permanent members of the Security Council. Throughout the cold war, realist concepts infused commentaries on world events. But the twelve-year hiatus from the fall of the Berlin Wall to the destruction of the World Trade Center also saw a growth of humanitarian interventions which marked a decline in the significance of state sovereignty. The US-led war on the Taliban in Afghanistan and against Saddam Hussein in Iraq reinforced questions about the fundamental aspects of international relations.

Definitions of sovereignty abound in the discipline of international relations, but they usually include at least the notion that it refers to the legal, administrative and political prescriptions that give states supremacy over their own internal affairs. We have moved a long way from Jean Bodin's moral conception of sovereignty to the critical conceptions of sovereignty as a 'principle of political supremacy' or 'form of domination'. Stephen Krasner even says that sovereignty is nothing but 'organized hypocrisy' and concludes that it has always enjoyed more prestige in principle than adherence in practice.[2]

The concept of sovereignty and its lineage with the state arose from the sixteenth-century Latin word 'status', which referred to the position or standing of the rulers of European territory after the Wars of Religion. In abstract terms the possession of sovereignty came to mean that no authority existed which could order the state how to act. The 1648 Treaty of Westphalia confirmed the notion of subject loyalty to the authority of the ruler, king or prince, and the concomitant principle that those in authority did not have to answer to any external authority, such as the Holy Roman Empire. All authority and legitimacy resided inside the state. In other words, domestically the doctrine came to mean the sole authority to issue decisions and obligatory commands. Externally it conferred autonomy and independence.

Traditionally, therefore, sovereignty referred to a bundle of characteristics, including territory, authority and recognition. It conveyed a sense of legitimacy or moral right to rule as well as the empirical properties of *de jure* and *de facto* power. But the fundamental point for our purposes here is that sovereignty described and justified the notion that states should not intervene in the internal affairs of other states. In that sense it became part of the conventional language of international affairs and international law.

Sovereignty has always been malleable, its significance for countries ever evolving and the notion of absolute sovereignty something of a myth. There is nothing new about debates concerning the definition of sovereignty or about the tension it brings to questions about contradictions in the international legal order and effective international action. The idea of indivisible sovereignty has always been under assault. Such concepts and organizational patterns as 'balance of power', 'collective security' with the League of Nations and the United Nations, regional organizations such as the EU, OAS, ASEAN or NATO, international organizations such as the World Court, ICC, War Crimes Tribunal Courts, and even non-state actors such as NGOs and multi-national corporations, all militate against the principle of indivisible state sovereignty.

Novel trade arrangements such as NAFTA go so far as to provide binational panels that can make binding decisions on Canada, USA and Mexico – even against the wishes of their governments. All federal systems involve some limitations on central state authority. And internationally, states can sometimes have authority without external recognition of their sovereignty: witness Taiwan, which in the1970s lost its recognition as a sovereign member of the United Nations and yet still remains a stable and effective state.

Dealing with this historical and conceptual issue may appear to be flogging a dead horse, but if sovereignty is not the foundation of modern international life, what is? The fact is that state sovereignty remains the most completely legitimate and accepted institutional form – even if it does not always describe reality. Or as President Bill Clinton sarcastically put it, 'It all depends what *is*, is.'

Despite the fact that weaker states have always been penetrable and penetrated, proponents of the state uphold sovereignty as necessary for the defence of the nature and legality of the international system. They claim it provides states with formal guarantees of their independence and allows for the development of principles on which to base orderly international relations. Despite the enormous disparities among states, it gives formal independence, and some reassurance and dignity, to smaller or weaker states. On the other hand, its opponents claim that sovereignty is a fiction used to limit humanitarian assistance and foreign intervention on behalf of people being neglected or massacred by their governments. Other opponents say that it is too often used to legitimize the power of the strong to coerce the weak.

What is unique today is that there has been acceleration in the use of new terms, and the misuse of old terms, by both academics and practitioners alike. Or perhaps we should put it in the form of a question, and ask whether the complex new vocabularies of semi-sovereignty, disputed sovereignty, divided sovereignty, subdued sovereignty, quasi-states, weak states, incomplete states, divided states, failed states and so on have enriched or reduced our ability to explain and evaluate international behaviour. Clearly, a gulf has also grown between the purely theoretical discussions about the topic and writings about specific events and policies in the so-called real world, particularly in the cases of the recent terrorist attacks in the United States, Madrid, London, Bali and elsewhere, in recent peacekeeping and military interventions, and lastly in the wars against Afghanistan and Iraq.

Many of these military actions are now at odds with the idea of sovereignty, and international law in this area has become confused.[3] The fact is, there are no relevant new international rules or laws, but there certainly are new practices. While international law and the structures of the most important international organizations are based on inviolable sovereignty, violations of that sovereignty are increasing throughout the world. Simply stated, a new practice of intervention has developed without a corresponding development in international law. This problem is conflated by terrorism, crimes against humanity and violations of the law of war.

This topic needs to be aired and debated. There are no easy answers to questions about whether or when the international community should breach sovereignty, even for the noblest of reasons. The subject is replete with moral, legal and conceptual issues, and intersects with problems about international relations theory and, in particular, with judgments about realism and idealism in international relations.

## Realities in international relations

In less than two decades the international security system has changed in an extraordinary fashion. The dynamics of world power have shifted, signalled by the end of cold-war rivalry, terrorist attacks on American soil, a war over terrorism, an increase in the role of international institutions in post-conflict situations, the development of an international human rights culture, and evolving concepts of 'security' itself. Moreover, at the economic and social levels, globalization has caused a growth in interdependence and this development has increased security problems inside both strong and weak states. Hijacking, shoulder-launched missiles, the threat of attacks with anthrax germs, and suicide bombings are only a few recent examples of the types of weapons that can be used in transnational terrorism. The state and its sovereignty have proven to be very fragile indeed.

The 9/11 terrorist attacks and the subsequent response of the coalition led by the United States have profoundly affected global politics, altering the geopolitical map almost beyond recognition. Leaders have had to decide how to respond to terrorist organizations without exacerbating the cycle of action and revenge between the West and the Islamists. Even before 9/11, the impact of globalization and the outbursts of enthusiasm for humanitarian interventions in Third-World countries had given rise to a mismatch between the conflicts that exist and the language and institutions for dealing with them.

To make the point as simply as possible – the cold war is over. Yet we still have no appropriate name for the new period characterized both by globalization and local conflicts. The Soviet Union has broken into independent republics. The monolithic Soviet military threat to the West that dominated defence thinking is gone. The threat of a strategic nuclear exchange has receded close to vanishing point. But other threats have arisen to alarm ordinary Westerners as well as bureaucrats and politicians. They include the recent terrorist attacks around the world, the possible failure of democratic and economic reforms in the former Soviet Union, the possibility of nuclear attack by terrorist states, and lastly, and most important, the ever present regional, ethnic and religious conflicts around the world.

Since the end of the cold war such local conflicts and threats have occurred with great frequency, the annual number remaining relatively constant for a decade. Depending on definition, there were about 82 armed conflicts in the year before 9/11 alone. 33 countries, mostly in Africa and central Eurasia, are at serious risk of continued violent conflict and instability for the foreseeable future. During the cold war, Western support for the developing world consisted primarily of propping up states and elites that were hostile to the Soviet Union. Today such practices are seen by many commentators and some governments as questionable. Human security requirements are considered to be as important as the security of states and their leaders, if not more so.

The end of the cold war left the state-dominated system in conflict with increasing globalization and also with enhanced concern for diversity within and across states. While there are 191 states in the United Nations, there are more like 10,000 nations in the world. 'State' and 'nation' and 'people' do not coincide in most countries. There are millions of Chinese, Russians, Albanians, Hungarians, Romanians, Turks, Kurds, Palestinians, Tamils, Ibos, Zulus and Tibetans in other peoples' countries – millions of Muslims, Buddhists, Hindus and Sikhs living on each other's laps in Asia. Such diversity also haunts Europe: almost all the states of central and Eastern Europe and many in Western Europe have sizeable ethnic minorities fomenting some level of social and political unrest. Especially, but not only, in poorer countries, these diversities are increasingly producing conflict with state authorities and elites. Armed conflict and humanitarian crises plague countries across Africa, Asia, Latin America, the Balkans and the former Soviet Union.

In many regions ethnic and religious conflicts are eroding the state system of government. We have both a unipolar international system and violent multipolarity. The problem is to link the two symbiotically and make the world safe for such diversity and diversity safe for the world.

## The security debate

With such conceptual confusion at the international level, it is not surprising that a security debate has been taking place throughout the world and especially within multinational organizations. As states and international organizations stumble from crisis to crisis, principles are struggling to keep up with new actions. There is an almost anarchical relationship between principle and policy and action. We have 'wars' on terrorism. We have preventive diplomacy, peacekeeping, peacemaking, peace enforcement, peace-building and even nation-building. The activities have expanded from wars and traditional peacekeeping to monitoring human rights, setting up and monitoring elections, delivering humanitarian aid and protecting civilians – in short, from fighting or separating the combatants to reconstructing their countries.

Western states are now deeply involved in nation-building in Bosnia, Haiti, Kosovo, Afghanistan, Iraq and several African countries. High-sounding diplomacy by both Europeans and Americans at the United Nations gives the impression that these tasks are proceeding well. Yet the world community finds it almost impossible to keep these fragile countries and the regions around them from collapsing into chaos, conflict and misery over and over again.

As we think about the futures of Afghanistan and Iraq in particular, we should bear in mind that our concept of security has broadened. During the past decade the definition used in international organizations has expanded to include not only security of persons and property, but also human rights, democratic government and possession of the basic necessities of life. Operations such as those in Afghanistan and Iraq include a variety of organizations from the military to suppliers of health, food, housing and even prisons. Security has become tied to wider concepts of democratization – free societies, free elections and free markets.

The most prominent institution plagued by this turbulence has been the United Nations. A former president of the United Nations Association in the United States, Edward Luck, put it like this: 'No one understands what's happening. It's happening much too quickly. There's not been time to shift institutions that were moribund into global miracle workers in the New World Disorder.' The problematic history of United Nations security activities is well known. The United Nations Charter is an optimistic document which calls on the Security Council to provide for the peaceful settlement of disputes and the collective use of force to deal with threats to the peace and acts of aggression. It allows for the use of force in only two circumstances – in self-defence or as authorized by the Security Council in response to 'a threat to the peace, a breach of the peace, or an act of aggression'.

The cold war paralysed the United Nations in even these primary functions. Eventually it made a number of improvizations to avoid East–West issues and to allow the Security Council to take some actions when peace was threatened or when a violent conflict seemed likely to escalate.

From this developed the concept of peacekeeping – the non-violent use of soldiers.[4] But, when the cold war ended, the United Nations began to undertake more robust military interventions and humanitarian activities. The question of whether the United Nations had the right to interfere in the sovereignty of weak and divided states was hardly discussed. Before the necessary arguments about concepts, policies and actions were clarified, 9/11 intervened and the United States attacked Afghanistan and Iraq. In other words, international terrorism and war were added to the grounds for intervention.

In the modern technological age a handful of terrorists can create havoc anywhere. Not even the world's only superpower can prevent the destruction of property and people in its own homeland. Elsewhere, the post-cold war revival of the power of ethnicity, tribalism and religion threatens to break down the barriers of the state system, especially in poorer regions of the world. Moreover, modern technology makes it more and more difficult for Westerners to comprehend and accept what they see in the world. Each passing day reveals more victims of avoidable disease, environmental catastrophe, human conflict and misery – more charred bodies to be counted, photographed and transmitted via satellite for the evening news, more irate internet chat groups.

Obviously the traditional notions of sovereignty should be abandoned only with great reluctance. But when? By whom? Who is to choose where intervention takes place? The General Assembly where all are represented no matter how weak? The Security Council that needs restructuring? NATO? The President of the United States? A coalition of 'willing' states?

The interventionist desires of some members of the Western public and their leaders need to be tempered. Of late, it has become fashionable to call for military intervention or outright vengeance to be visited upon the heads of all perceived aggressors. Cooler heads must prevail. But as the world becomes more united – with the expansion of global economics, global technology, global communications and global weapons – the inclination to overlook the principles of independence and sovereignty threatens to overwhelm world order.

## Limited sovereignty

Clearly, a new set of dynamics has overtaken international relations since the fall of the Berlin Wall and the Soviet Union. Sovereignty is being reduced in importance and belief in a kind of 'limited sovereignty' is developing. Intervention has become more and more acceptable. People have become used to the idea of the West intervening in the affairs of other people – in order to enhance humanitarian causes or their own state's national interests.

Many, if not most, of the problems of the post-cold war period emerge from transnational or trans-sovereign challenges. These new problems are difficult to address because they exist inside extant states or are trans-sovereign in nature, and because existing concepts and the institutions based on them are structured on earlier state-to-state relations and the East-West conflict in general. This has meant that the important concept of sovereignty has begun to erode. It is under attack from globalization forces, economic and trade liberalization, the changing nature of technology and American hegemony. In some cases these factors have caused states to collapse; in others they have given rise to transnational or trans-sovereign problems of refugees, disease, ethnic conflict, drug-smuggling, terrorism, violence and civil war.

At the same time, terrorist tactics have become more destructive and the United States has determined that it has the right to wage preventive war against states, groups or individuals who might harm American interests. That combination, as we have all seen, is lethal for both Americans and foreigners.

## International intervention

Reasonably, international organizations are in some policy confusion about how to react to these changed realities and beliefs about the hard-shelled nature of the state and sovereignty. Many commentators have come to think that the international community has a *right* to intervene in the internal affairs of states regardless of what the leaders of such states want. During the last decade alone, the Security Council agreed to intervene, without an invitation, in Somalia, Bosnia, Rwanda, Albania and Haiti because of humanitarian crises occurring in those countries. In the case of Liberia the United Nations gave agreement *ex post facto* to the intervention. In the cases of the no-fly zone over northern Iraq and the bombing of Serbia because of Kosovo, the Security Council did not commission the acts but came close to sanctioning them. And in the problematic cases of Russia's intervention in the states of Moldova, Georgia, Tajikistan and domestically in Chechnya, the United Nations did not protest. After the 2001 attacks in New York and Washington, the United Nations gave half-hearted approval for the United States to retaliate 'in self-defence' but as an organization it did not join the fight. The mantle of war was taken up by the United States, its NATO allies and a few other like-minded countries in Afghanistan, and by an American-led 'coalition of the willing' in Iraq.

Clearly, there is a high degree of selectivity here. In fact, there may be a growing belief that 'some' states may do whatever they please with their citizens while others may not. Saddam Hussein could not. UN Secretary General Boutros Boutros-Ghali put it like this: '[S]overeignty is no longer absolute...Sovereignty must be kept in its place.'[5] When discussing the need for intervention the influential *Economist* magazine thundered, 'National sovereignty be damned.' But these declarations were made only selectively – in reference to weak states. Few even mentioned the topic of sovereignty when Afghanistan and Iraq were invaded for crimes committed by their own citizens on their own territories.

### The old and new security dilemmas

During the cold war the 'security dilemma' was interpreted as being essentially about the East–West conflict and Western policy was based on protecting its own interests without aggravating relations with the enemy. The bipolar configuration of the cold war period generally reflected the realist principle that states attempt to increase their own security by enhancing their power and military strength, but in so doing they inherently make other states feel less secure. As each state looks out for itself in terms of survival and security, it frightens others, encouraging them to strengthen their own militaries, as power cannot be shared since it is essentially zero-sum in nature. As John Herz summarized it – in the anarchy of world states,

> Striving to attain security from [such] attack, they are driven to acquire more and more power in order to escape the power of others. This, in turn, renders the others more insecure and compels them to prepare for the worst.[6]

In short, each state's security is defined and rests on other states' insecurity.

The security dilemma that characterized the cold war years has not disappeared, but today it also concerns how to protect states against transnational challenges, and aid failed, weak and underdeveloped ones. The dangers generally come not from strong states but from those that are weak, divided and disintegrating. Almost all of the violent conflicts in the post-cold war period have been internal, not international wars. It was a feeble state that harboured bin Laden, not a strong one.

The *new* security dilemma therefore arises from the fact that an increase in even a superpower's military strength may not provide a corresponding increase in its security and may even be irrelevant. This is because the stronger states become, the more they open themselves up to increased challenges from globalization forces and to international terrorism from non-state actors. The fragility of the modern state can be seen in every walk of life from trade through transportation to telecommunications. The state is under challenge and, while it is not obsolete and will not disappear, its security can no longer be founded on weapons and soldiers alone. It requires new approaches to international politics and reforms in non-traditional security sectors such as policing, intelligence and foreign aid.

The current unstable and difficult situation is due to the simultaneous existence of both traditional state challenges, such as that posed by the rapid rise of Chinese power, and the new security threat, emerging from subnational actions, in particular from the Muslim world. It is this changing nature of security that must be confronted. The issue is not just about UN legitimacy or US actions; it is about the need for an overall commitment to multilateralism. Those who argue that the United States is now so powerful that its government is increasingly tempted to act alone in international affairs are obviously correct. Where they may err is in assuming that because America possesses this power it knows how to use it wisely. Moreover, other countries are equally powerful in economic and social fields. The US margin of superiority is not unassailable, and eventually American political leaders too will realize that in a turbulent and violent world collective action will be most effective in the long run. The advent of the *new* security dilemma indicates that even the most powerful country in the world cannot deal with its problems alone.

## Notes

1   See 'US Image Up Slightly, but Still Negative', Pew Global Attitudes Project, 23 June 2005. http://pewglobal.org/reports/display
2   Stephen D. Krasner, *Sovereignty: Organized Hypocrisy* (Princeton University Press, 1999).
3   Geoffrey Best, *War and Law Since 1945* (Oxford University Press, 1997).
4   Alan James, *The Politics of Peace-Keeping* (London: Chatto & Windus, 1969).
5   *Agenda for Peace* (31 January 1992); found at www.un.org/Docs/56/agsupp.html
6   John Herz, 'Idealist Internationalism and the Security Dilemma', *World Politics*, vol. 2 (1950), p. 157.

# 2
# Ideologies, Ideas and Political Slogans in the Formation of George W. Bush's Foreign Policy

Attempts to resolve the contradictions between concepts in American foreign policy and global realities gave rise to vociferous and polarized debates from the 1990s onwards. Politicians and analysts argued continually, using traditional concepts and tired clichés. The debates appeared to go nowhere. Some discouraged critics opined that this whole endeavour had produced a mental slum from which nothing could be rescued. However, such pessimism was misplaced. We do need a vocabulary and conceptual frameworks to determine which ideas are significant in understanding the pattern of world politics and how the United States approaches them. As Alexis de Tocqueville pointed out, politics is a reflection of habits of mind, not just institutions.[1] Intellectual constructs or theories of international relations are similar. The broad frameworks may not explain all the facts, but at any particular time those that are regarded as the most conclusive can have a significant effect on policies.

The dominant issues in the study of international relations in recent years have concerned the new world order and the role of the United States following the collapse of the Soviet Union and the discrediting of communism – events that forced Americans to rethink the configuration of the world and their significance in it. The concepts underpinning this discussion revolved around ideas that have been part of the cultural dialogue for several years – those that warn of a 'clash of civilizations' and others that debate the role of the United States as a single superpower or 'empire'. A second-level set of political issues concerns how these ideas are linked to US foreign policy. Conditions in the strategic environment clearly have an impact on policy, but to what extent is the United States' evolving view of itself as a hegemonic power determining its actions? To what extent is it simply providing justification for them? The hyperactive neoconservatives, for example, have been the most loquacious supporters of military action, with their stress on US 'exceptionalism' and their 'missionizing' belief in the use of power in the search for what they regard as democratic peace. Their ideas helped to seduce the United States into the instability of Afghanistan and the abattoir of Iraq because they provided focus and leadership for the inchoate popular determination in the United States to avenge 9/11.

This chapter does not attempt to repeat or assess the philosophical underpinnings of academic theories of international relations. Excellent studies such as John J. Mearsheimer's *Tragedy of Great Power Politics* and Stephen M. Walt's *Taming American Power* carry out this task with wisdom and verve.[2] Our purpose is to outline the ideas and words that have been employed by the Bush administration to explain its policies and to trace where they have come from. In fact, theories of international relations often fall well short of providing the ability to explain how and why an administration makes its policies. Looking for coherent policy and certainty in international relations can be futile because human characteristics such as greed and generosity, pride and idealism, arrogance and error may determine specific diplomatic choices. Life's vagaries and bad judgments can account for many decisions in international relations. Certainly they played a role in the US imperial follies in Vietnam and South America, and do so in Iraq today. But that is not all that counts. A wide range of ideas resonate in American foreign policy and we focus here on some of the most influential and representative of them, searching for those that shape and inform the Bush administration and provide coherence and justification for its policies. The debate over ideas among America's intellectual elite concerns competing ways of interpreting current realities and justifying policies in response to such 'facts'.

The unprecedented attack on the US homeland led the President and his advisers to focus on fundamental ideas and reinforced their tendency to see the solutions to international problems in military terms. The events of 9/11 generated extreme rhetoric about world order, the place of the United States in it and the superiority of US ideals of democracy and freedom. This rhetoric and the militaristic foreign policy based on it have provoked anti-Americanism throughout the globe, particularly among Muslims. President Bush describes himself as 'a uniter, not a divider' but, when he committed the United States to an open-ended war on a global scale, fears about his intentions became widespread.

We see the direction of recent US foreign policy as a conjuncture of five factors: dominant ideas or ideologies, the pivotal events of 9/11,

Bush's character and personality, the temptation to use the overwhelming military power of the United States, and the inability of major institutions, such as Congress or the armed forces, to resist this impetus. Thus, it is possible to discern the broad influences and continuities behind the decisions that led to the attack on Iraq and the failure to plan for an end to the war. Here we focus on the dominant ideas.

## A clash of civilizations

As the Soviet Union's decline became ever clearer in the 1980s and the cold war neared its end, analysts began to turn their minds to the shape that international relations would take after the bipolar system collapsed. According to one influential group of scholars, the global order was entering a new phase in which the crucial elements that would divide humankind and cause international conflict would be cultural. When the world was suddenly freed of its domination by the cold war clash between democracy and communism, it became a more varied and in some ways a more frightening place. The threat of war suddenly changed from a specific one with the Soviet Union to a multiple, uncertain one. Samuel Huntington's classic book *The Clash of Civilizations* is the most influential and thorough presentation of this argument.[3] According to his thesis, or 'map' as he calls it,[4] civilizations are the highest cultural grouping of peoples in the world. Differentiated by their traditions, religions, languages and collective histories, they provide the motivational factor in global politics. As global politics is being reconfigured along cultural lines, divisions over culture and religion, rather than the clash of ideologies, constitute the primary factor in the future of world order and security. Peoples and countries with similar cultures are coming together, while those with dissimilar cultures are becoming increasingly alienated. Alignments defined by ideology and superpower relations are giving way to alignments defined by culture and civilization, and cultural units are replacing cold war blocs as the fault-lines between civilizations.

According to Huntington, the existing civilizations include Western, Islamic, Sinic (primarily in China), Hindu, Orthodox, Japanese, Latin American and African. Conflicts are most likely to occur between or among states and groups representing these different civilizations, which will define the battlegrounds of the future. What ultimately counts for people is not abstract political ideology or even economic interest. It is faith and family, blood and belief that people identify with and are ready to fight, kill and die for.

Huntington's reasoning suggests that culture and religion may lead to wars and international terrorism. Suicide bombing, for example, is one of the most recent and effective tactics in the terrorist arsenal. In modern times, it can be said to have emerged in Sri Lanka and Lebanon in the 1980s and spread throughout the world, mostly in the Middle East and Asia. The phenomenon has been linked to Tamil Tiger nationalists and groups identified by religion such as Hezbollah, Hamas, al-Qaeda and the overall Islamic Jihad. In 2001 it appeared in the United States. In 2004 and 2005 it showed up in Madrid, London and elsewhere.

Some critics contend that Huntington's argument divides peoples too rigidly by crude differences. They dislike the notion of 'we' and 'them' in the analysis and they contend that this approach stereotypes cultures and religions, portraying the world in terms of Christians and Muslims, good and evil. Amartya Sen, the Nobel economist, has argued that such thinking robs us of our plural identities. It 'not only reduces us; it impoverishes the world'.[5] However, Huntington's political analysis is much more nuanced than his critics claim. He does not hold that his paradigm explains all events in global politics, only general attitudes or tendencies. Nor is he a warmonger. He holds that the United States should work to forge strong alliances with those cultures with which it shares a common ground and common inheritance in order to spread its values as widely as possible. For him, all civilizations will have to learn to live together and tolerate one another because in the globalized world there is ultimately no avoiding such relationships.

As for those civilizations with which the United States shares less common ground, Huntington argues that US policy should be cooperative when possible, but strong-willed and confrontational when necessary. He rejects the concept of a universalistic value system and the related global ambitions that have predominated in the West since the eighteenth century. The belief in the universality of any particular culture, he says, is false and dangerous. Empirically, Western culture is not universal because other civilizations adhere to different ideals and norms. Morally, the idea is unjustified because imperialism is the logical and necessary consequence of universalism. When the United States seeks to impose its values and traditions on other countries, thereby overriding local interests, culture and leadership, it is extremely dangerous and could even provoke a major inter-civilizational war. Huntington argues that instead of seeking the universality of Western culture we should accommodate the differences between civilizations and create a system of order and power that acknowledges their differences and dividing lines.

For Huntington, these claims were demonstrated by the Soviet–Afghan war of 1979–89 and the first Gulf War of 1990–91, both of which were quickly transformed into wars between civilizations. They marked the beginning of an era of cultural and ethnic conflict and fault-line wars between groups from different civilizations.

Huntington outlines three rules for the management of foreign affairs and the avoidance of inter-civilization wars. The first rule holds that the major core states should refrain from intervening in conflicts in other civilizations. Spheres of influence among civilizations should be recognized and respected, much as they were during the cold war domination of the United States and the Soviet Union. Second, where regions overlap and are prone to instability, such as in the former Yugoslavia, the Middle East, and Central Asia, core states must engage directly with one another in joint conciliation to contain or to halt fault-line wars between states or groups that are part of these civilizations. Third, despite his fundamental rejection of universality, Huntington argues that peoples in all civilizations should search for and strive to expand the values, institutions, and practices they have in common with peoples of other civilizations. This responsibility Huntington holds is necessary if we are to avoid the doomsday conflicts that could occur in the new world order. In his view, an international order based on civilizations is the best safeguard against world war since clashes of civilizations are the greatest threat to world peace.

The inevitable encounters between civilizations might be manageable, Huntington argues, if we can find some way to replace traditional forms of community and autonomy. Within most modern religions there exist communities that are emphatically against violence. If their voice is strong enough and the costs of hostility toward outsiders are fully recognized as unacceptable, these communities may defuse the most serious threats. Meanwhile, since no civilizations are prepared to withdraw from the exchanges that characterize the new global world, the West should continue to spread Western values wherever possible. In fact, Huntington goes so far as to claim that it must create a stronghold with which to defend its civilizational heritage. To this end he believes that the United States should reaffirm its Western identity and cooperate closely with its European partners to protect and advance the interests and values of their shared civilization.

There are, nevertheless, major problems with relating Huntington's theories to the world of diplomacy. What would non-interference in other civilizations mean? Was it interference in the Muslim world to drive Saddam Hussein's forces from Kuwait in 1991 in conjunction with

Saudi Arabia and other Arab countries? Was Bosnia-Herzegovina part of the Muslim world or the West and, if part of the Muslim world, should Western peacekeepers have abandoned it to its fate in the early 1990s? Is it interference in the Sinic world to negotiate about nuclear weapons with North Korea, as the government in Pyongyang repeatedly asks Washington to do? Similarly, is it interference to discourage Taiwan from declaring its independence from China? Is it interference in the Hindu and Muslim worlds to encourage India and Pakistan to abate their differences? Should the African countries be left to their fate and Western peacekeepers removed? Should we withdraw from international efforts to limit the spread of weapons of mass destruction? Even to pose these questions shows the extent of the difficulties in Huntington's analysis; the fact is that parties in one 'civilization' often beg for interference by parties in another, and each civilization penetrates others all the time through trade, emigration and ideas.

There is an 'open market' in ideas propagated through trade, the media and universities. In fact, Western cultural influences may be too pervasive. We appreciate Asian or African literature, food, music or architecture precisely because it is different from our own. There is already a danger that the world is becoming too much the same. Only the street signs tell us whether we are in Chicago or Shanghai, so similar is the urban architecture. We need to appreciate the values of other civilizations and encourage them to maintain their traditions. They will have to decide how much they need to adapt to global capitalism and, when attitudes to human rights clash, compromises will have to be found in the give-and-take of debate. We need to see differences of ideas and values as no more threatening than differences between cuisines – indeed such differences are enriching and it is homogenization which is impoverishing. Only thus can we reduce the likelihood of conflict between civilizations.

Despite Huntington's obvious humanity and concern for global peace, his influential book predicts the growing clashes between Western countries and those with Muslim and Chinese cultures in particular. 9/11 and the wars in Afghanistan and Iraq certainly buttress his claim that conflict will emerge along cultural lines. It was not Western Christians but 19 Muslim Arabs who initiated the attack on New York and Washington that unleashed the wars in Afghanistan and Iraq. It does not take much imagination now to envisage an all-out clash between rich, militaristic, Christian America and the politically volatile, energy-rich world of Islam. Whatever his own attitude to the phenomenon, Huntington's ideas have influenced those who believe that the United States must protect its own values in a sea of conflicting viewpoints. It underpins the principles which neocon-servatives in particular wish to foster and provides some justification for the actions and goals of the US administration. Among President Bush's supporters, the Christian evangelist Franklin Graham was one of the prominent church leaders who denounced Islam and encouraged the Bush administration to overcome it.[6]

## America as empire

The idea of America as an empire emerged after the Second World War as the great powers struggled to create a new post-war order, and the United States, together with the Soviet Union, quickly graduated to superpower status. After the fall of the Soviet Union, the United States became the world's only superpower, with its military posts round the world providing security for allies and operating as it wished without the constraints of other powers. Its hegemony encouraged the United States to act like an empire, imposing its views and constructing security cordons around the world.[7] It engaged in new imperialist ventures both economically and militarily. Some celebrate this new imperial nature of US power, others fear the threat it represents to established alliances and institutions and even to democracy itself. The argument has recently been taken up by a new school of empire studies.

The essential meaning of empire is that one country rules other parts of the world directly or through intermediaries – that is by indirect rule. Historically, empire referred to satrapies or viceroys or provincial govern-ors who governed as subordinate rulers, managing the colonial admin-istration of subjugated countries. Such systems provide major gains in legitimacy for local elites and lower administrative costs for the dom-inating country. In this view the Greek, Roman, and British empires are taken as prototypes of what the United States is becoming. The United States currently has about 5 per cent of the world's population, but spends closer to 50 per cent of all military budgets. For the moment, there is no counterbalancing power or combination of powers that can match it. The US military circles the globe with permanent bases and weapons caches. While its troops will eventually be withdrawn from the fragile states of Afghanistan and Iraq, American leaders will insist on leaving the countries in friendly hands – to a kind of 'comprador' class. In the long run such actions may only prop up weak transitional leaders who in turn will be overthrown by new nationalists. In the meantime, insurgents, successful or not, will attempt to destroy the empire and its colonial connections.

Americans often regard themselves as reluctant imperialists. To them the very concept smacks of eighteenth- and nineteenth-century European imperialism – or in French terms *'mission civilatrice'*. They don't like to think of their country as an empire; it makes them uneasy. Despite the history of how the United States became a country in the first place – by virtually wiping out an entire continent of indigenous people – Americans struggle to stay afloat in a sea of denial about their ambitions to empire status. Their presidents, including George W. Bush, have not hesitated to pronounce global ambitions and enact policies of extraterritorial significance, but the fact remains that for Americans generally the country is not an empire – and if by some chance it is, then, it is one of a kind.[8] It is not clear whether this is because the term empire is odious to American ears or because of an inability to face up to reality. As a presidential candidate George W. Bush said 'America has never been an empire ... We may be the only great power in history that has had the chance and refused.'[9]

For many, the concept of an American empire is becoming not only reasonable but unavoidable. Some contend that empire status is vital to prevent evil in the world – evil in the form of terrorism, tyranny and the like. As such they contend that the American empire is benevolent and their only fear is that it may become weak, overstretched or head for collapse. Critics of the United States as empire meanwhile focus on the negative aspects of a colossus determined and able to get its way in the world. They work to create forces to counterbalance this development. They often view America as a ruthless capitalist enterprise determined to maintain access to the sources of foreign energy that sustain its economy and way of life.[10]

In his books *Colossus* and *Empire*, historian Niall Ferguson argues that in both military and economic terms, America is nothing short of the most powerful empire in history.[11] In addition, he believes optimistically that the United States has an unparalleled ability and opportunity to take a role of positive global leadership and shape the world around its values of free markets, the rule of law, and representative government. He believes there is a 'liberal' form of empire which can benefit all peoples by enhancing prosperity and democracy, and by creating a kind of benevolent, negotiated order – upholding the rules of international law and coercing deviants with military power. He sees the United States as the natural inheritor of the British Empire and argues that the current international order needs its enlightened leadership – especially the many sovereign but failed states that need supervision. In this regard, George W. Bush follows the tradition of many other US presidents who have promoted the liberal ideal of the desirability to spread democracy around the world, especially in the Middle East.

However, Ferguson argues that Americans shy away from the necessary long-term commitments of sustaining an empire because of their short attention span and an extreme case of denial. For him, the United States is a superpower that is reluctant to accept the grand scale of its global responsibilities and refuses to allow realistic timescales and sacrifices for its overseas activities. Thus, it ventures into countries in order to restore order but, because of financial, political, and ideological hindrances, it departs before ever creating or restoring democracy and order.

In his enthusiasm for empire Ferguson barely considers whether the world's peoples want to be subject to the imperial control of this new American order. Thus, he overlooks how stability may be jeopardized by insurgencies and how, when combined with the growing domestic problems of economic instability and the increasing distrust of American citizens for their country's overseas ambitions, America's imperial ventures may end because of 'overreach' – the recognized cause for the fall of the world's previous great empires.[12]

Another example of the empire thesis is provided by the realist Robert D. Kaplan. In *Imperial Grunts*[13] he draws an analogy between America's role in the world today and its earlier conquests of Native Indians in the Wild West. This repugnant analogy which compares foreign lands to 'Injun Country' obscures what is a decidedly a pro-empire book. Kaplan surveys US military actions around the world with pride and little caution. He paints a vivid picture of how US troops on the ground carry out American policy on every continent. As he puts it, quoting a gleeful American soldier, 'you get to see places tourists never do. We're like tourists with guns'.

Yet another audacious thesis is put forward by Michael Mandelbaum in his volume *The Case for Goliath*.[14] He denies that the US is an empire but sees it rather as the world's *de facto* government or Goliath. He contends that the US is indispensable as a benign world government and even compares it to the sun that keeps 'the planets in their orbits by the force of gravity and radiates the heat and light that makes life possible on one of them'. For him the United States provides world government through diplomatic negotiations, world wide military deployments and rules for the global economy. The US pays while the rest of the world benefits but does not have to pay.

As an apologist for America and its foreign policy, Mandelbaum overlooks all the errors made by recent US governments. He dismisses US atrocities and skips over events such as the US invasion of Iraq, as though he were the sole judge of history. This might be satisfactory if his judgments were confined to the US homeland but he also decides whether or not US actions are good for other countries. For him the US provides services that are indispensable for the world and can only be judged positively. He contends that the US provides world security by stopping countries from attacking each other and in its role of a Goliath assures global access to oil. He ignores the facts that in recent years it has often been the US which has attacked other countries and that it is the leaders of states with oil, not the US, which should decide what to do with their own minerals. The US does enjoy international supremacy, but American scholars cannot decide on their own what is good for the rest of the world.

Whether the correct terminology is empire or goliath there is little doubt that the US does use its power to keep many countries subordinate. For Mandelbaum, however, all other governments favour this US role in the world. He never notices the cruelty of American power. Nor does he seem to understand that there can be a conflict between American interests and those of other countries – that, indeed, other countries may actually be hostile to American domination. Mandelbaum's polemic is perhaps the best example of US scholarly hubris.

Critical scholars such as Michael Mann, Benjamin Barber and Andrew J. Bacevich take these arguments about the United States as empire much further. They share the view that any empire built on military domination will eventually fail.[15] In his criticisms of US foreign policy, Bacevich, for example, documents both America's rampant military reach and its resounding uncertainty about what to do with it.[16] He quotes from Arthur Schlesinger Jr's *American Empire: Realities and Consequences of US Diplomacy:* 'Who can doubt that there is an American empire? ... an 'informal' empire, not colonial in polity, but still richly equipped with imperial paraphernalia: troops, ships, planes, bases, proconsuls, local collaborators, all spread around the luckless planet.'[17] Bacevich then robustly attacks the seduction of America into military adventures. It should be noted that even before the occupation of Iraq the United States already had over 750 military bases in more than 130 countries. Its military divides the world into geographical commands that span the globe, a fact that unequivocally points to the absurdity of US political rhetoric claiming that America never leaves 'occupying' forces in countries after military victory.[18]

Of the many other public intellectuals who are vociferous critics of the United States as an empire we highlight the work of two critics, or more precisely two scholars, one American and one French, who have contributed extensively to the debate on this issue.

The first of these staunch critics is Chalmers Johnson. For Johnson the American empire is not liberal but military. In his widely acclaimed book *Blowback*, he predicted that US interventionism abroad would create the climate for catastrophic terrorist attacks at home.[19] With a sometimes simplistic view of military hegemony, Johnson, in his more recent book *The Sorrows of Empire*, warns that rampant militarism could spell the end of American constitutional democracy.[20] His argument stems from the notion that US foreign policy revolves around a seemingly endless quest to accumulate military bases overseas. Military power has consolidated these far-flung bases in a new form of global and imperial rule. During the cold war United States bases were situated in locations best suited to thwart communist threats. Today they are increasingly clustered around large oil and natural-gas reserves.

Johnson claims that, because threats to the homeland were exaggerated, not only did America become more and more militarized over the past century, but that the Pentagon now far exceeds the State Department in terms of influence. Regional military commanders now have more power than ambassadors, and their influence is growing as they oversee the 'mercenaries' or private military companies whom the United States both arms and trains to defend the interests of the American empire. Johnson holds that the large defence budget and the massive troop deployments overseas starve domestic needs in order to feed the colonial machine. He thus fears that America faces the 'sorrows of empire': a state of perpetual war and the end of constitutional democracy, with a Pentagonized presidency and a bankrupt US economy.[21] In Johnson's view, the fall of the Soviet Union ended the US justification for overseas naval bases and military enclaves. However, 9/11 provided Bush with an excuse to expand the US military and also abandon its alliance partners, treaties and laws, and launch its imperial rule.

Similarly, the French journalist Emmanuel Todd sees the US as a muscle-bound giant with feet of clay, whose widespread military ventures obscure its noticeable decline. He argues in his book *After the Empire* that 'far from being on the verge of world domination, America is steadily losing control throughout the world.'[22] Todd is optimistic that democracy can spread, but not through American military power. He considers the trend toward democracy throughout the world to be inevitable and attributes it to educational rather than economic causes. In any case, in his opinion economic factors prevent the United States from being the vehicle for the spread of democracy.[23] He argues that the United States no longer has the economic and financial resources to back up its foreign policy objectives.

Over the past four years, the Bush administration has made massive tax cuts but failed to cut programmes accordingly, thus overreaching itself and becoming increasingly dependent on an influx of foreign capital to cover its exponentially growing budget deficits, particularly from China and Japan. In addition, the decline of America's industrial base has been matched by an increased dependence on imports, leaving the United States at the mercy of any combination of Europeans, Russians, Chinese and Japanese. Such dependence is a great weakness and has created the conditions in theory to strangle US imperialism.

Because of this economic vulnerability, Todd argues, the fundamental strategic objective of the US will be to gain control of the world's resources. He claims that the overthrow of the regimes in Iraq and Afghanistan is nothing but 'theatrical micromilitarism' intended to distract the other major powers from an awareness of America's imperial weakness. That weakness, he says, rests on the fact that its army is unable to hold territory without exposing the US citizenry to the 'unacceptable' deaths that are inevitable with occupation. Thus, given the economic turmoil the United States now faces, and the congruently increasing internal hostility that its foreign and domestic policies bring, Todd believes that George W. Bush and his neoconservative supporters will destroy the American empire.

As we have seen in these brief summaries, imperial status imposes significant burdens. It is buoyed up by the creation of sentimentalized myths about America's military as liberators and heroes who fight to preserve freedom.[24] These myths, expounded especially fervently by conservative Christians in the United States, support and sustain the military and provide cover for extending the perimeter of empire around the world. They predispose Americans to see US military power as inherently good and necessary to counter evil in the world. Great military power also provides the wherewithal to conduct an interventionist foreign policy based on self-interest, disguised or not.

But no matter how pure the motives of a dominant power, interventions engender wariness and hostility in other states. And history shows that intervention by a dominant power accelerates the rise of a combination of other powers as challengers. Acting alone as empire is also enormously expensive. The United States is undergoing a deep political and foreign-policy crisis because of the cost of its war in Iraq. Its military is being seriously stretched and degraded and it cannot recruit sufficient numbers of volunteers to sustain it. The Pentagon is being forced to reduce the number of its troops in Korea and elsewhere. It cannot afford to enforce global order alone.

Even hegemons need allies to share financial burdens, and to provide moral authority and legitimacy. They also need the assistance of an international order that provides transparency and enables victors to obtain the willing cooperation of the vanquished rather than hostility and terrorism. It is doubtful whether the American public will support an administration that continues to incur military obligations and the financial burdens of post-war occupations without the help and moral support of the international community. Indeed, unilateral military rule is dangerous and probably ultimately unsustainable in today's global order where, because of the imperatives of a global market, countries depend heavily on other states for most aspects of political and economic life. The collaboration of states in one sphere facilitates and necessitates interstate cooperation in others.

As we shall argue throughout this book, it is difficult to sustain an imperial democracy. But alas, this is what the Bush administration seems to have undertaken.

## The neoconservatives

American conservatives can be divided into three broad categories – realists, neoconservatives and nationalists. All three groups adopt, but also vigorously contest, the concepts of 'civilization' and 'empire' discussed above. All three embody combinations of dreamers and opportunists from both inside and outside the highest levels of government. The realists are characterized mostly by their concern for the realities of power while neocons seem to be more concerned with the art of the desirable than the art of the possible. The realists treat global power relations as given and the neocons believe that the United States should enlighten the world with its values of democracy, freedom and the goodness of American life. Neither is miscible with the nationalists. The nationalists favour an inward-looking, America-first agenda.

The neoconservatives' linkage of morality and force does not sit well with nationalist conservatives. As Patrick Buchanan put it, he despises intellectuals who would 'define morality for all peoples for all times'.[25]

Because of the conjunction of values and events that occurred in and around the Bush administration, the neoconservative agenda has been more influential than the other two traditions. The events of 9/11 provided the neocons with a unique opportunity to shape events to their interests. While they had earlier focused on opposition to communism, they now began to advocate a positive, aggressive ideological agenda, particularly about politics in the Middle East. Unlike other conservatives, their objective was to use state power to transform global politics rather than to conserve traditions and older alliances. Given an opportunity to fuse American military power to their principles, they helped to shatter the idea of a bipartisan foreign policy by giving impetus to the neoconservative idea of both supporting the concept of the United States as empire and promoting freedom and democracy abroad. Despite the seeming contradiction between these goals, the support for military force is always prevalent in their thought, as is the allure of empire. In fact, after the cold war they argued that an American empire was vital to sustain global order – but of course they thought it would be a benign empire that would be viewed by other peoples as bringing democracy to the world.

The neoconservative camp is wide, ranging from its founders including Irving Kristol and Norman Podhoretz through policymakers such as Paul Wolfowitz and John R. Bolton to in-and-outers such as David Frum and Richard Perle, and public intellectuals such as Donald Kagan, William Kristol, Robert Kagan, Charles Krauthammer and Francis Fukuyama.[26] All have broken with the traditional conservative distrust for broad principles in politics to list instead their own criteria for success, perhaps the most fundamental of which is the idea that America's national interests and moral purposes are the same.[27] This diverse group of men fostered the intellectual climate that gave sustenance to the new American militarism,[28] calling for a revolution in military affairs that would take advantage of technological changes to give the United States overwhelming military dominance.

Although they have existed for about three decades without an explicit organization, the neoconservatives share five ideals. These provide purpose to American foreign policy and are to be protected and advanced through superior military power. They can be summarized as follows:

*Moralism*  Seeing the world in absolutes and a conviction that there is a need to reassert American values.

*Realism*  The assertion that military power is the primary determinant in global affairs – indeed that it is the first and perhaps only option of power.

*Unilateralism*  Suspicion of internationalism and international organization.

*Focus*    A need to concentrate on Middle East and Islam above other
areas of the world.
*Leadership*    That men, not impersonal forces, determine the course of
history.

These ideas, outlined by Podhoretz in his influential magazine *Commentary*,
(1960–95), encouraged pugnacity, contempt for compromise and a
tough, realist perspective. Another generation of neocons took over in
the mid 1990s led by William Kristol in his new journal, *The Weekly
Standard*. Symbolically taking up residence close to the White House, the
new generation of neocons transformed themselves into establishment
figures using articles and talk shows to enter the public discourse. They
actively sought to have a direct impact on policy.

Among the influential neoconservative books of the past few years
is Robert Kagan's *Paradise and Power*, which examines power in international relations.[29] It is broadly representative of the neoconservative
ideas that have been influential in American foreign policy, and the
book has caused a considerable stir on both sides of the Atlantic by arguing that America's military strength has given its leaders not just the
capability, but also the responsibility, to act forcefully. It posits that
dependence on the United States and the experience of creating the
European Union through compromise and concession have created a
psychology of weakness and powerlessness in Europe. It concludes that
America is from Mars, Europe from Venus.

According to Kagan, the realities of power have produced views on
each side of the Atlantic so divergent that the two sides have parted
ways over fundamental beliefs and values in international relations. The
US desire to avoid casualties and its resultant willingness to spend heavily on advanced military technologies has placed it far ahead of Europe
as a military power. European expenditure on defence is about 2 per cent
of GDP, while that of the United States is above 3 per cent. With its older
demographic profile Europe is less prepared than the United States to
shift money for social welfare into military expenditures. Consequently,
Kagan says, the United States has become more willing than Europe to
go to war and is a better judge of the utility and necessity of military
force than Europeans are. As a concrete example of the new technological gap, Kagan argues, the United States had the power and willingness to use military strength to attack Iraq in 2003, while France and
Germany preferred a multilateral peaceful solution through diplomacy,

or UN action if necessary. In short, for Kagan and other neoconservatives, Europeans have become impotent in world affairs while the United States has become all-powerful and therefore can, and will, 'go it alone' when it chooses. The proliferation of American military operations and the Bush *National Security Strategy* are taken as proof of the US intention to maintain its pre-eminence and act unilaterally and pre-emptively.

Kagan's argument is a clever effort to defend American hegemony and its aggressive militaristic policy and blame it on the weakness of other countries, in particular European states. In our view, Kagan tries to justify the short-sightedness and wrong-headedness of recent American policy choices by arguing that the United States had no choice but to act alone in Iraq, as Europeans have become 'wimps'. Despite the evident popularity of this argument in many conservative circles in America, Kagan's volume contains organic fallacies and stereotypes that make it read more like a political party tract than a reasoned piece of analysis. Arguments based on the simplistic idea that 'Americans think; Europeans think the opposite' run throughout the book. But, of course, there is no single 'American view', and policies depend to a large degree on which political party is in power. Almost every Democratic Party spokesman has said that if Gore or Kerry and the Democrats had been in office they would have chosen a more comprehensive, multilateral United Nations route for solving the Iraqi problem and certainly would have allowed the inspectors more time to discover any WMD.

Moreover, there is no single European view. Despite efforts to formulate a joint security policy for the European Union, as of 2006 it does not possess a single, unified policy on major strategic questions. Europe divided into two camps over the attack on Iraq, with Britain, Spain, Italy, Netherlands, Portugal, Denmark and the former communist states of Central and Eastern Europe initially supporting United States action while France, Germany, Belgium and Russia opposed it. In fact, after a terrorist attack in Madrid, the Spanish elected a new government that immediately reversed the country's pro-American policy and pulled its troops out of Iraq.

Kagan's argument is also highly deterministic. It assumes that economic and military facts 'determine' opportunities rather than just provide them, and encourage certain foreign policy choices. As he put it, 'If this evolving international arrangement continues to produce a greater tendency to unilateralism, this should not surprise any objective observer.'[30] For Kagan in other words, American leaders were driven to attack Iraq by the situation: 'It is objective reality which has changed, not the American character.'[31] But the objective reality is that the international community, or a very large part of it, can be persuaded to follow the US lead only when US statesmen succeed in making a reasonable case for their policies. In the Iraqi example, the administration failed to persuade a majority in the Security Council that the situation had suddenly become so serious that military action was needed.[32] The Iraqi reality had not changed for the worse, only the US understanding and views of that reality. Saddam Hussein was not using chemical weapons against his own people, as in the past. We now know that Iraq was not producing WMD, as it had done before 1991, and Saddam Hussein was not implicated in 9/11. The neocons however encouraged President Bush to link Iraq with those events despite all the evidence to the contrary.

In the rose-coloured neoconservative view wars are simply a fact of life. Their consequences are not particularly troublesome. The deaths and problems in so-called triumphs – such as in Haiti or Afghanistan – are not even mentioned, though they took place well before Kagan's book was completed. This leads critical foreign commentators to argue that Americans and Britons are only interested in the deaths of their own countrymen and callously ignore foreign casualties.[33] Nor are the causes or the possible revival of the Vietnam Syndrome discussed in the neo-con literature, even though they played a major part in earlier American foreign policy (including in Bush Senior's decision not to occupy Baghdad after the liberation of Kuwait) and might again influence US foreign policy if losses and costs in Iraq, Afghanistan and elsewhere continue to mount.

In light of the Iraqi experience, it is questionable whether Washington has proved to be better than European capitals at judging military policy. Kagan attacks Europeans both for being too idealistic about the Third World and for being introverted and ignoring it. In fact, Europeans are often more realistic. They have learned from their colonial experience that permanent settlements cannot be imposed from the outside and will last only if they are accepted by the masses of the people concerned. They are also more sensitive to charges of neo-colonialism and anti-Muslim bias. It is not even true that the United States has always been more willing than the Europeans to use military force. In many recent cases in Africa, Europeans have been more prepared than the United States to send their troops; the Congo and Sierra Leone are two recent cases in point where European states dispatched peacekeepers in the hope of reducing the violence and facilitating a local settlement. In Bosnia, the Europeans had troops on the ground as part of UN peacekeeping forces long before the United States acted, and in Kosovo it was

Britain which sponsored the use of ground forces if air attacks on Serbia failed to bring Milosevic to terms.

Clearly, the use of force will be successful in the long run only if it paves the way to a political solution. Kagan mocks Europeans for encouraging compromises between Israel and Palestine. But how can such problems between antagonists (India and Pakistan, Turkish and Greek Cyprus for example) be resolved without compromise, and what is the US-backed Middle East 'road map' about if it is not about concessions and compromises? Israel has been prepared to use massive conventional power against the Palestinians, but this policy has not brought a resolution any nearer; rather it has created a generation of Palestinians willing to sacrifice their lives and kill innocent civilians so that they can vent their frustration and anger on the country they see as their oppressor.

Unlike the neoconservatives, as we argue below, we do not believe that it is feasible to attack all states that appear to be showing an interest in producing or maintaining weapons of mass destruction. Should India, Pakistan, Argentina, Brazil, Ukraine and South Africa have been attacked because we feared their nuclear policies? Are we now to initiate wars against Iran and North Korea? What happens if the public refuses to believe that these states are trying to develop WMD, particularly as no such weapons were found in Iraq? At best, the destruction of nuclear facilities can only delay the production of nuclear weapons, and it is only in persuading other states of the benefits of a non-nuclear stance that we can be successful in the long run.

Many Europeans opposed the use of force against Iraq not because they were wimps, but because they remained unconvinced – that the Iraqis were cooperating with terrorist organizations; that the United Nations had been allowed sufficient time to hunt for WMD; that the West has the right to replace any government it dislikes; and that the United States was necessarily capable of establishing a better government, let alone a democratic one, in Iraq. Even if some of these doubts and reservations were questionable, alliances have to be capable of managing disagreements without resorting to hectoring and public abuse.

Neoconservatives tend to assume US hegemony will continue forever. They neglect the consequences of 'imperial overstretch'. As a spokesman for them, Kagan assumes that the United States alone will continue to have precision-guided munitions which make it possible to fight wars while keeping civilian casualties to a minimum. In fact such weapons are already proliferating. He leaves aside the power of guerrillas to defeat even the strongest conventional forces. Have the lessons of Vietnam and Marxist Afghanistan been forgotten so quickly? He ignores the weakness of the US economy a decade ago when Saudi Arabia, Kuwait and Japan had to foot the bill for the first Iraq War. Similarly, he ignores the current US budget and balance-of-payments deficits and the steady rise of East Asian economic power.

Kagan's analysis of international relations is expounded by hardline conservatives and even by relatively moderate columnists such as Thomas L. Friedman for the *New York Times*, who for example argued at the time of the attack on Iraq that any country that opposed US actions was wrong. Friedman claimed variously: 'France is becoming America's enemy'; 'France wants America to fail in Iraq'; that France was 'malicious ... But then France has never been interested in promoting democracy in the modern Arab world, which is why its pose as the new protector of the Iraqi government – after being so content with Saddam's one-man rule – is so patently cynical.'[34] No wonder that the French government sent a letter to the administration protesting the 'organized campaign of disinformation' based on briefings by anonymous 'administration officials' in 2003.[35] Both Paris and Washington had supported Saddam Hussein in the past because they saw his regime as preferable to the alternatives. The judgement may or may not have been correct, but in politics the best is often the enemy of the good and perfectionists have often caused more bloodshed than realists and compromisers.

Like Kagan, British diplomat Robert Cooper in *The Breaking of Nations* argues that Europe is weak because it has chosen to 'abandon power politics'. Europe, he says, is ill-suited to both humanitarian intervention in failed states and pre-emptive action against rogue states, especially those seeking WMD. For Cooper there is a need to 'get used to the idea of double standards ... to revert to force, pre-emptive attack, deception, whatever is necessary'.[36] Clearly it would be impossible to build an international community or to enhance respect for international law on such a basis. World leaders have to work on the assumption that states abide by international agreements, respond appropriately when this is not the case and resort to the use of force only as a last resort when they are under threat. To abandon the idea of an international community because of a few terrorist incidents or because states fail to live up to their obligations is a gross overreaction and likely to lead to disastrous consequences.

In short, what has come from the neocons and their journalistic allies has been assertion, not analysis – but extremely influential assertion. The idea that the United States is exceptional, and that therefore on balance the world would be better off shaped by American values, runs through their thinking. While other countries have power in the economic and social fields such as treaty negotiations and peacekeeping, the US margin of superiority in conventional and nuclear warfare is unassailable. Kagan is obviously correct about military power and the US ability to use it. Where he and others err is in assuming that because America has this power it knows how to use it wisely or that it will achieve the ends the Bush administration seeks.

The consistent mistake of neoconservatives is to believe that the US can win wars alone, whether on countries or on terrorists. It needs allies as the world's only superpower just as it did when it shared its powerful status during the cold war. Shared decisionmaking, as in the United Nations Security Council, that requires negotiation and compromise is superior to unilateral decisions because its causes less resentment among the weak and distributes the burden of upholding the decisions taken. US power easily crushed Saddam's army, but without help from its allies, from Arab states and, above all, from the Iraqi people themselves, it can never build a peaceful and stable Iraq. The neocons ignore the vital importance of legitimacy in foreign lands, and the historical inability of the United States to stay the course and face years of occupation and hatred.

In sum, Kagan's diagnosis and prescription, as representative of other neo-cons, is seriously faulty. It is, however, the kind of reasoning that has informed and encouraged the Bush administration's foreign policy in Iraq and elsewhere. As we will show in later chapters, US power will last longest, be most effective and cause least damage and bitterness when it is used sparingly. Neocons rarely seem to understand or even acknowledge that US actions may do more harm than good.

Among the most articulate and influential of the neoconservatives who encourage the Bush administration are David Frum and Richard Perle. Frum, a journalist and Canadian, was the Bush speechwriter who coined the phrase 'axis of evil'. Perle has been a consummate inside/outside player since he served as a security advisor under Ronald Reagan. In their defence of the war on Iraq they have been joined by other commentators who are not known as neoconservatives such as William Shawcross whose book *Allies* defends Bush's policy.[37] But such writers tend to confine themselves to a defence of this war, whereas Frum and Perle want to change the whole pattern of US foreign policy to a more muscular approach based on idealistic principles of right and wrong – with the goal of fighting 'evil' wherever it is found.

Above all, neoconservatives believe that the articulation of moral clarity is fundamental to foreign policy, a clarity that is to be contrasted to the 'realpolitik' of the realist school of thought and more traditional commentaries. Until 9/11 such arguments were confined to the fringes of actual policymaking. The names William Kristol and Charles Krauthammer come to mind, but it is to Richard Perle and David Frum that we look for a defence of the actual policies of the Bush administration.

The main, perhaps the only, contention of Frum and Perle in *An End to Evil* is that the clash between Islamic fundamentalism and the West is only beginning, and that a war of ideas and guns must be mounted in defence of the latter.[38] They adopt the 'clash of civilizations' argument without even mentioning it. As they see it, the United States is the 'hope for the entire world' and if it has to act alone to provide a more just world then so be it. At home, these authors want to create a security state with tougher rules for immigration, while abroad they want to build a strong democracy in Iraq and directly confront North Korea, Iran, Syria, Libya and even Saudi Arabia. Since 9/11 these ideas have come to represent a large part of American foreign policy.

## From commentators and analysts to George W. Bush

The ideas of clashing civilizations, the United States as empire and, more directly, the neocon ideas about the absolute need for the United States to use military force – even preventive war – to serve their idealistic goals, inspired the Bush administration's foreign policy after 9/11. To explain the movement or causal relations between ideas and action is always difficult, but it is clear that these ideas were emblematic of the culture and ideas swirling around the Bush administration when 9/11 took place. To ascribe certainty to such claims would be preposterous. Since we can expect all politicians to dissemble in social situations we will need a careful reading of the historical record many years from now to build a more accurate account of such matters. But the congruence of the above ideas and the Bush administration's actions is certain. They created a positive climate for the war on Iraq by leading a public policy debate about American obligations and prerogatives in the new world order, and by lending respectability to the notion that the world's only superpower could and should use force before other alternatives were exhausted.

When he came to power, George W. Bush was a traditional conservative. At that time he did not accept the neocons' views. Like all presidential candidates he was essentially concerned with election strategy and the views of his opponents. He was fairly malleable, having few strong views on foreign and defence policy. George W. Bush is not a reader. Like his father he prefers to receive most information aurally, not by the written word.[39] New ideas are accepted only slowly. He came to power with only a rudimentary grasp of military affairs. He learned on the job from the ideas his staff and subordinates placed before him.[40]

Of course, as a Republican, he is a believer in traditional values – US ideals, the US Constitution, and belief that these values should be projected elsewhere. He is a traditional conservative who accepts that questions of global stability can be conveniently forgotten when it is in American interests. As he has put it, America is 'the greatest force for good in history'.[41]

There is a danger of too much conviction in politicians, and the new ideas adopted after 9/11 came from a near conversion. The neo-cons had an ideology but needed an accident of history to break free of the restraints on US power, and that happened with September 11. In fact, without the events of that momentous day it is fairly clear that George Bush would not have switched fully to the neocon position. In other words, 9/11 was useful in promoting the neocon ideas, in providing the Bush administration with justifications for its choices and certainly in providing a sense of urgency for its behaviour. As Bush put it, 9/11 'changed everything'. And, as William Kristol and Robert Kagan said, 'the road that leads to real security and peace … runs through Baghdad'.[42] Removing Saddam Hussein, they argued, would transform the political landscape of the Middle East. And so it has, but not in the way that they intended.

In the policy dispute over Iraq that took place among Bush's staff, the neoconservatives clearly won. Fear of terrorism provided a disposition for Bush to accept a war on Iraq, but it was not decisive. It was much easier to believe in the old idea of state-sponsored terrorism than the subversive suggestion that hatred for America could lead to terrorism. Thus, Bush accepted the neocon premise that the challenge of terrorism could be reduced by military means against the Iraqi state. Secretary of State Colin Powell argued for financial, legal, diplomatic and political actions but apparently not for war with Iraq. But on September 15 2003 at Camp David, Paul Wolfowitz made the case for taking military action against Iraq and won.[43] The doctrines of preventive war and permanent military supremacy became official US policy.

9/11 empowered the neocons. It also transformed Bush, and in his anger he accepted the need for American interventionism and declared a war on terrorism. It also led to his declaration in the State of the Union address on January 29 2002 that Iran, Iraq and North Korea constituted an 'axis of evil'. Bush shared with the neocons a bizarre mixture of idealism and realism: idealism in terms of the belief that the United States should help to spread democracy and liberalism, realism because of a tough or hawkish belief in the use of military power combined with a distrust of multilateral institutions such as the United Nations. Bush accepted the neoconservatives' assumption that the United States has unparalleled military strength, economic dominance and righteousness on its side.

Like the neocons, Bush has chosen a muscular strategy: act with allies when possible, act alone when necessary. He is a believer, with a near-messianic conviction, expressed in his often talked-about claim that 'you are either with us or you are with the terrorists', or worse, as in his implied assertion at the United Nations that, 'you are either with us or you are irrelevant'. Ideas often abhorrent to traditional conservative Republicans – intervention abroad, pre-emption, high government spending – have become acceptable in the war on terrorism. The marriage between George Bush's traditional conservatism and the more radical neo-cons resulted from a convergence of facts and convenience. The revolution in military affairs (RMA) had been supported by policymakers, such as Rumsfeld and Wolfowitz, and after 9/11 the administration used its combination of precision air power and agile ground forces to enforce global order, particularly in Afghanistan and Iraq.

George Bush came to office unfamiliar, like many Americans, with foreigners, world history and global geography. Even today, despite all the evidence and a number of official reports to the contrary, many Americans still believe Saddam Hussein was involved in or caused 9/11. But neocons are not so naïve. They are highly educated, sophisticated intellectuals who believe in a firm US security policy, particularly in the Middle East. The Iraq War represents a continuation of that philosophy. Bush shares with them the idea that the best way to prevent terrorist attacks is to stay on the offensive. Their shared fantasy is that establishing democracy in Iraq will have a domino affect and democratize the Islamic world. As one neocon had argued earlier, the fall of Baghdad would create in the Middle East a change that 'might prevent a future clash of civilizations'.[44]

Bush interprets the world through religious rather than ideological lenses. He has many allies in the Christian community. After 9/11, evangelists such as Franklin Graham, Jerry Falwell and Pat Robertson, who were already united behind the Bush administration, interpreted the attack as a war between Christians and the forces of evil. They claimed that the attack on Iraq was a 'just war', even though it was clearly a preventive action, and maintained that by aiding and harbouring terrorists Iraq had already attacked the United States.[45]

US determination to spread democracy to Iraq and the broader Middle East is not credible. Since there are twenty-two Arab states and none is even close to being free and democratic, this is a near impossibility. Moreover, Bush's dream is in contradiction to the march of events in that part of the world. America's reputation has evolved from a country admired by many in the Middle East for its democracy and anti-colonialism to one thought of today as an empire that supports authoritarian rulers (despite the lip service to the spread of democracy in the region), and aggressively pursues its economic interests, especially oil, and stations military units throughout the area. Realists may even argue that defending democracy may be a bad idea if it ignores other ideals and consequences – Pakistan, Egypt and Saudi Arabia are not democratic – but where would US policy be without their support on, say, terrorism?

Americans justify their wars in terms of values rather than sordid self-interest. But something must also be said about the importance of oil in the decision to go to war in Iraq. Oil does, indeed, play the central role today that coal played in the developed economies before the First World War. Without coal the industrial revolution would have been impossible in the form that it took; without oil it would not have been possible to spread that economic revolution around the world and produce the vast increase in wealth which has occurred since 1945. Virtually all means of transport depend on oil and it also generates much of the world's electricity. Were the oil supply to be seriously threatened, there would be a very good reason for all governments to be concerned and to do everything in their power to obviate the threat, including consideration of the use of military power. Cheap oil is the lifeblood of the American way of life – the means by which it is preserved. Even Democrat Jimmy Carter felt moved to claim in his 1980 State of the Union Address that

An attempt by any outside force to gain control of the Persian Gulf again will be regarded as an assault on the vital interests of the United States of America, and such an assault will be repelled by any means necessary, including military force.[46]

But it is a mistake to believe that access to oil has to be 'defended' by military force. The oil exporters want to sell oil at the highest price, though they are aware that, if they raise prices too much, they will cause a depression in the West, as they did in the 1970s, and thus cut consumption. Oil is useless unless it can be sold, and there is the ever-present danger that some technological breakthrough might reduce oil's significance, just as the importance of coal, water and wind power were previously diminished. Hydrogen power is constantly touted and the development of the fuel cell might make electric cars competitive. Thus, it may be unwise to place an unlimited belief in the conservation of oil for its future benefits.

Of course, this does not mean that the US administration did not think that it was vital to prevent Saddam Hussein from controlling Kuwaiti and, eventually, Saudi oil in 1991. What matters is not economic reality but rather what national leaders believe is essential to their nation's prosperity. The Japanese armed forces asserted it was essential for them to control China, Korea and other sources of raw materials and markets in the 1930s, though in fact raw-material exporters were desperate to sell their products and Japanese goods were so competitive they found no difficulty in securing markets. Moreover, even if we can dismiss the notion that Saddam Hussein would have cut off Western oil supplies, it is true that, had he controlled Kuwait, his wealth would have vastly increased and thus enhanced his ability to increase his military power and perhaps develop WMD. Such a near monopoly of oil supplies would also have created nervousness and thus instability in the market for oil.

It is always difficult to be certain about the motives for political action. What one can say with some confidence is that some people in the US administration believed in 2003 that it was vital to secure greater control over Iraqi oil, that Bush himself and his vice president, Dick Cheney, had been deeply involved in the oil industry and thus they needed no prompting to accept the centrality of oil for the United States. One can also assert that, in so far as securing oil was a prime motive, in the years after the invasion the administration's actions have had precisely the reverse effect. The insurgents have made it impossible to increase Iraqi oil production and thus have encouraged extreme price rises.[47]

After all the effort put into the war, Americans still have to face the fact that they consume one out of every four barrels of oil produced world-wide, while US reserves account for less than 2 per cent of the world's total. America's very way of life is increasingly tied to the politically unstable, increasingly hostile, energy-rich world of Islam.[48] It took little persuasion, therefore, for the United States to take advantage of 9/11 to use its military might to try to transform the entire area. It could not resist the opportunity to try to create a new political order in the region that would incorporate American values while also gaining primacy in the oil fields of Iraq. Left-wing critics will say that this was the only reason for the attack on Iraq. That would exaggerate its importance; however it certainly was one of the major reasons.

There are some who would contest the idea of linking ideas and policies, especially in the Bush administration. As Doonesbury put it, 'Bush doesn't think about anything – he just believes things so he's never conflicted by reality.' But politics is never so simple. The words and ideas that come out of President Bush's mouth *are* foreign policy.[49] The language of clashing civilizations, the concept of United States as empire, and the neoconservatives' rhetoric all underlie his convictions and actions. It is ironic that his messianic rhetoric about the need to spread democracy around the world parallels the corrosive rhetoric of Osama bin Laden and his call for world jihad.

## Notes

1 Alexis de Toqueville, *Democracy in America*, vols 1 and 2 (New York: Mentor, 1956 [1835, 1840]).

2 John J. Mearsheimer, *Tragedy of Great Power Politics* (New York: Norton, 2001); Stephen M. Walt, *Taming American Power: The Global Response to US Primacy* (New York: Norton, 2005).

3 Samuel P. Huntington, *The Clash of Civilizations and the Remaking of World Order* (London: Simon & Schuster, 1996).

4 Samuel Huntington, 'If Not Civilizations, What?', *Foreign Affairs* (November/December 1993), 187–94.

5 Amartya Sen, 'A World Not Neatly Divided', *New York Times*, 23 November 2001.

6 See Gustav Niebuhr, 'Muslim Group Moves to Meet Billy Graham's Son', *New York Times*, 20 November, 2001.

7 Arguments over the definition of empire persist. See Campbell Craig, 'American Realism Versus American Imperialism', *World Politics*, vol. 57, (2004) 141–71. There also remains the question of what is a hegemon. We follow the suggestion in Patrick Karl O'Brien and Almand Clesse (eds), *Two Hegemonies: Britain 1846–1914 and the United States 1941–2001* (Aldershot: Ashgate, 2002) that the United States is the sole example of geopolitical hegemony since the fall of Rome in that it can set conditions for peace and security of the world, has predominance in world economy, and manages security organizations such as NATO. See also Christopher Sandars, *America's Overseas Garrisons: The Leasehold Empire* (Oxford University Press, 2000) and Edward Thompson, *The Making of the Indian Princes* (London: Curzon Press, 1978).

8 Tony Judt, 'Dreams of Empire', *The New York Review of Books*, vol. 51, no. 17, 4 November 2004; found at www.nybooks.com/articles/17518

9 Cited in Niall Ferguson, 'Hegemony or Empire', *Foreign Affairs* (September/October 2003), 154–61, 155.

10 For a somewhat more positive treatment of the US as an empire see Dimitri K.Simes, 'America's Imperial Dilemma', *Foreign Affairs* (November/December 2003) 91–102.

11 Niall Ferguson, *Colossus: The Price of America's Empire* (New York: Penguin, 2004).

12 Brian Urquhart, 'World Order and Mr. Bush', *New York Review of Books*, vol. 50, no. 15, 9 October 2003, and Ted Widmer, 'The Lighter Side of Imperialism', reviews of *Colossus: The Price of America's Empire*; at www.powells.com/review

13 Robert D. Kaplan, *Imperial Grunts: The American Military on the Ground* (New York: Random House, 2005).

14 Michael Mandelbaum, *The Case for Goliath: How America Acts as the World's Government in the 21st Century* (New York: Public Affairs, 2005), p. xvi.

15   Michael Mann, *Incoherent Empire* (New York: Verso, 2003), and Benjamin R. Barber, *Fear's Empire: War, Terrorism and Democracy* (New York: Norton, 2003).

16   Andrew J. Bacevich, (ed.), *The Imperial Tense: Prospects and Problems of American Empire* (New York: Ivan R. Dee, 2002), and *The New American Militarism: How Americans are Seduced by War* (Oxford University Press, 2005).

17   Cited in Urquhart, 'World Order and Mr Bush'.

18   James Rubin, 'Base Motives', *The Guardian*, 8 May 2004; found at http://books. guardian.co.uk/review See also Christopher M. Gray, 'The costs of Empire', *Orbis* (Spring 2003) 7.

19   Chalmers Johnson, *Blowback: The Costs and Consequences of American Empire* (London: Little, Brown, 2000).

20   Chalmers Johnson, *The Sorrows of Empire: Militarism, Secrecy and the End of the Republic* (New York: Henry Holt, 2004).

21   Rubin, 'Base Motives'.

22   Emmanuel Todd, *After the Empire: The Breakdown of American Order* (New York: Columbia University Press, 2003), quoted in Gerald Horne, 'Book Review', *Political Affairs Magazine*; found at www.politicalaffairs.net/article

23   Rubin, 'Base Motives'.

24   John Willoughby, *Remaking the Conquering Heroes: The Postwar American Occupation of Germany* (New York: Palgrave, 2001).

25   Patrick J. Buchanan, *Where the Right Went Wrong* (New York: St Martin's Press, 2004).

26   Stefan Halper and Jonathan Clarke have splendidly demystified the neo-conservatives. See their *America Alone: The Neo-Conservatives and the Global Order* (Cambridge: Cambridge University Press, 2004), particularly pp. 40ff.

27   See, for example, Robert Kagan and William Kristol, 'Towards a Neo-Reaganite Foreign Policy', *Foreign Affairs* (July/August 1996), pp. 22–23.

28   Bacevich, *The New American Militarism*, p. 71.

29   Robert Kagan, *Paradise and Power: America and Europe in the New World Order* (London: Atlantic Books, 2003). Later Kagan somewhat adjusted his approach in 'America's Crisis of Legitimacy', *Foreign Affairs*, vol. 83, no. 2 (March/April 2004) 65–87.

30   Kagan, *Paradise*, p. 76.

31   Kagan, *Paradise*, p. 82.

32   *The Times*, 10 September 2005.

33   See the excellent analysis by Les Roberts, 'The Iraq War: Do Civilian Casualties Matter?', MIT Centre for International Studies (July 2005).

34   *New York Herald Tribune*, 19 September 2005.

35   *The Times*, 16 May 2003.

36   Robert Cooper, *The Breaking of Nations: Order and Chaos in the Twenty-First Century* (London: Atlantic Books, 2003).

37   William Shawcross, *Allies: The United States, Britain, Europe and the War in Iraq* (New York: Public Affairs, 2004).

38   David Frum and Richard Perle, *An End to Evil: How to Win the War on Terror* (New York: Random House, 2003).

39   For George Bush senior's literary leanings see George Bush, *All The Best: My Life in Letters and Other Writings* (New York: Scribner, 1999).

40   Bacevich, *The New American Militarism*, p. 148.

41  See Ivo H. Daalder and James M. Lindsay, *America Unbound: The Bush Revolution in Foreign Policy* (Washington: Brookings Institution, 2003).

42  Robert Kagan and William Kristol, 'Remember the Bush Doctrine', *Weekly Standard*, 15 April 2002.

43  Bob Woodward, *Bush at War* (New York: Simon & Schuster, 2002), pp. 83–4.

44  Victor Davis Hanson, 'Our Enemies, the Saudis', *Commentary* (July/August 2002).

45  'Washington Insight', *National Association of Evangelicals* (October 2002).

46  Cited in Bacevich, *The Imperial Tense*, p. 181.

47  'Petroleum Investments: Reality and Prospects', *Organisation of Arab Petroleum Exporting Countries, Monthly Bulletin* (July 2005).

48  *The Times*, 27 October 2004.

49  For the importance of language see Sandra Silberstein, *War of Words: Language, Politics and 9/11* (London: Routledge, 2002).

# 3
# The United States, Europe and the World

## From victim to pariah

Rarely has a superpower received more widespread, more genuine and more fervent tokens of support and sympathy than the United States did on September 12 2001. Rarely has the United States found itself more isolated, more disliked and more feared than it did in March 2003. It took a mere eighteen months for governments from Ottawa to Paris, from Wellington to Berlin, to distance themselves from Washington. In this they were merely reflecting domestic attitudes; many of the millions who took to the streets to protest against US policies toward Iraq in 2003 were the same people who had watched the events of 9/11 with horror and incomprehension.

The attack on that day shocked much of the world, just as its perpetrators hoped it would. It seemed more like a horror film thought up by Hollywood scriptwriters than a 'real' event; a villainous group, based in a poverty-stricken, land-locked country, planned to wound the only superpower and destroy the symbols of its wealth, power and prestige – the financial centre in New York, the Pentagon and the White House – and they did so by hijacking the emblems of globalization, Boeing jets, and ramming them, together with their hapless and terrified passengers, into the targets. It was filmed, like a Hollywood movie, and the scenes were transmitted instantly to television screens everywhere.

As the extent of the damage slowly became clear, thoughts turned to the consequences. Governments of all persuasions rushed to send their condolences to the United States and offer whatever help seemed appropriate; a day after the attack the UN Security Council passed resolution 1368 allowing the United States to use force against the attackers; NATO declared the terrorist actions an attack on all its member states under Article V of its founding treaty; President Putin of Russia insisted that the attackers must not go unpunished; and even the Afghanistan representative in Islamabad denounced the attack and denied that bin Laden and his followers were involved.[1] Newspapers spent days listing the victims and describing their backgrounds, interviewing their relatives and speculating on the nature of the terrorists and their motives. All other stories faded into insignificance.[2] And, as it became clear that al-Qaeda was responsible and that the Taliban government in Afghanistan would not hand bin Laden and his collaborators over to the United States, support around the world for military action against that land-locked country increased. Admittedly, Saudi Arabia and Iran refused the United States the use of military bases, but the key states of Pakistan, Uzbekistan, Kyrgistan and Tajikistan cooperated by permitting overflights or allowing US forces to be deployed there.

By the first week of October 2001, US and British aircraft were in action. At the same time their special forces assisted soldiers of the Northern Alliance who had been fighting the Taliban government in Afghanistan for years. At the end of October the United States began to focus its bombing attacks on the Taliban's front lines using massive fuel air explosives which flattened all buildings near the target zone. Many of these were guided to the Taliban by the laser designators of the special forces and, consequently, were all the more effective. Although they were originally weaker in numbers and equipment, the Northern Alliance began to move forward. Kabul fell on November 12, just over two months after 9/11. Bin Laden and some of his closest colleagues managed to escape but the regime which had protected them had been destroyed and its supporters scattered.[3]

There was controversy in the Western media about the civilian casualties being inflicted by the bombing, the danger of retaliation by victorious Northern Alliance forces on those who had supported the Taliban and the possibility that Muslims everywhere might see the war as a Christian crusade against their fellow Muslims.[4] But there was little opposition in the West to the war and fewer and less violent anti-Western demonstrations in Pakistan and the Middle East than many had predicted. The United States was careful not to cede operational control to NATO, but eventually Australia, Britain, Canada, France, Germany, Italy, Japan, New Zealand and Turkey sent ships or special forces to the region.[5] There was near unanimity in the West that Washington was acting within its rights to defend itself under the UN Charter, and much as it had to do as a superpower.

## The temptation of Iraq

If the United States had been satisfied to destroy the Taliban government, to set out to rebuild Afghanistan, to step up coordination with police and intelligence services everywhere against terrorist groups, and to lean on Muslim states whose charities supported al-Qaeda, then the pro-American coalition would have held together and Western leaders would have been impressed by President Bush's wisdom and resolve.[6] As the former British permanent representative to NATO put it immediately after 9/11, transatlantic solidarity against the terrorists 'would involve, for the United States a difficult act of self-restraint in order to mobilize a multilateral response'.[7] But there is always a temptation for leaders to 'push their luck', to take advantage of a momentary advantage or, in the strategic jargon, to 'go beyond the culminating point of victory'. This was particularly the case for George W. Bush because neither he nor a majority of the people of the United States were 'satisfied' with the fall of the Taliban. It was too easy a victory to dissipate their anger, and their urge to use their massive power was not assuaged. US casualties were negligible, and deaths and woundings among the Taliban were almost invisible to the US public because, given the nature of the war, they could not be filmed.[8]

Those who stood up against the American urge to wage a wider war, whether the French government or individual journalists and academics, met not with disagreement, but vilification. They became themselves the objects of displaced aggression because they were trying to stand between the United States and its intended victims. The extent of the emotion can be contrasted with US feelings in the 1960s towards the Western governments who refused to join in the Vietnam War and the academics and journalists who backed those governments' decisions. At that time, Lyndon Johnson's Washington was saddened but not infuriated by such rejection and condemnation.

Immediately after 9/11, Paul Wolfowitz and Donald Rumsfeld pressed Bush to use the opportunity to destroy Saddam Hussein's government in Iraq. Rumsfeld, in particular, protested that vilification of bin Laden made it more difficult for the United States to widen the war. He recognized that the destruction of the al-Qaeda leader would not be enough to satisfy the US people.[9] Saddam Hussein was a more substantial target because he had been attacked for years in the Western media. Modelling himself on Stalin, he had maintained power by killing or intimidating his opponents;[10] he had invaded Iran in September 1980, starting a war which lasted the best part of a decade and cost hundreds of thousands of lives;[11] he had seized Kuwait in August 1990 and, when he had been defeated, he had crushed the Shiites and Kurds who rose up against him. It was known that he had produced chemical weapons and used them in breach of international law against both the Iranians and the Kurdish villagers in Iraq who resisted his rule.

After Saddam's forces were thrown out of Kuwait in 1991, it was discovered that he had been illegally trying to produce biological and nuclear weapons. Under the agreement ending the war Iraq had promised to halt such programmes and to allow IAEA and UN inspectors to verify its actions.[12] But instead, it resisted inspection and, although the IAEA believed that the Iraqi nuclear programme had been ended, proof of this became much more difficult when inspections ceased in 1998. The only pressure which the United States and its allies could bring to bear was through the sanctions imposed on Iraq after its invasion of Kuwait, but these were slackened when their impact on the Iraqi people became ever clearer. Subsequently, Saddam Hussein used the money released by the agreed 'oil for food programme' to increase spending on palaces and other luxuries and to bribe UN and government officials around the world. He was a textbook villain, but he was also hostile to Islamic extremism and he succeeded in keeping the inherently fissiparous state of Iraq together and that was why, until his invasion of Kuwait, he had been regarded by Washington as preferable to his Islamist neighbours in Iran. His power and his defiance of the West also made him a hero to many Arabs.

Impelled by forces within US society, however, Bush began to listen to the suggestions by Rumsfeld and Wolfowitz that Saddam Hussein should be overthrown. Worse still, he announced in his State of the Union Address on January 29 2002 that Iraq, Iran and North Korea constituted an 'Axis of Evil' arming to threaten the peace of the world', thus hinting that an attack on one of these states would be followed by offensives against the others. The coalition that had supported the attack on Afghanistan dissolved as preparations for an attack on Iraq intensified.[13] The situation looked very different in Washington, the Middle East, Europe, Canada, China and Russia, Latin America, Australasia and South Asia, though the debate in one region had an impact on others. The administration played on American fears of terrorism, weapons of mass destruction and widespread anger at Saddam Hussein's defiance so successfully that popular support for the new policy remained strong in the homeland. Meanwhile, the threats to Iran and Iraq, together with the war in Afghanistan, led President Mubarak of Egypt to warn the United States, 'if you strike Iraq, and kill the people of Iraq while Palestinians are being killed by Israel ... not one Arab leader will be able to control the angry outbursts of the masses'.[14] Saudi spokesmen, representing one of America's closest allies, suggested that the United States, not Iraq, was threatening regional stability.[15] China and Latin America had long feared US hegemony and saw Washington's policy as further evidence of such tendencies; India and Pakistan were jockeying for Washington's support in their mutual struggle but neither could back such hegemonic ventures.[16]

It was in the West that the soul-searching was often longest and deepest.[17] It seemed hard and ungrateful to abandon the United States in its hour of need, and the three regimes labelled as partners in the 'axis of evil' appeared particularly unattractive. Many experts in the field believed that the United States was right to suspect Iraq and others of wanting to produce weapons of mass destruction and feared the use they would make of such horrific weapons.[18] But the majority of West Europeans, Australians and Canadians wanted war to be a last resort used only after all diplomatic and economic measures had failed to force Baghdad to prove that it had no WMD. Many could see no connection between Iraq and 9/11. Indeed sympathy for the Iraqi people had grown with their suffering.

There was also widespread suspicion in Western Europe of US Middle Eastern policy for being too sympathetic towards Israel. According to a poll published in May 2002, most French and Germans disapproved of US policies towards the region.[19] France had long regarded itself as the repository of wisdom on the Middle East, Germany was still burdened with its past and had only reluctantly used its forces for peacekeeping in former Yugoslavia, and Russia had gone along with the war on Afghanistan because of its own problems with Muslim fundamentalists, but none of these countries was prepared to support an attack on the *de facto* government of Iraq. Only 12 per cent of French people and 13 per cent of Germans believed the US should attack Iraq without UN authority and their governments were not going to support Security Council resolutions to that effect.[20] German Chancellor Schroeder declared, 'Under my leadership, Germany will not go to war with Iraq;' the French foreign minister, Dominique de Villepin, told the Americans, 'You cannot go out and do things alone.'[21]

On November 8 2002, after eight weeks of haggling, the United States and Britain managed to persuade the Security Council to support Resolution 1441 which declared Iraq to be in *material breach* of its obligations to disarm. Baghdad was warned that it would 'face serious consequences' if it refused to cooperate.[22] Washington and London were later to claim that this and earlier resolutions gave them the right to attack Iraq, if they were unsatisfied by Saddam's response; the French, Russians and Germans were to deny this. Ten days after the resolution, UN weapons inspectors returned to Iraq for the first time since 1998 but the director of the UN Inspection Commission, Hans Blix, still complained to the Security Council on December 19 about lack of Iraqi cooperation. By February 15

2003 Blix reported that, while cooperation had increased, he lacked evidence that the Iraqis had destroyed all their WMD and Colin Powell, the US secretary of state warned that the threat of force against Iraq had to remain in place.

Blix's account details the ensuing negotiations.[23] The French, the Germans, Canadians and others made clear that they continued to be hostile to war. The British searched for a compromise resolution in the Security Council which would list the precise actions Baghdad had to take to avoid a military strike. The US national security adviser, Condoleezza Rice, kept up the pressure by telephoning Blix to expound the US point of view. At the crucial March 7 meeting of the Security Council, Blix stressed that Iraqi cooperation had improved and some of its missiles had been destroyed, though he still lacked the documents on Iraqi disarmament which he would have liked. The French, Germans and Russians continued to argue that more time was needed for inspections, while Colin Powell expressed scepticism about the progress made. The British still appeared to be hoping that Iraq would make enough progress to satisfy Washington before the deadline.[24] But the United States was by this time set on war without further Security Council support. All through the negotiations US preparations for war continued. Already, on February 16 2002, senior US officials were briefing the press that the administration was determined to act.[25] On October 2 2002 Congress had passed a resolution authorizing the use of force against Iraq; troops, aircraft and ships poured into the region handicapped only by the refusal of the Turkish parliament to cooperate.

## The anti-Iraq coalition, 2003

The United States might have been totally alone, but Bush had two great strokes of luck. Many East Europeans harboured lingering fears of Russia, and the more assertive the United States, the more secure they felt in their belief that Washington would support them if they were threatened from the East. This was their most vital interest; the fate of Iraq was a sideshow. It was this support for the United States which led Rumsfeld on January 22 2003 to dismiss the French and Germans as 'old Europe' and to laud the newcomers to NATO from the former Eastern bloc.[26]

Bush's second lucky break was that in 1997 a Labour government had been elected in Britain after nearly two decades when the party had been in the wilderness. It was led by Tony Blair, a young, thrusting leader who was determined to move the party dramatically to the right. It abandoned the core of its earlier policies which had favoured nationalizing industry and increasing taxes. In foreign policy Blair stressed the need for a new and overtly 'ethical' policy while moving closer to both Europe and the United States. Blair and his colleagues wanted to crush the Tories by aping their policies, and their party members were so keen to be once again in power that they were careful to support Labour government policies on education, policing or immigration which they had devoted their youthful years to denouncing.

Had Labour been in opposition, its MPs would have lambasted US policies in lurid terms, but they were emasculated by their ambitions. In August 2002, 52 per cent of Labour voters opposed US policy on Iraq as against 35 per cent who were in favour but, by that stage Blair was already committed to following wherever Washington led. After 9/11 Blair made himself the spokesman and ambassador for the United States, circling the globe in support of the war on terror. Like the US president, Blair divided the world into good and evil; Milosevic had been evil, the Taliban had been evil, Kim Il Sung was evil and so, above all, was Saddam Hussein. The idea that each country has, to some extent, 'the government it deserves' because each government grows out of powerful elements in the society over which it rules was equally foreign to Bush and Blair. Hence their eventual consternation when they discovered that the arrival and continuation of their forces in Afghanistan and Iraq did not remotely meet with universal support in those countries.

Blair's backing for the attack on Iraq evoked more opposition in Britain than any war since Suez in 1956 or possibly the Boer War in 1899. There was the largest demonstration that there had ever been in London and the first full debate ever in the House of Lords on the legality of the decision to go to war. The majority of legal experts condemned the government's action, while its own legal advisers fled the debate. It was left to Baroness Ramsay of Cartvale to defend the government, to accuse her legal opponents of intellectual dishonesty and to denigrate all international lawyers. Rarely had the House been treated to such a breathtaking combination of arrogance, obscurantism and ignorance.[27] We now know that the attorney general, Lord Goldsmith, had warned two weeks before the war that it might be illegal and that the deputy legal adviser in the Foreign and Commonwealth Office resigned after describing the attack as a 'crime of aggression'.[28] No wonder Goldsmith avoided the Lords' debate so assiduously.

120 Labour MPs voted against going to war on February 26 and more threatened to do so, only to draw back for fear of toppling the government.[29] A number of retired diplomats including Sir Harold Walker, the former British Ambassador in Baghdad, Sir Patrick Wright, the former

head of the Diplomatic Service, Sir Brian Barder, Sir Alan Munro and Sir Nicholas Barrington had taken the unprecedented step over previous weeks of voicing their opposition publicly.[30] But Blair's luck held. For the first few months after the attack public opinion, which had been sceptical of a military offensive without UN support, rallied round the government and armed forces as soon as the fighting began.[31] And, since Saddam Hussein had been overthrown with relatively few allied casualties, it proved difficult for critics to argue that the war had been wholly bad, even if the government had to shift its ground and argue that, while no weapons of mass destruction or evidence of links with al-Qaeda had been found, there was plenty of evidence of the brutality with which the former ruler had maintained himself in power.[32] Meanwhile, Blair refused to apologize for his earlier mistakes and for months continued to maintain that there was still a possibility of finding WMD.[33] It was in July 2004 that, in his official report, Lord Butler exposed the flimsiness of the intelligence on which the decision to go to war had been based.[34]

In the meantime, the occupation of Iraq bogged down into fighting insurgency, and the fury of the US people abated as they comprehended where the administration had led them. But their attitudes may have doomed them psychologically after 9/11: inherently, many could not be satisfied until their forces had drawn blood and suffered casualties. In Britain, Labour's satisfaction with gaining office in 1997, combined with Blair's determination to bind Britain to the US chariot, prevented the US from being isolated internationally.

## Why Europeans often disagreed with the United States

While Europe and the United States have common interests, the Europeans no longer 'need' the United States as they did in the cold war years. They are no longer threatened by the massed tanks of the Warsaw Pact or by communist subversion. Indeed for years before 1990 many Europeans felt that the Soviet threat had been declining and, as it declined, so they became more critical of US policy. Many now believe that US policies towards the Muslim world threaten their own security, making them more of a target for al-Qaeda. Thus, while they were profoundly sympathetic to the United States immediately after 9/11, in the months that followed they drew opposite conclusions from the event and the transatlantic gap widened.

To some extent these European attitudes are, as neocons such as Robert Kagan have argued, a consequence of the difference between the military power which Washington can wield and that possessed by the Europeans.[35] When provoked, the United States had the option of crushing the Taliban in Afghanistan *and* Saddam Hussein's government in Iraq. If either had harboured terrorists who attacked a European state it is most unlikely that the Europeans would have responded by trying to overthrow the government of the attacker. They might well have retaliated with economic and diplomatic pressure, or even with a bombing attack, but they would not have invaded.

This is not, as sometimes suggested, because Europeans are more pacifically minded than Americans; in 1990 the British were much more supportive than the Americans of a war against Baghdad because they believed it was right to liberate Kuwait from Iraqi forces. If the Europeans were more hesitant about upsetting the governments of Afghanistan and Iraq after 9/11, it was because of their historical experiences. The Belgians, British, Dutch, French, Germans, Portuguese and Spanish all had non-European colonies in the nineteenth century and all came to doubt their right and competence to dominate such peoples. They also doubted their mandate and ability to convert the subject peoples to a foreign way of life and government. Even so, they left behind legal and political systems fashioned on their own models. In India, Malaysia and Singapore the former colonial peoples were able to modify these to suit their own cultures, so that their systems of government still have recognizable Western features. More often, however, the European implants were swept away by military coups, civil wars or reversion to traditional forms of control.

Of course the United States had a similar experience in the Philippines after taking the islands from Spain. Its armies had to fight a prolonged and dirty guerrilla campaign to overcome resistance there, and by the 1930s it had already decided that it would liberate its colony. In South Vietnam, when the United States took over from the French as the main supporter of the right-wing government in the late 1950s, its presence evoked such bitter nationalistic as well as communist hostility that it was compelled to withdraw its forces in 1973 and to abandon its embassy in Saigon two years later. This humiliating reversal affected US politics for almost two decades, but Americans did not lose their belief that the United States had a right, and perhaps even a duty, to direct other states onto the democratic–capitalist path. It was simply its *ability* to do so which came into question. Moreover, as we will see below, the Vietnam War proved the exception to a string of US victories, whereas the Europeans looked back on successive defeats and disasters. History taught the Europeans caution; it left the Americans confident that they knew how the world could and should be governed.

The United States has often pursued the most idealistic goals to great effect. In its idealistic mood, it helped to found the League of Nations and the United Nations, and to establish international tribunals for war crimes at Nuremberg, Tokyo and the Hague. It also encouraged the growth of the Common Market and subsequent European Union, even though it knew this would become an economic and, potentially, a strategic competitor. Yet, to win the cold war, it crushed left-wing governments in Latin America and tried to assassinate hostile foreign leaders.[36] After 9/11 the contrast between liberal ends and brutal methods became pronounced. The administration wanted to impose democracy unilaterally on the world and insisted that the international institutions, which it had helped to found, were feeble and multilateral organizations slow and inefficient.

## The growth of US military power

The temptation to adopt this view after 9/11 was all the greater because the United States had such immense military power. Its conventional forces were not just stronger than those of the next most powerful countries: they were stronger than all the other major states combined. The gap widened when the cornucopia was opened to the US military after 9/11, giving them a vast array of new weapons. Today the most 'usable' forms of long-range, conventional military power are cruise missiles, large, long-range transport aircraft and bombers, precision guided munitions (PGMs), stealth aircraft and aircraft carriers. Together these enable their possessors to intervene far from their own shores, and the United States alone has them in great abundance. Of all the countries in the world, land-locked Afghanistan was perhaps the most 'secure' from US attack, yet, as we have seen, in the autumn of 2001 Washington was able to bomb it and encourage an uprising which, within a few weeks, overthrew the government. In every aspect of high technology warfare the United States is a decade or more ahead of its rivals. Of course, technological breakthroughs might negate or reduce the US lead, but, for the moment, there are no signs of such major changes and the PGM revolution is still working to the US advantage.

George Bush argued in June 2002:

As we defend the peace, we also have an historic opportunity to preserve the peace. We have our best chance since the rise of the nation state in the seventeenth century to build a world where the great powers compete in peace instead of prepare for war ... America has, and intends to keep, military strengths beyond challenge – thereby, making the destabilizing arms races of other eras pointless, and limiting rivalries to trade and other pursuits of peace.[37]

This forecast might be true, as far as conventional weapons are concerned, if people everywhere accepted US power as beneficial. But they do not and it defies common sense and experience to believe that they would. Instead, many feel, as one of Blair's former Ministers put it, that 'the biggest political problem in the world is the overwhelming power of the US'.[38] Bush's comments sound uncannily similar to the sort made a century ago by German spokesmen and they have had the same consequences in terms of alienating the international community. As Count von Balestrem put it while celebrating the Kaiser's birthday on 27 January 1906:

> We must be strong if we are to suppress all those who would like to disturb the peace. In any case the powers will take care not to move if they know they will be beaten by the first army in the world and a fleet which is increasing every day.[39]

Just as Kaiser Wilhelm's Germany built up its armed forces, so the United States poured money into defence in 2003 and 2004, making a mockery of Bush's claim that US hegemony would avoid arms races. According to the International Institute for Strategic Studies in London, the United States spent $1,391 per head on defence in 2003, the Russians $455, the European NATO members $426, the Chinese $43 and the Indians $15. Between 2001 and 2003, US defence spending rose from 3 per cent of GDP to 3.7 per cent and from $305,500 million to $404,920 million, nearly twice as much as all NATO members in Europe, and US expenditure is expected to grow to $508,150 million in 2009, quite possibly exceeding the whole of the rest of the world put together.[40]

Even before 9/11 the United States had begun to use its power more actively as it became aware of how significantly the restraints had disappeared since the collapse of the Soviet Union in 1990. The trajectory of its policy is clear. In January 1968 at the low point of US strength during the Vietnam War, Washington did not retaliate when North Korea seized its intelligence vessel, the *Pueblo*, in international waters and kept the crew hostage for eleven months. In 1990 it hesitated to use force to expel Iraqi troops from Kuwait, and the ensuing war was always less popular there than it was in Britain. But in 1995 the United States overcame the reluctance of its European allies to use air power against the Serbs, and bombed Serb forces to compel them to come to the negotiating table at

Dayton. In 1999 it bombed Serbia itself to force Milosevic to halt the ethnic cleansing of the inhabitants of Kosovo, and in 2003 it bombed the Taliban forces in Afghanistan. All of these actions had moral justification, even if the legal basis of the attack on Serbia was cloudy to say the least. But the restraints declined with each use of force. The US public had come to see such actions as routine even before 9/11, while the Europeans had become steadily more cautious; in other words, during the course of the decade attitudes to the initiation of warfare on the two sides of the Atlantic had been reversed.

## The end of the balance of power?

When a superpower adopts strongly unilateralist policies, it encourages others to follow suit. Thus, for example, if it adopts a policy of waging preventive wars, other states may do the same. Such behaviour also provokes fear and, consequently, distrust among foreign governments so that the whole international atmosphere deteriorates. This has been the scenario on a number of occasions in the past. To take a major example, when Germany adopted a preventive war strategy in the 1860s, all other states had to mobilize their forces as quickly as possible in a crisis, thus making every incident of this sort more tense and unstable. Furthermore, after Wilhelm II became Kaiser, he spent heavily on his army and navy, and his militaristic and unpredictable initiatives drove Russia, France and Britain into an entente against his country. To insist that international affairs are ruled by force and fear, and that anyone who disagrees is an unrealistic idealist, is thus to create a world in which all states rightly look to their safety.

Statesmen and commentators traditionally were thus only too well aware of the temptations which power gives to governments and peoples. Herbert Butterfield encapsulated this in his 1949 essay, *Christianity and History*, where he pointed out that

> It was clearly understood in [the past] ... that if you placed a great power in a position to act with impunity over a considerable part of Europe, then though it had been righteous hitherto – kept on the rails by the general balance of the world and by its calculations of what was prudent – it would now become an unrighteous power. Either it would be dazzled by new vistas of temptation or it would be desperately nervous to find itself the object of general suspicion.[41]

Unfortunately, as Max Beloff pointed out two decades later, 'the balance of power is not, in the mid-twentieth century, a phrase likely to arouse the enthusiasm of an enlightened public'.[42] Thus, when the Soviet Union collapsed and the United States became the sole super-power, Western publics did not immediately realize the temptations which the new imbalance would provide. Euphoria over the end of the cold war, and the general belief that the United States would be restrained in the use of its forces by its own public, masked the real and present danger of the temptations of power – a danger for the United States itself almost as much as for other states.

Given the history of international relations, and particularly of imperi-alism, it is hardly surprising that citizens of smaller states feel safer when there is a balance of power. But it is remarkable today, so overwhelming is US dominance, that this is the case even among America's allies. Inter-national relations theorists have often argued that smaller allies act like jackals, waiting for their great power ally to destroy the enemy and then joining in the exploitation of the spoils. European companies would, indeed, have been happy to participate in programmes for the reconstruc-tion of Iraq, had order been restored after March 2003, but European publics would have been ashamed to see these economic benefits as a justification for the war.

In spite of the constraints which make weaker states dependent on their great-power allies, the governments of several weak states were pre-pared to risk their economic and political interests by refusing to sup-port the 2003 war against Iraq. New Zealand and Chile opposed the war even though they were in the middle of free-trade negotiations with the United States. Chilean President Ricardo Lagos explained later that 'it is not only a question of ethics, but in this kind of world that is global, you are going to need some kind of rule of law ... And the only way is by the United Nations and the multilateral institutions.'[43] Turkey's refusal to allow US forces to launch attacks on Iraq from their territory was particu-larly galling because it threw US plans into disarray. The United States had expected compliance since it had long supported Turkey's position on entry into the European Union. Washington subsequently 'pun-ished' Turkey by reducing or ending contact between the Pentagon and the Turkish armed forces.[44]

What can the United States do to reduce the natural popular antag-onism and fear which its power evokes in other countries? The Americans could cloak their raw strength within international organizations; after all, even within states we try to hide power by, for example, making judges wear wigs. But the Bush administration has done the opposite. It spares no opportunity to disparage the United Nations and similar bod-ies. Of course, strong states feel that international law and institutions

are unnecessary constraints on their actions, but in the long run all benefit from such institutions. Bush told Bob Woodward that his unilateralism would not matter if US actions were successful:

> Action – confident action that will yield positive results provides kind
> of a slipstream into which reluctant nations and leaders can get behind
> and show themselves that there has been – you know, something
> positive has happened towards peace.[45]

Unfortunately, this is not what has occurred in Iraq.

## The United States' unipolar moment

US attitudes towards state power have always oscillated wildly – sometimes supporting international measures to limit aggression, but on other
occasions vehemently rejecting any constraints on their own power.
During the Napoleonic Wars and the First World War, the United States
strongly protested against British and French measures to restrict neutral
trade, yet they themselves imposed even tougher measures against neu-
trals when they joined the war in 1917. At the end of that war, US
President Woodrow Wilson was one of the staunchest supporters of the
newly-formed League of Nations, yet it was the US Senate which undermined the organization by refusing to ratify the treaty. In recent years, it
was the United States which revived war crimes trials to deal with human
rights abuses during the collapse of Yugoslavia, but now the United States
refuses to accept the International Criminal Court that would make such
trials a permanent feature of the international scene. In many ways it was
the United States which alerted the world to the threat to the environment, yet now the United States leads the opposition to the Kyoto Protocol.
For much of early US history successive administrations rejected 'entangling alliances', yet during the cold war their successors formed more
alliances than perhaps any state in history.

While Bill Clinton was president, he was able to expand NATO into
Eastern Europe, and broker peace agreements in Bosnia and Northern
Ireland without creating hostility and resentment. But George Bush has
given the impression that America's allies are obliged to follow its lead,
whether that leadership is wise or foolish. Thus he has refused to apologize to allies, even on those occasions when US policy has been clearly
in the wrong. For example, the administration made no attempt to apologize for feeding the United Nations false information over Iraq's possession of weapons of mass destruction. It remained hostile to France

throughout 2004 even though the French position on the war with Iraq had been vindicated. Donald Rumsfeld, Bush's defence secretary, believed that by expanding US power he could force the Europeans, Chinese and Russians to conform and to accept US dominance. However, given the intense distaste for US power which has manifested itself, it is more likely that the Chinese and Russians are simply abiding their time before challenging US political hegemony.

By its aggressive stance since 9/11, the United States has encouraged foreign publics to forget the occasions when it has played the role of stabilizer and intermediary on the international scene. It was Washington which encouraged the Indians and Pakistanis to draw back when they seemed to be on the brink of war after the terrorist attack on the Indian parliament in December 2001.[46] It is Washington which reins in the Taiwanese when they provoke Beijing by threatening to declare independence. It was US officials who coerced the Serbs and Bosnians to compromise at the Dayton peace conference.[47] It is the United States which has made the most effort to find a settlement between the Palestinians and Israelis.

In none of these cases were US interests directly at stake except in the general sense that it benefits from peace. Rather, the United States tried to moderate the hostile moves of other states whose interests were directly involved. Problems arise when Washington is a prime-mover in a crisis because its supreme power gives it the ability to dismiss all intermediaries and moderating influences with contempt. There is thus a startling contrast between the cautious and diplomatic US efforts in New Delhi or Taipei, and US policy under George W. Bush towards Pyongyang, Baghdad or Teheran. We have, of course, seen such contrasts before. In Europe in the nineteenth century, a weak Britain generally played the role of cautious balancer. However outside Europe, with no state to balance its own power, it expanded its frontiers aggressively until they bumped up against the Russian or French Empires, or against local guerrillas in Afghanistan or Southern Africa strong enough to raise the cost of conquest. Since 9/11 US leaders have allowed themselves to be tempted into making the same mistakes and the military and economic consequences will be with us for years to come.

In 1988 Yale University historian Paul Kennedy published *The Rise and Fall of the Great Powers*, causing a stir in the United States and elsewhere with its claim that great powers normally decline because they overextend their strength. He argued that

> The United States runs the risk, so familiar to historians of the rise
> and fall of previous Great Powers, of what might roughly be called

'imperial overstretch'; that is to say, decisionmakers in Washington must face the awkward and enduring fact that the sum total of the United States' global interests and obligations is nowadays far larger than the country's power to defend them all simultaneously.[48]

Kennedy's publication date was well chosen to create a stir, but badly chosen from the point of view of prophecy because the United States was just coming into its own as the centre of a unipolar system. However the imperial overstretch, against which Kennedy warned, has grown under George W. Bush. As Kennedy pointed out:

> The growing foreign challenges to this position have compelled [former great powers] to allocate more of their resources into the military sector, which in turn squeezes out productive investment and, over time, leads to the downward spiral of slower growth, heavier taxes, deepening domestic splits over spending priorities, and a weakening capacity to bear the burdens of defence.[49]

Every one of these forecasts has proven accurate. The war in Iraq costs the United States far more than the Bush administration predicted. In July 2002 the costs were being projected by the Pentagon at $80 billion.[50] By January 2005 Bush was seeking more billions for the campaigns in Afghanistan and Iraq, thus bringing the costs to $280 billion since 9/11, an increase of 250 per cent. Some commentators claimed that, taking inflation into account, this amounted to half the cost for the United States of the First World War or the Vietnam War.[51] The federal US budget deficit of £220 billion in 2004 and the balance of payments deficits led to a rapid decline in the value of the dollar in 2004. Even then, many US industries have remained uncompetitive. In the circumstances, the Chinese, with an economy which grew at 8% in 2002 and 9.1% in 2003, will have simply to maintain their progress and national unity for long enough to be able to ally with the other malcontents who object in principle to external interference in a country's affairs to balance US power within their regions.[52]

Europeans do not want to see such a development.[53] They demonstrated their sympathies with the US people after 9/11. Most of them will remember what they were doing when they saw the ghastly television pictures of flames engulfing the Twin Towers and people jumping from the doomed buildings, just as they remember what they were doing when the Berlin Wall was destroyed. But the impact of 9/11 was subtly different in Europe from the United States. Older people remembered the Second World War and knew that the scale of the destruction then in Warsaw,

Hamburg, Leningrad, Coventry or Dresden was vastly greater than the suffering in Washington and New York. As well, the Europeans have been habituated to terrorist attacks; the Germans have suffered from Baader–Meinhof, the Italians from the Red Brigades, the Spanish from ETA and the British from the IRA. While no single attack from these groups was as destructive as 9/11, the British had, for, example, lost more people in the war against the IRA and the attacks had killed Prince Philip's uncle and come near to killing their prime minister on a number of occasions.

It was not simply the tragedy of 9/11 which shocked the United States. Its people could stoically accept losses; it was the insult to their pride that an attack could have come from such an apparently insignificant source which galvanized them into action. When Hurricane Katrina hit New Orleans in 2005, it was feared for a while that tens of thousands might have died. Yet Vice President Cheney continued with his holiday, Condoleezza Rice, the national security adviser, went to a Broadway show and President Bush could barely stir himself into action. The contrast with the immediate response to 9/11 was dramatic and deeply shocking to many foreigners but it demonstrated that it was the type of tragedy which mattered, not just its extent.[54]

Western Europeans generally welcomed the accumulation of power by the United States during the cold war because of fear of the Soviet Union. The US image was all the more favourable because the United States was not only the arsenal of all the allied countries in the Second World War but itself provided almost all the manpower in the Pacific and much of it in Western Europe and North Africa. In a study published during the period, pollsters asked people to choose adjectives to describe foreigners; despite their recent defeat and occupation, the Germans chose the most favourable terms for the Americans, calling them progressive, generous, practical, intelligent, peace-loving and hardworking. In contrast, they described the Russians as cruel, backward, hardworking, domineering, brave and practical, and the British as intelligent, self-controlled, conceited, domineering, practical and progressive.[55]

But the positive image of the United States has dimmed as its power has grown since the collapse of the Soviet Union. Presidents Roosevelt, Truman, Eisenhower and Kennedy were heroes to much of the European public, unlike Johnson, Nixon, Reagan, Clinton and the two Bush presidents. Carter alone of recent presidents was widely admired in Europe in the same way as his pre-1963 predecessors, perhaps because he seemed both engaged with the world and tormented by its problems.

Nevertheless, Europeans have much more in common with the United States than with any of its potential enemies. For more than half a century they have benefited from NATO and other transatlantic organizations.

West Europeans may be less aware of this than the Poles, Romanians and Bulgarians (who have seen only too much of the alternatives), but they understand that America protected the West from the Soviets and that Western European countries continue to spend less than the United States on defence. Sheltering behind NATO, they have overcome the bitter Franco-German antagonisms of the past. Even now their peoples have no ambition to rival US defence spending. Against whom would such spending be directed except the United States itself? They could easily defeat Russian conventional forces now that the Soviet Union has collapsed and, if the Islamists represent a threat, it is not of a conventional military nature. Those Americans who grumble about the inadequacy of European defence spending have to explain why the Europeans need to spend much more than they have done since the end of the cold war.

What Europeans want is an administration in Washington which acts as leader of a coalition, which appears to give courteous consideration to arguments from even the smallest of its allies, which fosters international organizations, which submits its soldiers to tribunals if they are accused of war crimes, and which pays attention to the threat of global warming. If or when a balance of power begins to re-emerge with the economic decline of the United States and the rise of the Asiatic powers, Washington will need European support. The United States will also regret that it did not foster an international system based on rules rather than raw power. It may not need international law now but it will do as its eclipse accelerates and as the Asian giants increasingly challenge it in international affairs. It also needs national leaders like Franklin Roosevelt, Harry Truman and Dwight Eisenhower, who can earn the admiration and affection of the European peoples. But by then the bases of power may have shifted away from the United States and it may be too late.

As we will show in the next chapters, the United States already has a number of major challenges to meet, including Islamist terrorism and the rise of China. Washington needs to deal with these without succumbing either to the temptation of preventive war or to infringing its own democratic, legal traditions, embroiling itself in demoralizing anti-guerrilla wars in the Third World or proclaiming lofty ideals while practising devious and transparent realpolitik.

## Notes

1   See, for example, 'La Nouvelle Guerre', *Le Figaro*, 12 September 2001.
2   See 'The Face of Hate' in the Friday Review of *The Independent*, 14 September 2003, and the photographs of the dead on the front of *The Times*, 15 September 2001.
3   *Strategic Survey 2001/2001*, pp. 229ff.

4  *The Times*, 29 September 2001, 3 July 2002 and 29 October 2001.

5  *The Times*, 7 November 2005.

6  *The Times*, 20 and 25 September 2001.

7  Sir John Goulden letter to *The Times*, 18 September 2001.

8  See Michael Ignatieff, *Virtual War: Kosovo and Beyond* (London: Chatto & Windus, 2002), for the importance of the media in modern warfare.

9  Bob Woodward, *Bush at War* (New York: Simon & Schuster, 2002), p. 81; Richard A. Clarke, *Against All Enemies: Inside America's War on Terror* (New York: Free Press, 2004), pp. 33–34.

10  Kanan Makiya, *Cruelty and Silence* (London: Jonathan Cape, 2003).

11  *Strategic Survey 1983–1984*, p. 76.

12  Philip Towle, *Enforced Disarmament from the Napoleonic Campaigns to the Gulf War* (Oxford: Clarendon, 1997).

13  Sifry, Micah and Cerf, Christopher, *The Iraq War Reader: History, Documents, Opinions* (New York: Touchstone Books, 2003), p. 250; there was also friction over duties in Afghanistan, see 'Europeans Chafe at "Picking up the Pieces" after US', *Financial Times*, 21 February 2002.

14  *The Times*, 28 August 2002.

15  *Los Angeles Times*, 22 September 2002; see also *The Times*, 30 July 2002.

16  *The Hindu*, 26 January and 20 March 2003.

17  *The Times*, 30 April, 11 June and 8 August 2002.

18  Richard Butler, *Saddam Defiant: The Threat of Weapons of Mass Destruction, and the Crisis of Global Security* (London: Weidenfeld & Nicolson, 2000).

19  *The Times*, 21 May 2003.

20  *The Times*, 30 January 2003; *The Guardian*, 11 February 2003.

21  See also *The Times*, 1 May 2002.

22  *The Times*, 8 April 2002.

23  *The Times*, 15 February 2003; Hans Blix, *Disarming Iraq* (New York: Pantheon, 2004), p. 177.

24  Blix, *Disarming Iraq*, p. 245.

25  *The Times*, 16 February 2002.

26  *Strategic Survey 2003–4* (London: IISS/Oxford University Press, 2004), p. 105.

27  *Parliamentary Debates (Hansard), House of Lords*, 17 March 2003.

28  *The Guardian*, 23 February 2005.

29  *The Times*, 27 February 2003; *The Guardian*, 27 February 2003.

30  Letters to *The Times*, 20 February and 16 April 2002; 26 February and 17 March 2003.

31  MORI, 'Ratings for Blair and IDS rise in the first weekend of the war', 28 March 2003, http://www.mori.com/polls/2003/t030324.shtml; 'End of the Baghdad Bounce', 8 June 2003, http://www.mori.com/polls/2003/t030528. shtml

32  For later polling figures see *The Times*, 17 September 2004 and *The Times*, 9 February 2005.

33  Simon Jenkins, 'Why Blair Can't Issue the Mother of All Apologies', *The Times*, 9 July 2003.

34  *Review of Weapons of Mass Destruction: Report of a Committee of Privy Councillors*, HC 898 (London: Stationery Office, 2004).

35  Robert Kagan, *Paradise and Power: America and Europe in the New World Order* (London: Atlantic Books, 2003).

36  John Ranelagh, *Agency: The Rise and Decline of the CIA* (London: Weidenfeld & Nicolson, 1986).

37  Sifry and Cerf, *The Iraq War Reader*, p. 270.

38  'World's Biggest Problem Is the US, Says Meacher', *The Times*, 20 June 2003. Michael Meacher had served for six years as Minister for the Environment.

39  Quoted in Maurice Paleologue, *The Turning Point: Three Critical Years* (London: Hutchinson, 1935), p. 320.

40  *Military Balance 2004–2005* (London: IISS/Oxford University Press, 2004), pp. 262 and 353.

41  Herbert Butterfield, *Christianity and History* (London: George Bell, 1949), p. 32.

42  Max Beloff, *The Balance of Power* (London: George Allen & Unwin, 1968), p. 3.

43  'Global World Needs Rule of Law', *The Hindu*, 30 January 2005.

44  'Turkish Media Project – US and the Middle East', 9 June 2005, Middle East Media Research Institute.

45  Woodward, *Bush at War*, p. 341.

46  *The Times*, 31 December 2001; *The Hindu*, 2 June 2002.

47  Richard Holbrooke, *To End a War* (New York: Random House, 1998).

48  Paul Kennedy, *The Rise and Fall of the Great Powers* (London: Unwin Hyman, 1988), p. 515.

49  Kennedy, *Rise and Fall*, p. 533.

50  *The Times*, 31 July 2002.

51  *The Times*, 26 January 2005.

52  *Military Balance 2004–2005*, p. 322.

53  'US Image Up Slightly, but Still Negative', Pew Global Attitudes Project (23 June 2005), 3.

54  'The Shaming of America', *The Economist*, 10 September 2005.

55  William Buchanan and Hadley Cantril, *How Nations See Each Other: A Study in Public Opinion* (Urbana: University of Illinois Press, 1953).

# 4
# New Challenges to US Hegemony: China and the Muslim World

International relations are in some ways like a pentathlon in which competitors can rival each other in different types of events. The United States predominates in almost every competition from finance to air power, from diplomatic influence to nuclear weapons, and from its all-pervasive media to its ubiquitous warships. Of course it has weaknesses; as explained elsewhere in this book, its armed forces have never excelled at counter-insurgency and its constant budget and balance of payments deficits make it dependent on foreign investors. But, unlike the participants in the pentathlon, states and other agents do not have to compete in every event; they can pick the game at which they are most adept. It was not surprising that al-Qaeda challenged the United States by using terrorism; this is the one area where an actor, however weak, can attack a hated enemy, however strong.[1] In retrospect what is more surprising is that only rarely has an insurgent movement struggling against a Western state resorted to attacks on the latter's homeland. Upton Close from the University of Washington noted in 1926: 'there is not the bud, thus far, of an offensive against the white man in his own countries'. And there were only isolated incidents over subsequent decades. For example, Uddham Singh hunted down the British officer he held responsible for the massacre of 379 Indians at Amritsar in 1919 and murdered him at a public meeting in London in 1940. Singh is still a hero to many in South Asia but his example has rarely been followed.[2] The publicity given to 9/11 will ensure that changes.

Communism once presented the Western world with profound ideological as well as military challenges. Some Westerners believed that the communist world represented a superior way of life. Traitors within Western governments even supplied the potential enemy with confidential information. The West had to live with the problem, improve its

Intelligence services and vet applications for official positions. Now the communist threat has evaporated and been replaced by that of Islamist ideology. It is to this challenge and the revival of an old problem in the shape of China that this chapter will turn.

Over the next decades these two issues will confront US administrations with what seem likely to be two of their most serious external political and security problems. In time other states, such as India, will follow China's example because of their vast and industrious populations. China now presents the traditional difficulties of adjustment which rising powers thrust before the dominant one. Germany's growing strength forced Britain to adapt its policies before the First World War and the United States compelled it to change its priorities afterwards.[3] Inevitably such periods of change and accommodation are also ages of friction and uncertainty but, as the Anglo-American example demonstrates, they do not necessarily lead to violent conflict. The Islamist movement presents the West with a non-military, ideological problem, which has already led to the disaster of 9/11 and to a series of other bloody incidents including the planting of bombs on commuter trains in Madrid and London. Just as China will have to be treated with great diplomatic skill, if growing tension is to be avoided, so the Muslim world will have to be handled with considerable tact if the seizure of the US Embassy in Iran, the Salman Rushdie affair and 9/11 are not to be harbingers of yet more extreme violence and greater challenges to the international order. We look first at the way the West gradually adapted to the challenge of communist China and then at the Islamist problem to show the diplomatic and political methods which are going to be needed.

## The challenge from China

It took more than twenty years after the communists had seized power in Beijing in 1949 before they and the authorities in Washington made a major effort to understand each other and come to terms. In 1972 they found a common interest in resisting what each saw as a threat from Moscow. Once they had begun to discuss their differences, they started to see what they had missed through all the years of hostility. Today their continued disagreements over Taiwan, trade and human rights should not be underestimated, even though it is clear that over the last three decades both Washington and Beijing have striven to avoid confrontation and to minimize tensions.

In contrast, the early history of US relations with the Chinese communists was characterized by lack of patience and understanding on both sides. In part this was a consequence of US support for the Kuomintang against the communists in the Chinese civil war. It was easy for the communists to forget that such support was always half-hearted and that Washington had made extensive efforts to persuade both sides to compromise over their differences.[4] The failure of this diplomacy and the communist victory soured relations, but it was the advance of UN forces in Korea towards the Chinese frontier in the autumn of 1950 that perpetuated the hostility for the next decades. What Washington saw as a reasonable measure to eradicate the North Korean communists, who had invaded South Korea, Beijing regarded as a threat to its security and responded by intervening on a massive scale. Washington and Beijing had no direct diplomatic links in the 1950s and 1960s, and there was a series of crises which could easily have exploded into total wars.[5]

When French forces were besieged at Dien Bien Phu by Vietnamese guerrillas in 1954, the US chiefs of staff considered threatening China because it was regarded as the source of communist aggression. It was left to President Eisenhower and Prime Minister Churchill to try to lower the tensions. Eisenhower pointed out that US intervention against China would lead, in turn, to Soviet involvement and the outbreak of a world war.[6] Churchill admitted that Indochina might fall but he did not foresee any threat to Japan, Australia or the rest of South-East Asia. Vice President Nixon, one of the leading 'hawks', expressed himself as 'astonished that Churchill, who had understood the communist problem so well in 1946, could have made this statement'.[7] The following year a crisis over Taiwan brought the United States 'closer to using atomic weapons than at any other time in the Eisenhower administration' according to the president's biographer.[8] A further Taiwanese crisis broke out in August 1958 and the administration again considered using tactical nuclear weapons against Chinese airfields.[9] It was small wonder that the two sides viewed each other with hostility and that, in Henry Kissinger's words, 'US policymakers considered China as a brooding, chaotic, fanatical and alien realm difficult to understand and impossible to sway', while the Chinese, on their side, believed the United States saw Indochina as a springboard for aggression against themselves.[10] China's reputation for fanaticism increased in the 1960s with the cruel and bizarre Cultural Revolution when Mao encouraged young extremists to attack established officials and teachers, to humiliate the People's Liberation Army, to destroy historic monuments and to tyrannize over the general population.[11]

Sino-US relations changed abruptly and dramatically after President Nixon's epochal visit to Beijing in February 1972. Washington saw an opportunity to compensate for the economic and military weakness caused by the Vietnam War if it established relations with Beijing. At the same time, the Chinese wanted a counterweight to what Kissinger called 'the relentless Soviet military build-up in the Far East'.[12] The visit showed the futility of the previous Western policy which had isolated China, making it more paranoid and xenophobic. In contrast to his earlier attitude, Nixon now told the Chinese:

> There is no reason for us to be enemies. Neither of us seeks the territory of the other; neither of us seeks domination over the other; neither of us seeks to stretch out our hands and rule the world.[13]

It is probable that all the excesses of the Great Leap Forward, the Hundred Flowers and the Cultural Revolution would have occurred in any case, leading to the death of millions of innocent Chinese. But the hostility of the West encouraged Maoist extremism; his latest biographers have, for example, argued that it was the rush to produce nuclear weapons and so deter the West that led to the mass famines of the 1950s.[14] Moreover the ideas, current in the West in the late 1940s and 1950s, that the Chinese were successfully propagating guerrilla movements in Malaya, Indochina and Africa were baseless. When such wars broke out, it was primarily because of local factors, and because guerrilla leaders such as Ho Chi Minh in Vietnam were at loggerheads with Beijing, or isolated like Chin Peng in Malaya.

Nixon made important concessions during his visit to Beijing to appease Chinese views over Taiwan. Above all, the United States acknowledged:

> That all Chinese on either side of the Taiwan Strait maintain that there is but one China and that Taiwan is part of China. The United States does not challenge that position. It reaffirms its interest in a peaceful settlement of the Taiwan question by the Chinese themselves.[15]

Nixon was impressed by China's power and determination, and commented in his memoirs:

> We must cultivate China during the next decades while it is still learning to develop its national strength and potential. Otherwise we will one day be confronted with the most formidable enemy that has ever existed in the history of the world.[16]

In other words, apart from its concerns about Soviet strength, the United States was now being deterred by Chinese power – actual or potential.[17] Subsequent US presidents have tried to follow Nixon's advice but progress has been uneven. In the mid-1970s the Nixon administration was weakened by the Watergate scandal, and the Chinese government by Mao's decline, the temporary rise of the 'Gang of Four' and Chinese suspicion of US–Soviet detente.

It was not until 1979 that, following Deng Xiaoping's visit to Washington, President Carter formally recognized Beijing and broke off diplomatic relations with Taiwan.[18] The United States began to withdraw its forces from the island but it continued to provide enough arms to deter a Chinese attack. Beijing was particularly sensitive when Ronald Reagan was elected president because of his long-standing and vocal anti-communism and the way in which he continued to treat the Taiwanese as official representatives. Reagan's first secretary of state, General Alexander Haig, recalled later that he felt the president's hardline view of China was the most important issue separating them and one of the key factors in his resignation.[19] In this atmosphere the Chinese threatened in 1982 to break off diplomatic relations unless arms sales to Taiwan were ended, but Reagan's second secretary of state, George Schultz, refused to give way under pressure. Eventually, a compromise was reached under which the United States agreed to reduce sales gradually and the Chinese promised not to attack Taiwan.[20]

Over the next years, the Straits problem was, paradoxically, exacerbated by Taiwanese achievements. Taiwan not only became one of the most successful capitalist countries with a GDP per head of over $14,000 in 2000,[21] but it also established a proud and stable democracy. The electors chose the leader of the Democratic Progressive Party (DPP), Chen Shui-bian, over the ruling party, the KMT, in March 2000 because Chen's party wanted to push as far as possible towards the formal independence which Beijing had always denied. Subsequently the DPP has oscillated between moderate statements to placate the mainland and nationalistic assertions of Taiwanese individuality.[22]

At the same time, their own greater freedom encouraged the mainland Chinese people to become ever more demonstrative in their determination to prevent their government allowing Taiwan to 'secede'. Officials tell Western visitors that it would be impossible for a government to survive in Beijing if it permitted this to occur. There has been a prolonged debate in the West about whether states can accept that one of their provinces, which is determined to break away – as Quebec might become in Canada or Scotland in Britain – could be prevented by force.[23] Thus the Netherlands and Belgium divided in 1830, Norway and Sweden in 1905 and the Czechs and Slovaks went their own ways after the end of the cold war, an event that reached its culmination with the relatively peaceful disintegration of the Soviet Union. On the other hand, the Americans fought their bloodiest war to ensure that the Confederate States could not secede in the 1860s, and Serbia tried to dominate the remains of Yugoslavia by force in the 1990s. China is hardly, therefore, unique in attempting to maintain its territorial integrity by military means and repressing what it sees as secessionist activities in Tibet and the predominantly Muslim areas of its territories, just as it threatens war should Taiwan make a formal declaration of independence.

The hope must be that peace between Taiwan and China will be preserved until the two societies find some loose form of confederation which would satisfy both sides. Alternatively, the Chinese could eventually adopt a *laissez-faire* attitude, but unfortunately, this is a distant prospect; China was so traumatized and humiliated by Western attacks on its integrity in the nineteenth century and by Japanese assaults in the twentieth that its nationalism is particularly determined and forceful. As its strength increases so do its pride and nationalism, and these increases will continue to be the main source of tension between Beijing and Washington. On the other hand, the United States needs to keep on good terms with Beijing, not least because of the damage which confrontation could do to the international economy. China represented some 3.2 per cent of global output in 1980 and 13.6 per cent in 2005. Nearly a quarter of world economic growth in 2004 took place in China and a large proportion of the US debt is in Chinese hands, giving China the largest foreign exchange reserves in the world by October 2005. Thus it is not so surprising that, when US aircraft inadvertently bombed the Chinese Embassy in Belgrade during the war against Serbia over Kosovo, Secretary of State, Madeleine Albright took the unprecedented step of going to the Chinese Embassy in Washington in the middle of the night to apologize to the ambassador.[24]

US interests in maintaining good terms with Beijing have to be balanced against sympathy for the Taiwanese. Washington could not allow a long-time friend and a democracy of 22 million people to be crushed by a nation of over 1000 million without loss of credibility. On its side, China has been deterred from attempting an invasion of what it sees as a breakaway province by the strength of Taiwan and by the difficulty of staging an attack without first gaining command of the sea and air. It is also rightly nervous that the United States would intervene to help the Taiwanese and of the devastating impact on the world economy to which even major friction between Taiwan and China would give rise. But the US stance on the issue bewilders most Chinese; they cannot believe that US sentiment towards Taipei determines its policy; they do not understand the Western belief in allowing peoples to choose their own fate, particularly given recent events in Afghanistan and Iraq. Chinese leaders often maintain that US policy towards Taiwan is determined by some deep Machiavellian plot to subvert their society.

Such paranoia is enhanced by spasmodic US support for human rights within China. The issue was particularly critical in May 1989 when thousands of pro-democracy student activists congregated in Tiananmen Square in Beijing, apparently inspired by Mikhail Gorbachev's reforms in the Soviet Union. The students were joined by workers from the area who were also demanding democratic rights. For a while the students and workers could not be forcibly dispersed without great embarrassment because of the meeting of the Asian Development Bank in Beijing and the Sino-Soviet summit. The emboldened demonstrators began to demand the resignation of Prime Minister Li Peng and even of the leader Deng Xiaoping.[25] On May 20 the government declared martial law and on the night of June 3/4 the army moved in and cleared the square, killing at least some hundreds and possibly thousands of demonstrators. Western leaders, including George Bush Senior, responded by introducing economic sanctions and condemning the repression but, in contrast to the cold war years, they left the door open to rapprochement and maintained contacts. They had learned that isolating China was counter-productive. President Bush wrote apologetically to Deng:

> As you know, the clamour for stronger action remains intense. I have resisted the clamour, making clear that I did not want to see destroyed this relationship that you and I have worked hard to build. I explained to the American people that I did not want to unfairly burden the Chinese people through economic sanctions ... Any clemency that could be shown the student demonstrators would be applauded worldwide.[26]

The conclusion is a general one that can be applied to the Muslim world as much as the Chinese. The initial reaction when one group encounters an apparently hostile state or people is to respond in an equally hostile fashion. Incidents between the two groups exacerbate tensions and misunderstandings. Thus, while relations between the United States and China have improved over the last decades, relations between the West and the Muslim world have become increasingly strained. It is these countries which now appear 'brooding, chaotic, fanatical and alien', to echo Henry Kissinger's words. Moreover, it will take even more tact to moderate this hostility than the United States has displayed towards

China over the last thirty years because tension with China was felt largely at the state level in the early years, whereas friction between the Muslim world and the West is today largely between peoples.

## The Muslim challenge

It would have been easy after 9/11 for the Bush administration to fall into the trap of condemning the Muslim world as a whole. All of those involved in the attacks were Muslims and most came from Saudi Arabia, which is the centre of the Muslim faith and has been America's closest ally in the region. They represented a minority Muslim movement whose members openly loathe the West and its mores, and want to weaken and subvert all major Western institutions. The danger was that this movement would be taken as representative of the general Muslim attitude, not least because attacks on the West by Islamists had been increasing since the overthrow of the Shah of Iran in 1979. That Islamist revolution was followed by the Iranian decision to hold US Embassy officials hostage in breach of centuries-old diplomatic protocol and by vitriolic diatribes against the West in general and the United States in particular. Nothing similar had been heard since the Cultural Revolution in China.

Nevertheless, after 9/11 the Bush administration wisely tried to avoid appearing hostile to Muslim peoples and denied that its subsequent attacks on Afghanistan and Iraq, its increased surveillance of Muslims within the West, and its confrontation with Iran over Teheran's alleged nuclear weapons programme, were motivated by hostility to Muslim peoples or their religion. Unfortunately, however, Washington's actions were interpreted this way by many Muslims, including a majority who were not Islamists, because most of those targeted by the United State were, in fact, their co-religionists.[27] While the Bush administration gave reasons for its attack on Afghanistan and its measures to protect the security of the homeland which satisfied many moderate Muslims, its explanation for the invasion of Iraq in March 2003 was much less convincing.

Furthermore, the White House claimed that the overthrow of the Iraqi government was part of a long-term plan to help move the Muslim countries of the Middle East towards democracy, the hypothesis being that the Arab peoples wanted to be democratic and 'Western' – they were just waiting to overthrow their reactionary governments which were preventing modernization and economic growth. But, as Bernard Lewis has pointed out, it is precisely this modernization and economic change which have disorientated some Muslims and alienated them from the West.[28] Islamist terrorists have often lived in the West and been educated in its colleges; like their leader bin Laden, they have become alienated by Western society. The more they have come to know about secularism and modernization, the more they have been repulsed. Perhaps modernization and democratization are, in the long run, inevitable, but, if so, they will bring a very long period of upheaval across the Middle East before stable democratic governments are established there. And such governments will not be imposed by outside powers.

However one may explain the phenomenon, it is undeniable that the Muslim world has been resistant to the forces of modernity. It was the president of Pakistan, General Musharraf, who told his fellow Muslims in February 2002: 'Today we are the poorest, the most illiterate, the most backward, the most unhealthy, the most unenlightened and the weakest of all the human race.'[29] Similarly, it was a Pakistani journalist who in July 2003 claimed that fewer than 16 per cent of Muslim-majority states were democratic, while, so he added, in the non-Muslim world 80 per cent of all UN members had established democratic political systems. He continued: 'Within the Organization of the Islamic Conference, there is little or no social justice, no political reform and no meaningful social progress. The entire OIC is overwhelmed by social, political and economic ills.'[30]

The writer believed that democracy was entirely compatible with the Muslim religion but, plainly, many Muslim states have found democratic transition very difficult.

Thus a ferocious debate is under way in the Muslim world between such reformers and the Islamists. Among the modernizers, the Egyptian writer Sayyid Al-Qimni has argued that all Muslims share some responsibility for terrorism:

> When we let terrorism grow and flourish, when we allowed Islamist thought to infiltrate our media and schools … [t]he virus thrived when we allowed the current of hatred to be directed against the very interests of the people, when we charged the souls with the current hatred for the advanced Western countries to the point where our peoples now hate everything associated with the West – even freedom, dignity and democracy – instead of hating those Islamic sheikhs and armed militias who have dragged our honour in the mud for the whole world to see … Proper education and teaching create an individual who loves life, – not one who hates life and thus destroys himself and others – The universities have forgotten their role as the

primary place for scientific research, that is, to examine the country's ills, whether in medicine or in the field of culture, in order to fight against them – The universities have abandoned their field of expertise and assumed the role of the mosque.[31]

His last point about Muslim universities is particularly ironic because many scholars believe that the idea of the university originated in the Muslim world.[32] Conversely, the traditionalists argue that the West is trying to destroy Muslim societies and therefore that its ideas should be utterly rejected. When the Kuwaiti parliament finally agreed in May 2005 to allow women to vote and run for office, one conservative MP argued that 'According to Islamic jurisprudence, the woman has no political rights'. He went on: 'By pressurising the Arab and Gulf countries, the Western countries are trying to impose the violation of Islamic law in order to ruin society.'[33] Another MP argued: 'We must pay no attention to the external demands that call on us to give women political rights. They must know that the situation of women in Kuwait is better than their situation in the advanced democratic countries.' Such comments reflect the sensitivity of these issues and the anger which pressure to conform to Western standards and behaviour arouses among Muslim conservatives.

When hostility to the West's intentions and behaviour is increasing and Islamism spreading, openly fomenting democratic revolutions across a wide swath of the Muslim world is bound to enhance the anger and paranoia. Former Malaysian Prime Minister Mahathir Mohamed told the Islamic Conference of Muslim leaders on October 16 2003:

Today we, the whole Muslim ummah, are treated with contempt and dishonour. Our religion is denigrated. Our holy places desecrated. Our countries are occupied. Our people are starved and killed. None of our countries are truly independent. We are under pressure to conform to our oppressors' wishes about how we should behave, how we should govern our lands, how we should think even … There is a feeling of hopelessness among Muslim countries and their people. They feel that they can do nothing right. They believe things can only get worse. The Muslims will forever be oppressed and dominated by the Europeans and Jews.[34]

Rarely has a national leader expressed so comprehensively and passionately the frustrations felt by many of his people and their anger against those who criticize their way of life and beliefs. Of course, his view would also be regarded as at most a half-truth to a good many other

Muslims because it assumes a homogeneity of feeling which is imagined rather than real. As the battle between the modernizers and the Islamists demonstrates, Muslim societies have to find a variety of ways to reconcile their religion with contemporary problems.[35] Apolitical Muslims frequently protest against the tendency to assume that the most radical and politicized are also the best representatives of their faith or that particular organizations represent all Muslims. As one British Muslim pointed out, 'the only Muslims who are consulted are those who choose to drag Islam into the political sphere and relate it to issues such as the Israeli–Palestinian conflict'.[36]

Nevertheless, it is clear that the Muslim world is involved in a tumultuous struggle between modernity and conservatism equivalent in some ways to the sixteenth-century Reformation in Europe and the centuries of change which followed. When the Reformation began Europeans assumed, as many Muslims do today, that religion ruled every sphere of life. By the time it ended:

> Religion had been converted from the keystone which holds together the social edifice into one department within it ... To the most representative minds of the Reformation as of the Middle Ages, a philosophy which treated the transactions of commerce and the institutions of society as indifferent to religion would have appeared, not merely morally reprehensible, but intellectually absurd ... By their successors in the eighteenth century the philosophy of Indifferentism ... is held in practice as a truism which it is irrational, if not actually immoral, to question ... Thus the conflict between religion and those natural economic ambitions, which the thought of an earlier age had regarded with suspicion, is suspended by a truce which divides the life of mankind between them.[37]

It is easy to forget both the violence which this process engendered in Europe over the decades and the length of time which it took to become fully effective.

R.H. Tawney, the British historian quoted above on the interaction between religion and capitalism, wrote of the 'storm and fury of the Puritan revolution'. Such storms and furies are likely to be greater in the Muslim world than they were in Europe because modernization is associated by the Islamists with the alien and arrogant West rather than with indigenous, and therefore marginally more acceptable, changes within Muslim states. How much more would many Western ancestors have resented secularization had it come from the Muslim world or from the

Incas of Peru? Second, the dominance of the news media by the West has encouraged the adoption of conspiracy theories in the Muslim world that attempt to identify 'the real truth' behind the Western version of events.[38] Thus an Egyptian historian, Professor Zaynab Abd Al-Aziz, could solemnly tell Saudi Iqra Television on May 26 2005 that the Second Vatican Council in 1965 had set out to impose Christianity on the whole world, that the struggle had been delegated to the United States by the World Council of Churches and that the Bush administration had deliberately destroyed the Twin Towers on 9/11 as part of the plan, making sure that 4000 Jews had absented themselves from their places of employment in the buildings on the grounds that they were ill.[39]

Paranoid claims of this sort, fear of Western power and the pressure on the Muslim world to change mean that for the next decades Muslim politics are likely to continue to be tormented. Some will resent 'Westernization' and their polities will be subject to paroxysms of violence. The reaction against modernization was brilliantly evoked by the West Indian writer V.S. Naipaul in his 1981 account of travels through Iran, Pakistan, Malaysia and Indonesia. Many of those he encountered could hardly find words to express the anguish and disorientation they were feeling, the comfort which relying entirely on the Koran for guidance brought them and the hopelessness which they felt about their countries. Many hated the West for its godlessness, its tolerance of immorality and its materialism. At the same time, they tried desperately to leave their own countries to gain education, prosperity and security among the foreigners whom they denigrated and despised. The discovery that Osama bin Laden himself had in 1995 applied for asylum in Britain underlined the point admirably.[40]

Over the coming decades, the West will be blamed by the Islamists for the problems and torments which afflict the Muslim world. It was criticized for sending troops into the Muslim world to protect Kuwait in 1991, at the same time that it was criticized for not helping the Kurdish and Shiite rising against Saddam Hussein. In the future, it will be blamed for supporting Arab leaders by meeting them and arming them, and for not assisting them adequately because it has not given them enough arms or listened carefully enough to their views; for trading with the Muslim world and for not importing enough of its goods; for spreading the culture of Hollywood and CNN even though there is little Western governments can do to inhibit this process. It will be criticized for articles published in Western journals that express outrage for punishments laid down in the Koran and at the enforcement of dress codes in Muslim states. It will be attacked for propagating contraception and for not doing enough to combat poverty in the Third World.

Oil exacerbates the problem because many Arab Muslims believe that the West plunders their raw materials and that this was, for example, the prime motive for the Iraq War in March 2003. They also see that, unless the technology changes dramatically and demand for oil subsides, the rest of the world will become increasingly dependent upon the Middle East for oil over the next decades. According to the Organization of Arab Petroleum Exporting Countries, 60% of proven reserves lie in the region and these will last for another 85 years at current production levels. Europe will become even more dependent on the area as its own production is in decline, while the United States will remain vulnerable because it is more dependent than the Europeans on oil fuel.[41] The combination of Western dependence and Arab resentment is without historical parallel and is potentially highly destabilizing.

In the past Western peoples and their leaders expected to coexist with the Muslim countries. Indeed they hardly noticed that they were Muslim until the overthrow of the Shah of Iran by Ayatollah Khomeini in 1979, the fatwah against Salman Rushdie in February 1989 and the attacks on the Twin Towers on 9/11. The West was religion-blind, but the Muslim world was not. The more the Muslim world adopts Koranic codes and rejects secularization, the more the two civilizations will denigrate each other, just as the Chinese Red Guards denigrated capitalism and democracy in the 1960s. The more the two worlds know about each other, the more the hostility between them will increase. V.S. Naipaul's visit to 'the believers' did not turn him into an admirer of their way of life. On the contrary, he was appalled by the rage of political Islam.[42] Western peoples ignore punishments inflicted in Muslim countries because they do not know much about them, but they will know more. When a film of public hangings in Iran was smuggled to the West in June 2005, it evoked outrage. But that was precisely the sort of reaction which former Malaysian Prime Minister Mahathir would characterize as an arrogant attempt to tell Muslims how they must think and how they must run their countries.[43] Conversely, Muslim peoples know of Western encouragement of contraception, and tolerance of pornography, abortion and homosexuality. They deprecate the breakdown of Western family life and the denigration of religion in the Western media. The gap between these two 'civilizations' is much greater than that between the communist world and the West during the cold war. It is growing and will grow wider.

Before the nineteenth century, wave after wave of European invaders broke over Asian society, spreading Western culture, economics and political control. In the twentieth century this process was halted; Japan resisted through its industrialization and growing conventional strength, China resisted through boycotts of Western goods and then through Maoist insurgencies, India resisted primarily through Gandhi's non-violent actions. Today the resistance is expressed through Islamist terrorism. When a clash between societies is accompanied by basic disagreement over values, it is more intense and the outcome is liable to be all the more violent.

At the start of the cold war there was a prolonged argument between the doyen of American newspaper columnists Walter Lippmann and the then young diplomat and writer George Kennan who was serving in Moscow. Kennan argued that the United States had to concentrate on improving its own society, containing the communist world and waiting for change to come from within it. Lippmann doubted whether the United States had the resources and determination to contain Soviet expansionism for the decade and a half which he predicted was necessary. We can now see that Kennan was right to insist that the West had the stamina to coexist and compete with the communist world; in fact it managed such coexistence for half a century until communism disintegrated of its own failings.[44]

There are many distinctions between the present situation and the cold war. Plainly the Muslim world has far deeper historical roots than the communist world had in the twentieth century; the confrontation between East and West was often military and the outcome was determined by whether democratic capitalism or communist dictatorship could provide more prosperity for their peoples. The outcome of the present confrontation will be decided by much more complex factors. Over the next century the West will have to demonstrate more patience and tolerance when dealing with the Muslim world than it showed when dealing with communism. Then it was deterred by the danger of nuclear war from intervening openly inside the communist countries, even when they broke into rebellion against Moscow, as Hungary did in 1956 and Czechoslovakia in 1968. Instead it intervened covertly through abortive intelligence operations and, much more successfully, through radio propaganda. Now it must practise more restraint when dealing with Muslim countries if it is not to provoke terrorist attacks on Western societies. The threat of terrorism is the weapon of the weak, just as the Soviet nuclear force was the weapon of the strong, but terrorist attacks are far more likely, partly because they are more difficult for

Western governments to deter. We need to find substitutes for deterrence and containment which will be equally appropriate over the coming decades for dealing with the Muslim world.

Western peoples are realistic about the prospects; 72% of Britons told pollsters in April 2004 that they were expecting a terrorist attack. And in July 2005 the first attacks, and attempted attacks duly came.[45] What was most disturbing for British people was that the suicide bomb attacks on London trains and buses were mounted by four British-born Muslims, three of them from Leeds, and that none of them appeared to have a police record or even a reputation for extreme hostility to Western society. In fact three, at least, had travelled to Pakistan and they had probably been planning the explosions for a very long time. In reaction to the bombing there were a number of attacks in Britain on mosques, and columnists reported hostility growing towards Muslims.[46] There was also a widespread feeling that police powers for arresting suspects should be increased. 88 per cent were in favour of tighter controls at ports and airports; 89 per cent called, unrealistically, for baggage checks at train and bus stations.[47]

During the cold war, Western governments were criticized from the right for not doing enough to subvert and confront communism, and from the left by those who believed that Soviet society was superior to its Western counterpart. There were, however, very few occasions when the disputants actually came to blows or used violence against each other. Today we have already witnessed numerous violent episodes between the Muslim communities living in the West and the host communities.[48] An independent committee set up to look into the problem in Britain reported in June 2004:

> The cumulative effect of Islamophobia's various features ... is that Muslims are made to feel that they do not truly belong here ... On the contrary they are seen as 'an enemy within' or a 'fifth column' and they feel that they are under constant siege.[49]

The problem is certainly not confined to Britain.[50] Nevertheless, moderate Muslims have pointed out that their co-religionists have been allowed to do many things in the West which are prohibited to Christians in the Muslim world and that the West has shown forbearance in the face of Islamist terrorism:

> As a result of these actions ... millions of the new generation of Muslims in Europe have become a source of fear and anxiety for decisionmakers

in European countries ... In their extremism [the fundamentalists] are preventing the new generation of Muslims from internalizing the principles of freedom and enlightenment that have existed in European societies for over a century.[51]

Over the next decades Western governments will continually face occasions when foreign Muslim terrorists attack their cities or their people abroad,[52] when Muslims living in their own societies are caught planning or carrying out terrorist actions, when local Muslims murder politicians because they believe they are hostile to their religion,[53] when Muslim clerics preach hatred of Western society in mosques within the West, when Muslim countries stoke the hostility of Western media because of their persecution of Christian minorities, the severity of their punishments or the dictatorial nature of their governments. These occasions are going to evoke strong public demands on governments to reduce liberty within the West and to intervene with military forces in Muslim countries even though such interference will be ineffective and provoke more hatred.

As in the cold war, the West has already had to increase expenditure on intelligence services – services which are likely to be much more useful over the next decades than the accumulation of vast conventional forces which are of limited relevance to meeting the threats and which can sap Western economies. Governments in the United States, Britain and other countries have already taken unprecedented measures to meet the new difficulties even though they have had to reduce the fundamental freedoms of their people in order to do so. They have also discriminated against Muslims, or have seemed to have been doing so. As a Pakistani columnist pointed out:

> Post 9/11 people with Muslim identities have been targeted and screened, more on the basis of racial and religious association with the 'bad guys' than because of anything they might have done. This is not just perception but reality.[54]

Another commentator from the same country quoted reports from the Council on American–Islamic Relations listing the occasions when Muslim passengers had been mistreated by US immigration or prevented from boarding airliners because, so they were told, other passengers were 'not comfortable travelling with Middle Eastern men'.[55] Obviously Western governments are in danger of further alienating Muslim minorities living in the West as well as those who simply wish to travel from their countries on legitimate business.

The Muslim world, like the communist world during the cold war but for different reasons, will have to be left to work out its own destiny. In the end the Russian and East European peoples saw not only that Western society was becoming richer but that the 'Asian Tigers' were also overtaking them. As a result, communism lost the support of its people and rotted from within. It will be up to Muslim peoples whether they choose democratic capitalism or some modification of that form of society, or whether they prefer to insulate themselves to the maximum extent possible from the outside world. In the meantime, we should remind ourselves that the desire to protect one's culture and religion is not ignoble. It is, rather, the methods which the Islamists have chosen to use which are ignoble and threaten to create conflicts between religions and peoples.

George Kennan argued in 1948 that the West would be victorious in the cold war if

> The United States can create among the peoples of the world generally the impression of a country which knows what it wants, which is coping successfully with the problems of its internal life and with the responsibilities of a world power, and which has a spiritual vitality capable of holding its own among the major ideological currents of the time.[56]

The competition between the communist world and the West was often frightening, but it compelled Western people to look at their own societies afresh; were communist criticisms of the gap between rich and poor fair? Had the Soviets really found a way of developing their economies more quickly? Were Soviet educational and health systems preferable to their Western equivalents?[57] The friction between the West and the Muslim world could be equally profitable if it persuades Western societies to look again at their own deficiencies. Eventually the Muslim world will find a *modus vivendi* with many aspects of modernity as it has done in the past. The West has to have the patience to wait and the empathy to understand the attitudes of other peoples.

The challenges from China and other powerful countries represent the continuation of issues related to the traditional security dilemma while those of the Muslim world represent genuinely new types of problems. The United States and the West in general will need to be very astute to handle the difficult combination of challenges. Recent actions of the US administration, especially in Iraq, do not inspire confidence. Perhaps future administrations will possess the wisdom to avoid the temptations and confront the global necessities of the twenty-first century without a knee-jerk retort to militarism.

## Notes

1  *Quadrennial Defence Review Report* (Washington: US Department of Defense, September 2001), p. 5.
2  Upton Close, *The Revolt of Asia: The End of the White Man's World* Dominance (New York: Putnam's, 1927, p. 321; Alfred Draper, *The Amritsar Massacre: Twilight of the Raj* (London: Buchan & Enright, 1985); Rajni Bakshi, 'Resurrection of a Patriot?' *The Hindu*, 23 January 2000.
3  Aaron L. Friedberg, 'Britain and the Experience of Relative Decline, 1895–1905', *Journal of Strategic Studies* (September 1987); Correlli Barnett, *The Collapse of British Power* (Gloucester: Alan Sutton, 1987), pp. 254–6.
4  Dean Acheson, *Present at the Creation: My Years in the State Department* (London: Hamish Hamilton, 1970), p. 209.
5  Harry S. Truman, *The Truman Memoirs: Years of Trial and Hope*, vol. 2 (London: Hodder & Stoughton, 1956), p. 410.
6  Stephen E. Ambrose, *Eisenhower The President 1952–1969* (London: George Allen & Unwin, 1984), pp. 205–6.
7  Richard Nixon, *The Memoirs of Richard Nixon* (London: Sidgwick & Jackson, 1978), p. 152.
8  Ambrose, *Eisenhower*, p. 231.
9  Ambrose, *Eisenhower*, p. 483.
10  Henry Kissinger, *The White House Years* (London: Weidenfeld & Nicolson, 1979), p. 685.
11  Gordon A. Bennett and Ronald N. Montaperto, *Red Guard: The Political Biography of Dai Hsiao-Ai* (London: George Allen & Unwin, 1971); and Ken Ling, *Red Guard: Schoolboy to Little General in Mao's China* (London: Macdonald, 1972).
12  Nixon also said he was influenced by General de Gaulle; see Richard Nixon, *1999: Victory Without War* (London: Sidgwick & Jackson, 1988), p. 244. Kissinger saw the problem in terms of the balance of power: *White House*, pp. 685–8 and 693.
13  Nixon, *Memoirs*, p. 566.
14  Jung Chang and Jon Halliday, *Mao: The Unknown Story* (London: Jonathan Cape, 2005), p. 415.
15  Nixon, *Memoirs*, p. 576.
16  Nixon, *Memoirs*, p. 577.
17  Nixon, *1999*, pp. 244–45.
18  Zbigniew Brzezinski, *Power and Principle: Memoirs of The National Security Adviser 1977–81* (London: Weidenfeld & Nicolson, 1983), ch. 11.
19  Alexander Haig, *Caveat: Realism, Reagan and Foreign Policy* (London: Weidenfeld & Nicolson, 1984), p. 195.
20  George P. Schultz, *Turmoil and Triumph: Diplomacy, Power and the Victory of the American Idea* (New York: Scribner, 1993), ch. 22.
21  *Military Balance 2002–2003*, p. 301.
22  *East Asia Strategic Review 2001* (Tokyo: National Institute for Defense Studies, 2001), p. 2003; *East Asia Strategic Review 2003*, p. 194.

23   See Robert and Doreen Jackson, *Politics in Canada* (Toronto: Prentice-Hall, 2005).

24   Madeleine Albright, *Madam Secretary: A Memoir* (London: Macmillan, 2003), pp. 417–18.

25   *Strategic Survey 1989–1990*, pp. 126–8.

26   George Bush, *All the Best: My Life in Letters and Other Writings* (New York: Lisa Drew/Scribner, 1999), p. 430.

27   The editorial in the *Friday Times* (Lahore) (15–21 July 2005) even managed to see Bosnia as an example of Western imperialism alongside Afghanistan, even though the West protected Muslims in Bosnia; see '9/11 and Now 7/7'.

28   Bernard Lewis, *The Crisis of Modern Islam: Holy War and Unholy Terror* (London: Weidenfeld & Nicolson, 2003), p. 103.

29   *The Times*, 18 February 2002.

30   Farrukh Saleem, 'Islam and Democracy', *Friday Times*, 25–31 July 2003.

31   'Special Dispatch – Egypt/Reform Project', 13 June 2005, Middle East Media Research Institute.

32   William Dalrymple, 'The Truth about Muslims', *New York Review of Books* (4 November 2004).

33   'The Public Debate on the New Amendment Granting Kuwaiti Women Political Rights', Middle East Media Research Institute, 24 June 2005.

34   *The 9/11 Commission Report: Final Report of the National Commission on Terrorist Attacks upon the United State* (New York: Norton, 2004), p. 562.

35   Virginia Hooker and Amin Saikal, *Islamic Perspectives on the New Millennium* (Singapore, Institute of Southeast Asian Studies, 2004).

36   Letter from Ibrahim Sargin, 'Social Integration of British Muslims', *The Times*, 19 August 2005.

37   R.H. Tawney, *Religion and the Rise of Capitalism* (Harmondsworth: Penguin 1961), pp. 273–4.

38   For the attractions of conspiracy theories, see Daniel Pipes, *Conspiracy: How the Paranoid Style Flourishes and Where it Comes From* (New York: Free Press, 1997).

39   'Special Dispatch – Egypt/Saudi Arabia', 10 June 2005, Middle East Media Research Institute; see also the Special Dispatch no. 974 from the same institute,31 August 2005.

40   V.S. Naipaul, *Among the Believers: An Islamic Journey* (London: André Deutsch, 1981); *The Times*, 29 September 2005.

41   'Is the Era of Cheap Oil Over?' *Organisation of Petroleum Exporting Countries Monthly Bulletin* (August – September 2005); *The Times*, 15 October 2005.

42   Naipaul, *Among the Believers*, p. 331.

43   'Smuggled Film Shows Public Hangings', *The Times*, 2 June 2005.

44   George F. Kennan, *Memoirs 1925–1950* (London: Hutchinson, 1968–1973); Walter Lippmann, *The Cold War: A Study of US Foreign Policy* (New York: Harper & Row, 1972).

45   *The Times*, 13 July 2005.

46   *The Times*, 11 July 2005.

47   *The Times*, 12 July 2005.

48   *The Times*, 27 November 2004.

49   The Times, 3 June 2004; *The Hindu*, 30 May 2005.

50   *Friday Times*, 23–29 July 2004.

51  Ahmad Abu Matar, quoted in 'Special Dispatch: Reform Project', 10 June 2005, Middle East Media Research Institute.
52  *The Times*, 24 November 2004 and 23 and 24 June 2005.
53  *The Times*, 3 May 2005, 8 November 2004 and 14 November 2005.
54  *Friday Times*, 12–18 March 2004; see also *The Hindu*, 21 December 2003, and *The Times*, 2 March 2005.
55  *Friday Times*, 3–9 June 2005.
56  Lippmann, *Cold War*, p. 6.
57  Such soul-searching began very soon after the Russian Revolution; see E.J. Dillon, *Russia Today and Yesterday* (London: Dent, 1929).

# 5
# Military Power and Democratic Transition

Just as great wealth gives people freedom of choice and encourages them to hope that they can buy happiness, so great military power tempts strong states to believe that they can shape weaker states in their own image. In the nineteenth century the colonial powers tried to spread their civilization to Africa and Asia, but it was only later when the Asians and Africans found this cultural intrusion incompatible with their own civilizations that its ultimate effects, if any, could be seen. Similarly, for four decades after 1945 the Soviet Union was able to impose communist governments on Eastern Europe, a process that led to rebellions in 1956 and 1968. However, the overextension of its territorial control and the consequent strain on its resources contributed greatly to the Soviet Union's collapse at the beginning of the 1990s. Since the Soviet demise, America's leaders have come to believe that they can persuade states in the Middle East and elsewhere to adopt democracy, and are ready to consider the use of force against key states that resist their demands.

This chapter argues that military power, like great wealth, is limited in what it can achieve, and is less effective at changing the world than its possessors may believe. Its success depends upon self-discipline, restraint and good judgement. Unfortunately, the possession of great military power often encourages precisely the opposite behaviour because of the self-destructive temptations that accompany it. We also contend that liberal democracy is no panacea, that it cannot be imposed on unwilling states, and that the West must have the patience to leave weaker states to determine whether or not to accept the limitations it imposes on their governments. Finally, we conclude that several factors – the reluctance of the US army to become involved in further insurgencies, the increasing power of China, Washington's reliance on India and Pakistan to combat terrorism and the decline of the US economy – will combine in the long run to inhibit future US interventionism.

## The uses and abuses of military power

The greatest mistakes in US foreign policy over the past half century have tended to arise not because of evil intentions but because of Washington's overwhelming military power and the misjudgments by successive administrations about how that power should be used. The Kennedy, Johnson and Nixon administrations believed in the 1960s that they were struggling in Indochina against a communist minority that was trying to impose itself on the majority, just as the Bolsheviks had imposed themselves on the Russian people in 1917. But the analogy was poor; despite, or because of, the authoritarian nature of the Bolshevik party, intervention by Britain, Japan, the United States and France had failed to defeat the Bolsheviks in 1918 and, 1919. Instead it added to the calamity of civil war between Russian peoples, who died in hundreds of thousands. US intervention similarly failed in Indochina after the Second World War. In that case, the Vietnamese communists were also nationalists, and were more effective at winning over the peasants than the conservatives in South Vietnam and the non-communist governments in Laos and Cambodia. The US effort to defeat them in battle led to the deaths of hundreds of thousands of Vietnamese and tens of thousands of Americans.

Ironically, one of the main 'lessons' to be learnt from these disasters is that although the communists were victorious in the 1970s, in the long term they had to become part of the capitalist world economy. Western economic power triumphed where its military power was discredited. Much more importantly, in the Soviet case, Western military power could only deter its expansion but not change the nature of the regime or free its satellites. The West had to practise what the distinguished diplomat and historian George Kennan called firm and vigilant containment of communism for fifty years. During both the first Berlin crisis in 1948–9 and the Cuba missile crisis in 1962, a catastrophic war could easily have broken out, but the fear of nuclear annihilation preserved the peace until the Soviet Union was unable to compete economically or politically, and collapsed under the strain.

In Iraq in 2003 the US and British governments underestimated local nationalism. Some 25,000 Iraqi civilians had already died by the middle of 2005 without any clear sign that the anti-American insurgency would be defeated and order restored.[1] Both in Vietnam and in Iraq the Americans expected to be popular because they believed they were rescuing people from tyranny. And, no doubt, many Vietnamese and Iraqis did feel that way and were delighted to be protected respectively from the communists or from Saddam Hussein. Certainly, the Shiites and Kurds who turned out in their millions, at some risk to their lives, to vote in elections held in Iraq in 2005 demonstrated their rejection of the past regime. But others mounted insurgencies and were prepared to die to prevent what they saw as the threat of US domination over their country, just as so many Vietnamese had died for the independence of their country after the Second World War.

Unfortunately, the Bush administration ignored the Vietnam precedent. Instead, before March 2003, it focused on the way the Allies were able to rebuild Germany and Japan after the Second World War and turn them into model, peaceful and tolerant democracies. In 1945 the Allies were uncertain how they would be welcomed by the Germans and Japanese, not least because both nations had fought so determinedly long after there was any chance of them fending off their enemies, let alone achieving victory.[2] Consequently, they expected to keep thousands of troops in the occupation forces, only to find that there was virtually no opposition. In Japan it seems likely that the order from the emperor to cease fighting, combined with the exhaustion of the war and the US decision not to prosecute the emperor for war crimes, were decisive. In Germany the utter moral and political bankruptcy of the Nazi regime became steadily clearer as its genocidal policies were exposed after the Allied victory. In both cases it was evident that the occupation forces were prepared to stay, as long as they believed it was necessary to remove the threats the Axis had presented to world order and to use whatever means were necessary to reduce Japanese and German military power.

However, again the comparison is false. Afghanistan and Iraq today are very unlike Germany in Japan in 1945. There is no figure in Iraq who commands the loyalty that the Japanese emperor enjoyed among his people up to 1945. Rather, Iraqis can blame Saddam Hussein for their problems and thus feel perfectly capable of maintaining order without external intervention now that he has been overthrown.

Allied power gradually wore down the Axis states in the Second World War, destroying their cities, interdicting their trade, reducing their peoples to starvation and demolishing their armed forces. They had no heart for further violence. In Iraq, in contrast, the pressures which had been held in check for years by Saddam Hussein's authoritarian government suddenly vented in March 2003 in attacks on the country's museums, hospitals, and government officials. There were precedents for such violence, not least in the Korean peninsula after 1945 when the Korean people vented on each other the fury which they had been unable to unleash on their Japanese occupiers. The lesson is that release from an authoritarian government after a long and destructive war may be peaceful but sudden emancipation without such a war may shock the emancipators with the volcanic eruption of violence that they have inadvertently produced.

The occupation forces in Iraq in March 2003 were in exactly this position. The mood was ecstatic after their easy victory over the Iraqi army. US General Wesley Clark summed up the euphoria on April 11: 'If there is a single overriding lesson it must be this: American military power, especially, when buttressed by Britain's, is virtually unbeatable today. Take us on? Don't try ! And that's not hubris, it's just plain fact.'[3] Unfortunately for the allied forces, Iraqi insurgents did not accept it as 'plain fact', and General Clark must soon have hoped that everyone had forgotten his words as Iraq turned into a quagmire for US forces, while Afghan resistance and disorder also continued. It is not impossible in 2005 to imagine Western forces eventually departing from Kabul and Baghdad as ignominiously as US forces did from Vietnam in 1973 and 1975.[4]

Ever since the French defeat at Dien Bien Phu in 1954, there has been a potential balance or stand-off between the conventional power of the West and the proven ability of Third World countries to defend themselves by guerrilla warfare against Western intervention. Unfortunately, Western leaders are periodically convinced that new scientific developments have changed the situation and given them superiority. The French believed that aircraft could supply their forces in Dien Bien Phu and destroy the guerrillas who attacked their armed camp there, just as British forces had been supplied in Burma during the Second World War. They were wrong. The Americans hoped that helicopter and fixed-wing gunships, napalm and superior firepower would overwhelm General Giap's forces in Vietnam in the 1960s. They were wrong. The Russians hoped that their Hind helicopters would defeat the insurgents in Afghanistan in the 1980s. They were wrong. The threat of insurgency should have the same deterrent effect on modern developed countries as nuclear weapons had during the cold war. Alas, statesmen in the First World, especially American leaders, have ignored this principle.

Raw military power evokes strong and violently conflicting emotions. An impressive parade of troops, a flight of advanced warplanes, an armada of warships evoke nationalistic pride in the state to which they belong, but they evoke fear or rage among potential enemies. Indeed the more power they represent, the greater may be the frustration and hostility. Reports from Fox News, CNN and the World Service of the BBC showed US tanks driving across the Iraqi deserts in March 2003, fighter-bombers flying off the decks of US carriers in the Gulf, and Tomahawk cruise missiles launched from submarines and warships. This may have bolstered the pride felt by US citizens in the power and the professionalism of their forces, but we know from Pew polls the extent of the hostility among Muslim peoples that US policies have evoked. As an example, only 13 per cent of Pakistanis and Indonesians had a favourable opinion of the US in 2003.[5]

All these peoples have a tendency to identify with America's enemies rather than to sympathize with Washington's motives for intervening in Iraq. Such identification with groups, which are of the same religion or ethnicity, is pervasive in the modern world. When South Africa was ruled by the National Party's white government, blacks everywhere felt somehow diminished; when Palestinians are humiliated by Israeli troops, Arabs burn with anger and identify with the downtrodden; when Muslims are defeated by the United States and its allies in Afghanistan or Iraq then Muslims elsewhere sympathize with the defeated.[6] Some who had grown up in the West volunteered to fight against the country that had been their home. Some even joined terrorist groups or gave them support (see Chapter 7).

The conclusion is obvious. Western military power should be used defensively when Western democracies and other friendly states are threatened. It can also sometimes be used in tasks such as peacekeeping operations; it has, for example, prevented Greek and Turkish Cypriots from killing each other for the last thirty years, though it has not ended their mutual hostility. In other words, in this respect, as in others, military power is better at preventing violent change initiated by others than at producing deep changes in social and political attitudes in other peoples' lands. Thus, it stopped the ethnic cleansing of the Muslims in Bosnia-Herzegovina and Kosovo in the 1990s and it abated the recent conflict in Sierra Leone and other conflicts in Africa. Most commentators regretted that it was not used quickly enough to prevent the horrific massacres in Rwanda in April 1994. One balanced study concluded in 2004:

> A humanitarian intervention is justified if it stands a reasonable chance of success. If the protection aims cannot be realistically achieved, or if the cure is likely to be worse than the disease, there is little reason to resort to armed force.[7]

But peacekeepers intervene in others' countries on sufferance. They nearly always fail to understand local politics, and their intervention is generally perceived by some of the parties to the dispute as grossly unfair. The information available to Western leaders about such conflicts is very limited and often partial.[8] Peacekeepers usually need to arrive quickly to prevent a conflict from escalating, but rapidity and careful thought are incompatible. Moreover the peacekeepers also need to be ready to leave as soon as the local people are able to manage the situation.

In sum, military power, like wealth, can easily be overrated by those who possess it. Just as great wealth only benefits those who use it to achieve non-material goals, great power is of limited value in shaping the world in one's own image; this applies no less in a well-run democratic country than it does under a genocidal government, such as Nazi Germany or the Soviet Union. In particular, as we argue in the next section, it cannot be used to spread democracy.

## Military power and democracy

When a superpower does not restrict the use of its power to situations that have widespread international support and where there is no alternative, it further increases its isolation and the hostility towards it. A couple of samples from the non-Western press illustrate this. When George W. Bush was re-elected in November 2004, the editorial writer in a friendly and intelligent Pakistani journal commented:

> Most people believe that President Bush will continue to wreck international law and order, alienate world opinion, fuel anti-Americanism across the globe and give succour to Islamic terror ... Osama bin Laden will be gloating over his successful strategy of dividing America and the rest of the world.[9]

Similarly, a columnist in the austere *Hindu* newspaper, based in Madras, wrote:

> Though the most democratic of all nations, 'unimaginably perfect' in the views of many, the US moves on unscrupulously supporting its allies and brutally dominating the global economy to the detriment of the rest of the world. American motives might seem humanitarian but they differ little from the mechanisms of a totalitarian state ... The nature of American institutions seems to give it licence to intervene anywhere in the world.[10]

Thus has the use of military force without UN support, and more generally without convincing people across the world of the justice of the cause, alienated those who might have supported the United States in its war on terrorism and occupation of Iraq.

Not only are the means mistaken but the objectives are also often equally misguided. In recent years, US commentators have taken for granted that democracy is the ideal form of government, that democracies are inherently peaceful, and that the United States is, because of the particularly democratic nature of its government and people, ideally fitted to guide other nations.[11] In fact, however, democracy is no panacea for domestic or foreign problems.[12] Usually when a colonial power has made moves towards granting democratic 'freedom' to its colonies, antagonism has increased between the different national groups whom it ruled. Impending release from authoritarian governments also encourages sectarian violence, and there are rational explanations as well as irrational forces that encourage this tendency. In India in the 1930s and 1940s the move towards independence from Britain meant increased hostility between Hindus and Muslims leading to the division of the subcontinent into India and Pakistan, mass killings and numerous wars.[13] Similarly, independence in Cyprus meant genocidal warfare between Turks and Greeks, ethnic cleansing and the eventual partition of the island. In Israel it meant more than half a century of war between Jews and Palestinians with no end in sight for the conflict in 2005. Fortunately, through the good sense of statesmen on both sides, Singapore and Malaysia were able to separate peacefully when they gained independence in the 1960s, but there were riots in Malaya and threats exchanged across the Straits. Each side in these disputes liked to blame the colonial power for pursuing a policy of 'divide and rule' but, in fact, the parties were involved in a conflict for power to determine who would dominate the independent state which was emerging.

Democracy has to be based on the rule of law, a conviction that the government will not persecute individuals or groups out of spite or for party advantage, a sense of fair play, the willingness of the minority to admit that the other party has won the election and an understanding among the majority that it needs to avoid driving the minority to desperation and thus violence. These preconditions emerge only very gradually and thus nationalist parties struggling against colonial powers realize that their rivals might dominate after independence and threaten their very survival. In the past this has usually increased tensions and led to inter-communal violence. Thus it was not surprising that, after the collapse of the Soviet Union in the early 1990s, there was violence in

Tajikistan and Georgia, and a war between Armenia and Azerbaijan.[14] Similarly, when communist authority declined, Yugoslavia collapsed in a welter of violence and ethnic cleansing. The Serbs were determined to retain their predominant position while the Kosovans, Croats and Bosniaks were equally determined to end it. Jack Snyder of Columbia University rightly concluded from his study of the problem that 'a country's first steps towards democracy spur the development of nationalism and heighten the risk of international war and internal ethnic conflict'.[15]

In Iraq today, democracy could succeed only if the urge for violence were repressed and the Shiites in the south, the Sunnis in the centre and the Kurds in the north put the development of a new constitution above their own interests. If they do not do this, they will eventually tear Iraq apart just as the inhabitants of Yugoslavia destroyed their country in the early 1990s (see Chapter 9).

While democracy often exacerbates national tensions in weak states, it does not necessarily improve the formulation of foreign policy. The assumption to the contrary is all the more surprising because, while British, German or French foreign policy has often been criticized, the criticism has not usually encompassed the structure of their governments and the nature of their polity. On the other hand, the most distinguished critics of US foreign policy have, over the years, blamed the democratic nature of the US political system for the faults they discerned in its policies. Their arguments are worth recalling as a counterweight to the underlying assumption in current US policy that American democracy is so perfect that everyone should share in it.

From de Tocqueville in the 1830s to Fulbright in the 1960s, observers have noted the tendency for the United States and its citizens to oscillate between arrogance and uncertainty, cooperation and isolation.[16] Both Homer Lea, the pre-eminent American civilian strategic analyst before the First World War, and the US Secretary of State at that time, John Hay, claimed that popular control prevented the United States from signing or observing international treaties. Thus, in Lea's words:

> [A]s the government of a nation passes under the control of the populace, it passes, to a certain degree, beyond the pale of peaceful association with other nations. It enters into a condition of arrogant unrest, an isolation, insolent and impatient as to the rights of others. Out of these demeanours come wars.

Not only are potential enemies further antagonized but the views of friendly states are dismissed for, as Lea noted, 'foreign nations are without votes or lobbyists, their demands are of little or no importance to the average politician'.[17]

Writing in 1967, Senator William Fulbright believed he detected the atrophy of the Senate's role in foreign affairs and the aggrandisement of the presidency which led to mistaken decisions over Cuba, Santo Domingo and Vietnam.[18] Nearly two decades later the distinguished US diplomat and historian George Kennan wrote:

> The most difficult task of all will be that which confronts any American statesman who undertakes to conduct such [diplomatic] discussions; how, namely, to make the results intelligible and acceptable to an American public confused by many past appeals to its emotions, unaccustomed to be asked to confront soberly a series of highly complex realities, and informed primarily by commercial media of information whose dedication is to the over simplification and dramatization of reality rather than education of the public to recognition of its bitter complexities.[19]

Whether the alleged mistakes made by Washington were ascribed to excessive popular control, the increase in presidential power or the inability of the electorate to understand international affairs, the point made was that the democratic system itself was at least partly responsible.

Congress has notoriously often blocked long-considered US foreign policies, such as adherence to the League of Nations, yet it has totally failed to prevent some of the greatest mistakes, including intervention in Vietnam and now in Iraq. The system lacks the stability that professional civil services have traditionally given to parliamentary democracies. This means that the whole diplomatic world has to wait for several months every four years while a new administration is established. Then it has to pause while a working relationship or balance of power is established between the various senior officers. The US system has the considerable advantage that it draws on a far greater range of talents than the parliamentary system where prime ministers have to emerge from within the assembly. No British prime minister since Wellington has had the military experience of Eisenhower or the diplomatic experience gained by George Bush Senior. The highest US officers have frequently been immigrants – Henry Kissinger, Zbigniew Brzezinski and Madeleine Albright, to name but the most distinguished. No other democracy has employed its new citizens so effectively.

But the disadvantage of the US system is that presidents can lack all experience of government or knowledge of international affairs. In an increasingly professional age this is a hazardous way of appointing the most powerful man in the world. US presidents come up against national leaders who have sometimes been honing their skills in office for decades; thus Harry Truman was suddenly confronted with the most ruthless of all, Joseph Stalin,[20] and John Kennedy was faced with Nikita Khrushchev who had survived Stalin's purges to claw his way to the top of the Soviet political system.

In recent years foreign publics have not warmed to incumbents in the White House. This may be because of the way they are reflected in the media, which, it may be said, are always keen to disparage and diminish. In fact however national media are usually much more critical of their own leaders than of foreign ones; Margaret Thatcher, Mikhail Gorbachev and Kim dae Jung were all much more highly appreciated abroad than at home. US presidents have been subjected to a unique degree of foreign criticism. Simply put: Ronald Reagan and George W. Bush would not have been elected in Europe, and European publics distrust their power of judgement.

## Coalition-building or unilateral action?

The suspicion of American leadership makes it difficult for administrations to assemble 'coalitions of the willing' to deal with issues they consider vital. After 9/11, when the Bush administration was tempted into taking unilateral action against terrorists and 'rogue states', it believed that other states would follow if these actions were successful. This attitude was summed up in a very revealing comment by President Bush to Bob Woodward:

> I believe in results ... The world is watching carefully and would be impressed and will be impressed by the results achieved ... It is a way for us to earn capital in a coalition that can be fragile. And the reason it will be fragile is that there is resentment towards us ... Well, we're never going to get people all in agreement about force and the use of force ... But action – confident action that will yield positive results provides a kind of slipstream into which reluctant nations and leaders can get behind and show themselves that there has been – you know something positive has happened towards peace.[21]

The assumption was that successful US strategies would gain support, however reluctant other states might be initially to back Washington in its Iraqi policies. Judged historically, the assertion that others would follow a successful US initiative is a partial truth. After the Second World War, European security institutions preceded NATO and the Europeans wanted the United States to build on these.[22] In other words the policy preceded the success of the alliance. On the other hand, in the 1990s the East Europeans were enthusiastic to join NATO precisely because it had deterred and eventually 'defeated' the Warsaw Pact, thus partly justifying Bush's form of argument that nothing succeeds like success. Conversely, in the case of the Vietnam War, the greatest failure (before Iraq) of US security policy since 1945, very few states could be persuaded to join the enterprise, not least because they believed it was likely to fail and they were unsure whether the cause was just or legal.

After 9/11 most states were willing to support the US military action against Afghanistan – the Europeans without hesitation, and even the Pakistanis despite the difficulty of reversing their policy which had favoured the Islamist Taliban government. Moreover, they took a number of risks in doing so, the Pakistanis with their internal stability, the Europeans with their military forces which they offered to help the US war effort. The Taliban army was hardly likely to be able to challenge the US in open conventional warfare but the US was itself reluctant to risk large numbers of ground troops in Afghanistan in 2001. The Afghans had also demonstrated their traditional abilities as guerrillas when they defeated the Soviets in the 1980s, and the Western media were sometimes inclined to exaggerate historic Afghan successes in the autumn in 2001.[23] However the Europeans were prepared to take the risks involved in declaring 9/11 to be an attack on them all because they believed that the US was morally right to respond militarily to the destruction of the Twin Towers. In other words, states and peoples do not judge only by success, as Bush implied, but they are willing to take greater risks to the extent that they believe that a cause is just and legal.

Conversely, when President Bush criticized the 'axis of evil' in January 2002, the coalition fell apart because its members felt that the United States was succumbing to a unilateralist temptation. But, while many states had shied away from involvement in the Vietnam War because they had seen how successful guerrillas had been against the French and British, and feared involvement in a doomed enterprise, in 2002 many were fearful of the opposite – namely that the United States might be successful in its military ventures, enshrine its dominance and become yet more assertive. There was an inherent contradiction in Bush's thinking, as his comment to Woodward revealed; he rightly suggested that states naturally like to become involved with successful ventures, but he also talked about 'resentment' against the United States without recognizing that such resentment might overpower any desire to 'bandwagon' with a successful state. In practice, fear of US actions grew in the Muslim world and opposition mounted in Europe after the Afghan war, not because of fear of failure, but because of anxiety about American success.

Many states were also concerned about the justice and legality of the US attack on Iraq in March 2003. Had the administration justified it purely in terms of the repression used by Saddam Hussein against his own people, this would have left opinion deeply divided. There is nothing in international law to justify an attack on these grounds, because the founders of the United Nations were afraid that such a provision would become an excuse for unjustified intervention and undermine the independence of states. If Saddam Hussein had actually been engaged in genocide at that time, there might still have been a legal case for invasion in 2003, but the Iraqi leader was not killing his own people in any numbers before the invasion.[24] Alternative justifications therefore had to be found.

There was concern that a successful attack might have led to others of the same kind because Bush was just as vehement in his criticisms of North Korea as he was about Iraq. Bob Woodward recorded:

> I thought he might jump up he became so emotional as he spoke about the North Korean leader. 'I loathe Kim Jong Il!' Bush shouted, waving his finger in the air. 'I've got a visceral reaction against this guy, because he is starving his people. And I have seen intelligence of these prison camps – they're huge – that he uses to break up families, and to torture people.[25]

Bush went on to attack those, including presumably most South Koreans, who believed that the North Korean government should not be precipitously undermined, even if this were possible, because of the dislocation it would cause. Thus the general public was quite right to suspect that the US appetite would 'grow with eating'; Tony Blair had to reassure the British people constantly that the Pentagon was not being tempted into some new attack against Syria, Iran, North Korea or another state which had alienated the US administration.

Admittedly, in 2003 and 2004 the United States did manage to involve some states in the struggle against the insurgency in Iraq, despite their reluctance and the unpopularity of the conflict. The Japanese and South Korean governments bowed to US pressure and allowed their forces to go there, as long as they were protected from suffering casualties by Kurdish or other troops. The Ukrainians joined in the operation but, having poor training and weapons, ran away as soon as they were threatened.[26] The spectacle emerged of an administration so arrogant that it had dismissed allies as irrelevant immediately after 9/11 now begging them for the mere semblance of assistance. The governments committing troops were aware that the United States badly wanted coalition forces to remain as a political face-saver and they tried to use their presence in Iraq to gain other benefits. When President Roh Moo-Hyun made a surprise visit to South Korean troops stationed at Irbil in northern Iraq in December 2004, South Korean commentators said that he hoped to gain support for the emollient South Korean stand towards North Korea. In other words, attack on one partner in the 'axis of evil' was threatening to undermine attacks on the others.[27]

The Bush administration is 'learning the hard way' that its allies are independent, will not necessarily 'fall into line', and have ambitions and views concerning the international situation which may differ markedly from Washington's own. As the United States slides ever deeper into the mire of insurgency, it becomes more dependent upon the goodwill of Iraq's neighbours, such as Iran and Syria. President Bush had hoped to encourage other states to fall in behind the United States after its successful attack on Iraq, but has had to go cap in hand to friendly but reluctant states, even to hostile and suspicious Arab countries. Washington desperately needs allies to deal with Afghanistan and Iraq and it cannot find loyal allies unless it wins them over. Hectoring, boasting and browbeating does not work in the long run and may undermine governments friendly to the United States. Many believe that the involvement of Spanish forces in Iraq led to the Madrid bomb attacks in March 2004 and helped secure the election victory of a socialist government committed to withdrawing forces from the conflict.

## The importance of restraint

Foreign concerns with US unilateralism are all the greater today because there are so few institutional and physical restraints on American power. No state was able to deter US intervention in Afghanistan and Iraq or to warn the administration effectively against the threats President Bush made against Iran and North Korea. Opposition in Congress was muted by fear of public obloquy and the US public rallied behind President Bush whatever action he took in the early stages.[28] Bush himself seems to have been too inexperienced to understand the possible effects of his plans to invade Iraq as the first stage in an effort to 'reform the Muslim world'. Former President Jimmy Carter summed up the problem:

> It's just become almost unpatriotic to describe Bush's fallacious and ill-advised and mistaken actions. The press have been cowed, because they didn't want to be unpatriotic. There has been a lack of inquisitive journalism. In fact it is difficult to think of a major medium in the United States that has been objective and fair and balanced, and critical when criticism was deserved.[29]

The United States would not have fallen so easily into the error of believing that it could impose democracy on other states if its leaders had been aware of the economic costs of failure. Warfare should be, and be seen to be, extremely expensive. In the nineteenth century warfare often cost the European powers very little and the consequence was that they were constantly at war with weaker states.[30] Either they fought against groups that could not resist effectively because of the inadequacy of their armaments, such as the African tribes, or they fought against countries from whom indemnities could be exacted after victory. Thus the British forced indemnities from the Chinese after defeating them in the Opium Wars and the Japanese forced the Chinese to pay for the full costs of their defeat in 1895, as well as for expanding the Japanese army and navy.[31]

The Prussian statesman, Bismarck similarly compelled the French to pay the full costs of their defeat at German hands in 1871. The effect of this system of spoliation was to discourage treasuries from protesting strongly enough against the potential economic impact of warfare. Similarly, the essential restraint which their treasury ministers should have offered to the US and British leaders in March 2003 was undermined by the way in which the 1991 war against Iraq was paid for by Saudi Arabia, Kuwait and Japan, by the success of the US and British economies in the 1990s, and by the cheapness of the victories in Bosnia, Kosovo and Afghanistan.

If Washington has been unable to practise self-restraint over recent years, three factors will compel it to change its policies in the future: the US army's distaste for involvement in anti-guerrilla operations, China's growing strength and the increasing problems in the US economy. We deal with the failure of US anti-guerrilla operations below in Chapter 9, but the fact is that the US army never wanted to become involved in Iraq; it was the US Air Force which, intoxicated with its apparent power to 'shock and awe', led the charge against the Iraqis. It was left to the US army to deal with the power vacuum, which the destruction of Iraqi forces initially created, and the guerrilla insurgency that ultimately ensued.[32]

As we point out in Chapter 9, while the United States has dominated debates on nuclear deterrence since 1945, it has no tradition of anti-guerrilla warfare to rival or emulate the anti-guerrilla codes developed by Sir Charles Gwynn and Sir Robert Thompson for the British army, despite the valiant efforts by Edward Lansdale in the 1950s and Bruce Hoffman and others in more recent times.[33] This is not for want of military experience; anti-guerrilla campaigns were fought against the Native Americans in the nineteenth century, against the Filipinos after the Spanish–American War and again in the 1940s, and above all against the National Liberation Front in Vietnam between the early 1960s and 1973. Like any other armed force, the training, mores and structure of the US army reflect the society from which it has sprung. US society is dynamic, technological, problem-solving, impatient to find solutions. As a senior British official, who had worked in Southern Iraq after the invasion, put it later:

> The British (and apparently the Danish) civil bureaucratic tradition is to identify and anticipate potential difficulties and try to forestall problems through a process of debate and brain-storming – which could, to American eyes, appear insufficiently single minded or even defeatist. The US 'can do, will do' approach, on the other hand, could seem to pay insufficient regard to the consequences of their methods. They had greater scope to remove obstacles by simply overwhelming them with resources.[34]

These factors make the armed forces resistant to thinking about the subtle and time-consuming interaction between military and political processes that are so necessary in anti-guerrilla operations. Put crudely, the Americans 'don't do' guerrilla warfare or don't do it successfully, and it is unclear whether Iraq will make them change.

Second, there is, as already pointed out in Chapter 4, a marked divergence between the cautious US policies followed towards China and the Indo-Pakistan dispute, and those pursued in the Middle East. In 1945 the great powers acquired permanent seats on the Security Council because they were so powerful they *could not be overthrown or 'disciplined' without a world war*. The number of great powers has, by this definition, expanded to include Japan and India. It may be joined in time by Pakistan and Brazil. There is, then, already a balance of power of a sort between China and India on one side and the United States on the other. As we pointed out in the previous chapter, the United States desperately wants to avoid a confrontation with China over Taiwan and other issues, not least because of the economic relationship between the two countries and the way in which the Chinese have financed US economic profligacy.

Washington needs the cooperation of both India and Pakistan in its struggle against al-Qaeda, and thus it behaves with great caution in South Asia. When India and Pakistan mobilized against each other on the Kashmir border in 2002 after an attack on the Indian parliament, the United States and Britain worked to defuse the crisis. There is a greater chance of inter-state war in Asia than in any other region of the world because of maritime and territorial disputes between South Korea and Japan, China and Taiwan, the two Koreas and China, China and the South East Asian states, and India and Pakistan.[35] The United States is the key to stabilizing the area because it cannot afford to see the outbreak of hot wars in the region and it has the power and influence to discourage them.

The third factor that inhibits US power is its economy, which faces increasing problems. Its GDP has fallen with the collapse of the dollar in 2004/5 against other currencies. Indebtedness to China and Japan grows ever larger, and the budget deficit has expanded massively under George W. Bush to 4.4% of GDP in 2005. When Bush came into office the administration forecast a budget surplus over the next 10 years of 1.1 trillion dollars. By its profligacy it has turned this into a deficit of the same amount.[36] Indeed the precariousness of the US economy threatens the entire world economy. Financial journalists habitually refer to George W. Bush's government as the most fiscally irresponsible US administration since the Second World War, but the problem is a more general one. The United States is spending more than it can afford on defence and in the long run this will have to be reduced.[37] Disasters such as the hurricanes in the Gulf Coast in the fall of 2005 require massive expenditures at home. This will eventually mean no more expensive adventures of the Iraqi type. In 1988 Paul Kennedy pointed to the dangers that the United States would face if it continued to overspend on its military competition with the other great powers.[38] His thesis seemed to be undermined because the collapse of the Soviet Union masked the extent of the problem and gave the United States more than another decade of hegemony, but the precipitous fall in the value of the dollar has already shown that this will not last.

In the next chapter we argue that the recent US policy of preventive warfare is counter-productive and will have to be abandoned. It is just the most assertive of recent US military policies and reflects the fallacious emphasis on military power which, we have shown, has mired Washington in the disaster of Iraq.

## Notes

1  Letter from Lord Ramsbotham, General Sir Hugh Beach, Lord Garden and others, *The Times*, 27 July 2005.
2  For the ways in which the allies were received in Germany, see Lucius D. Clay, *Decision in Germany* (London: Heinemann, 1950); Noel Annan, *Changing Enemies: The Defeat and Regeneration of Germany* (London: HarperCollins, 1995); Ulrike Jordan (ed.), *Conditions of Surrender: Britons and Germans Witness the End of the War* (London: Tauris/German Historical Institute, 1997).
3  *The Times*, 11 April 2004.
4  Frank Snepp, *Decent Interval: The American Debacle in Vietnam and the Fall of Saigon* (Harmondsworth: Penguin, 1980).
5  Pew Global Attitudes Project, 23 June 2005. http://pewglobal.org/reports/display
6  'Egyptian Parliament Member Praises Killing Americans', Middle East Media Research Institute, 27 July 2005.
7  Katariina Saariluoma, 'Operation Allied Force: A Case of Humanitarian Intervention?' Athena Papers, Partnership for Peace Consortium of Defence Academies (September 2004), p. 85. See also Karin von Hippel, *Democracy by Force: US Military Intervention in the Post-Cold War World* (Cambridge: Cambridge University Press, 2000), p. 204.
8  Madeleine Albright, *Madam Secretary: A Memoir* (London: Macmillan, 2003), pp. 150–5; Marrack Goulding, *Peacemonger* (London: John Murray, 2002).
9  *Friday Times* (Lahore), 12–18 November 2004.
10 *The Hindu*, 26 December 2004.
11 See, for example, the comments by Albright, *Madam Secretary*, p. 512.
12 See, for example, F. Gregory Gause III, 'Can Democracy Stop Terrorism?', *Foreign Affairs* (September/October 2005). In recent years there has been a timely scholarly debate in the United States on the general issue of democratic peace, particularly in Michael W. Doyle, 'Three Pillars of the Liberal Peace', *APSR*, vol. 99 (August 2005); Bruce Bueno de Mesquita *et al.*, 'An Institutional Exploration of the Democratic Peace', *APSR*, vol. 93 (December 1999); and Sebastian Rosato, 'Explaining the Democratic Peace', *APSR*, vol. 99 (August 2005).
13 Nirad C. Chaudhuri, *Thy Hand Great Anarch! India 1921–1952* (London: Hogarth Press, 1990), p. 810.
14 *Strategic Survey 1992–1993*, pp. 75ff.; *Strategic Survey 1993–1994*, pp. 191ff.
15 Jack Snyder, *From Voting to Violence: Democratization and Nationalist Conflict* (New York: Norton, 2000), p. 352.
16 *Democracy in America*, p. 223.
17 Homer Lea, *The Valor of Ignorance* (New York: Harper, 1909), p. 143. For later concerns about the US ability to understand and respond appropriately to international affairs, see Walter Lippmann, *Public Opinion* (New York: Free Press, 1997 [1922]).

18 J. William Fulbright, *The Arrogance of Power* (London: Jonathan Cape, 1967), ch. 2.

19 George F. Kennan, *The Nuclear Delusion: Soviet–American Relations in the Atomic Age* (London: Hamish Hamilton, 1984), p. xxx.

20 Harry S. Truman, *Year of Decisions 1945* (London: Hodder & Stoughton, 1955), p. 342.

21 Bob Woodward, *Bush at War* (New York: Simon & Schuster, 2002), p. 341.

22 Duff Cooper, *Old Men Forget* (London: Rupert Hart-Davis, 1953), ch. 22; Sir Nicholas Henderson, *The Birth of NATO* (London: Weidenfeld & Nicolson, 1982); Joseph Smith (ed.), *The Origins of NATO* (University of Exeter Press, 1990).

23 *The Times*, 18 September 2001.

24 That is not to deny that Saddam Hussein had killed tens of thousands of Iraqis in the past; see Kanan Makiya (Samir al-Khalil), *Cruelty and Silence* (London: Jonathan Cape, 1993).

25 Woodward, *Bush at War*, p. 340; see also 'Bush Envoy Stuns Diplomats with Attack on Kim Jong Il', *The Times*, 1 August 2003.

26 Mark Etherington, *Revolt on the Tigris: The Al-Sadr Uprising and the Governing of Iraq* (London: Hurst, 2005), pp. 190–3.

27 *Korea Now*, 11 December 2004, pp. 14–15.

28 Woodward, *Bush at War*, p. 60.

29 *The Hindu*, 7 November 2004.

30 Brian Bond (ed.), *Victorian Military Campaigns* (London: Hutchinson, 1967).

31 Michael Hurst, *Key Treaties for the Great Powers* (Newton Abbot: David & Charles, 1972), vol. 1, pp. 269 and 431; Gotara Ogawa, *Expenditures of the Russo-Japanese War* (New York: Oxford University Press, 1923).

32 James F. Dobbins, 'America's Role in Nation-Building: From Germany to Iraq', *Survival* (Winter 2003–4), 87ff.

33 Sir Charles Gwynn, *Imperial Policing* (London: Macmillan, 1934); Sir Robert Thompson, *Make for the Hills* (London: Leo Cooper, 1989); Cecil B. Curry, *Edward Lansdale: The Unquiet American* (Boston: Houghton Mifflin, 1988).

34 Hilary Synnot, 'State-Building in Southern Iraq', *Survival* (Summer 2005).

35 See, for example, 'China Tests D-Day Invasion of Taiwan', *The Times*, 7 July 2004; 'Korea Resolute on Dokdo Sovereignty', *Korea Now*, 2 April 2005.

36 *Strategic Survey 2004–2004* (Oxford: IISS/Oxford University Press, 2003), p. 232.

37 *Financial Times*, 20 April 2005.

38 Paul Kennedy, *The Rise and Fall of the Great Powers* (London: Unwin Hyman, 1988), pp. 514ff.

# 6

# The Temptation of Preventive War

As the last chapter showed, to the consternation of most of its closest allies, US outrage at 9/11 combined with the strength of its armed forces tempted the Bush administration to overthrow the Iraqi government. But the temptations of power extend well beyond this. As the world's only superpower, the United States could be enticed into making even more preventive attacks on other states that appear to be developing the capability to threaten the United States sometime in the future. 9/11 has dramatically increased that temptation.

The justification offered for this new strategy of preventive war is twofold. First of all, rogue states, such as North Korea, Iran, Libya and Iraq under Saddam Hussein, have been attempting to obtain weapons of mass destruction and particularly nuclear weapons. Such states cannot be deterred, as the Soviet Union and Communist China were deterred, and thus they might make use of nuclear weapons either against the West or against neighbouring powers. Moreover, they might pass their WMD on to terrorist movements. Terrorists have become more ruthless, as 9/11 demonstrated all too clearly, and they might use WMD to obliterate a whole city or group of cities. In these circumstances, the United States must strike before the cycle begins by destroying the nuclear facilities being constructed by the rogue states. These dangers, or alleged dangers, have to be examined one by one to assess the extent of the threat.

To show that a rogue state will be more dangerous than China and the Soviet Union were in the past, we have to demonstrate that their leaders are more irrational than Stalin, Khrushchev, Brezhnev and Mao were when they were in charge of their countries or that the new leaders come from cultures where deterrence would not operate. No one has yet done this successfully. Certainly, there is no evidence that Kim Jong II in North Korea, Saddam Hussein or the rulers of Iran are or have been more ruthless than their communist predecessors. Stalin killed some twenty million of his own citizens, Mao probably more. Khrushchev was certainly less ruthless, though he had worked for Stalin at the height of the purges, which meant that he was prepared to kill in order to survive. Dictators generally have a great sense of self-preservation, and the communist dictators listed above were not likely to unleash a nuclear holocaust that would have obliterated their whole country. This was the case even though they had under their control more nuclear weapons than any rogue state is likely to acquire in the next decades. Had they launched a preventive war, the communist dictators had just a very outside chance that they might degrade the US nuclear force and thus damage their enemy while suffering less damage themselves – but they showed no sign whatsoever of falling for this fallacious and horrific logic. Why North Korea or Iran might be tempted into launching a first strike with any puny nuclear forces that they might produce has never been demonstrated or even seriously argued.

It is, of course, possible that some cultures might produce leaders who cannot be deterred. But, again, this has not been widely asserted let alone proven. Even Muslim fundamentalist governments, such as the Iranian, have not proved impervious to all the usual demands of statecraft. Kim Jong II's government has certainly behaved eccentrically in the past – kidnapping young Japanese and carrying them off to North Korea, and attempting to blow up the South Korean cabinet in Rangoon. But its nuclear weapons acquisition policy has been carefully modulated to gain the maximum economic advantage from the international community, to attract Washington's attention and to increase the government's prestige.

The greatest danger would seem to come not from rogue governments' indifference to nuclear deterrence but from their inability or unwillingness to control their nuclear arsenals. These might then spread to terrorist movements. The best evidence for this danger comes from Pakistan where the head of the nuclear programme, Dr A.Q. Khan, sold equipment to produce weapons and related information to Libya, Iran and North Korea. The Pakistani government claims he was acting alone, and the choice of countries suggests that they are right, or partly right. It also demonstrates that he was not motivated primarily by politics. A wealthy man, he appears to have wanted to be wealthier still so that he could contribute to Pakistani charities and increase his own popularity.

Plainly the Pakistani nuclear programme has been the most dangerous to date. But Pakistan is not rated a rogue state by the United States and there has been no suggestion that the United States should either try to overthrow the government there or destroy its nuclear facilities. Neither the United States, nor any group of countries, could successfully dominate a country the size of Pakistan and put in power a 'more responsible' government. What the Pakistani example shows is that proliferation in the Third World is extremely dangerous and will remain so, but that the way to deal with the problem is by bolstering the Nuclear Non-Proliferation Treaty and the conventions against the spread of WMD.

For many years the United States was the prime-mover in efforts to do this. Successive administrations defended such treaties on the grounds that they were inherently stabilizing, and as a useful side-effect they also favoured the stronger countries that already possessed WMD. However, in the 1990s Washington came to believe that such agreements were inadequate, following the discovery after 1991 that Iraq, which was a party to the international agreements, was systematically breaching them. Saddam Hussein's government was trying to produce chemical, biological and nuclear weapons and it had openly used chemical weapons in the war against Iran in breach of the 1926 Geneva Protocol. At the same time, fears were growing that North Korea was also secretly developing nuclear weapons. These evasions, together with nuclear tests by India and Pakistan, which were not parties to the Non-Proliferation Treaty, sapped US confidence in arms control even though South Africa, Brazil, Argentina and the new states established on the ruins of the Soviet Union adhered to the Non-Proliferation regime during this period.

Following the events of September 11 2001, the United States vowed that it would pre-empt attacks by terrorists and rogue states and threatened to use force to prevent other states developing weapons of mass destruction.[1] In the *US National Strategy to Combat WMD*, published in December 2002, the administration laid out the extent of the threat as it saw it. It emphasized the importance of counter-proliferation, meaning the use of force to prevent states acquiring WMD, and it threatened to use 'overwhelming force' against states which employed WMD on the United States or its friends and allies. It promised to develop the capability to 'detect and destroy an adversary's WMD assets before these weapons are used'.[2]

Although the strategies are often confused, a distinction has to be made here between preventive war and pre-emption as both legal and political terms. A *pre-emptive* strike is one delivered to forestall an imminent enemy attack. A *preventive* war is fought to stop a long-term increase in the power of a potential enemy. The first action is legitimate under international law, the second is not. The reasons are obvious: the balance between states changes all the time and thus to allow preventive war would give scope for constant fighting. For example, the Chinese economy is currently expanding rapidly and this will increase the country's military power. At some stage in the future, China might feel strong enough to oppose US wishes, but that does not give Washington the right to attack it first. On the other hand, a state cannot be expected to wait idly by when it knows that enemy forces are preparing to launch an attack in the next few hours or days. However, in their December 2002 paper and elsewhere the US administration has argued that the spread of weapons of mass destruction makes it necessary for the United States to carry out both preventive and pre-emptive wars. In his State of the Union speech on January 29 2003, President Bush said:

> Some have said we must not act until the threat is imminent. Since when have terrorists and tyrants announced their intentions, politely putting us on notice before they strike? If this threat is permitted to fully and suddenly emerge, all actions, all words and all recriminations would come too late.[3]

## Modern precedents for pre-emptive and preventive wars

Preventive war is an extremely dangerous and destabilizing strategy. The persuasiveness of this argument has been generally recognized ever since the First World War, and the modern international legal system was developed precisely to discourage it. Any state that wages preventive wars encourages other states to do the same and makes international relations much more tense and unstable. It leads states to invent threats so that they can wage aggressive wars, as the Nazis did in the 1930s. It encourages armed forces to tell their governments that they must mobilize and strike first, as many of the European armed forces did in August 1914. It encourages states to spend more on their armaments so that they cannot be destroyed in a first strike, thus unleashing arms races around the world.

The central international organizations, such as the League of Nations and the United Nations, were designed to reduce the temptation for states to launch either preventive or pre-emptive strikes. The military advantages of such attacks were obvious but, by definition, they shortened the time for statesmen to find diplomatic solutions to a crisis. The German and Japanese attacks, which touched off and widened the Second World War, brushed aside the legal barriers to deliberate aggression that had been assiduously built up in the League of Nations Covenant and the

Kellogg–Briand Pact. The League's founders had also tried to avoid inadvertent wars arising from crises which statesmen were unable to manage. They believed this had happened in August 1914 when Austro-Hungarian threats against Serbia led Russia to mobilize its forces, and the German army then insisted on mobilizing against both Russia and France. By that stage, statesmen were unable to reverse the process of mobilization without causing chaos in their forces, making them vulnerable to enemy attack.

To try to prevent such escalation from happening again, the drafters of the Covenant of the League of Nations included in Article 12 the stipulation that

> the members of the League agree that, if there should arise between them any dispute likely to lead to rupture they will submit the matter either to arbitration or judicial settlement or to enquiry by the Council, and they agree in no case to resort to war *until three months* after the award by the arbitrators or the judicial decision, or the report by the Council.

Precisely because of the failure of such diplomatic barriers against surprise attacks between the two world wars, the great powers relied on technology to prevent similar acts of aggression during the nuclear age. The United States, the Soviet Union, Britain and France developed 'secure second-strike nuclear systems' to ensure that other states could not attack them first in the hope that consequently they would avoid retaliation. At enormous cost, nuclear armed missiles were put in underground silos, sent to sea in submarines, or carried in bomber aircraft so that they could survive a nuclear strike by a potential enemy.[4]

## Israel's preventive war precedents in the Middle East

While political leaders have worked assiduously to discourage preventive attacks on their own forces, it has been highly unusual for a democracy to adopt or even give serious consideration to implementing a preventive strategy in peacetime. This, however, has not stopped military officers from occasionally advocating it.[5] Israel is the unique example since 1919 of a democracy consistently adopting both a preventive and a pre-emptive strategy. In 1956 the Israeli government decided to wage war before the Egyptian forces could make full use of weaponry procured from the Eastern Bloc. It also hoped to expand its territory to provide greater defence in depth.[6] Moshe Dayan, the Chief of Army Staff, wrote later:

> It was clear to us in Israel that the primary purpose of this massive Egyptian rearmament was to prepare Egypt for a decisive confrontation ... Egypt's purpose was to wipe us out, or at least to win a decisive military victory which would leave us in helpless subjection ... We considered that it would take the Egyptian army from 6 to 8 months to absorb and digest most of its new weapons and equipment ... I [urged] military action as soon as possible.[7]

Eleven years later the Israeli government again became convinced that the Arab states were preparing for war because President Nasser had ordered the UN peacekeeping forces that were separating the two states to leave his territory, closed the Straits of Tiran and begun a military buildup in Sinai. The Israelis, therefore, decided to strike first and succeeded within hours in obliterating the Arab air forces. Having secured command of the air, they were able to dominate the battlefield and seize control of Jerusalem, the west bank of the Jordan and Sinai. These actions made Israel the pre-eminent military power in the Middle East.[8]

Again, on June 7 1981 the Israelis staged a preventive air attack on an Iraqi reactor at Al Tawita, south-east of Baghdad. Their secret service had, apparently, already tried to destroy the French-built reactor at La Seyne-sur-Mer before it was delivered to the Iraqis in April 1979.[9] While there was general international condemnation of the Israeli preventive action and considerable scepticism of their claims about Iraqi ambitions to acquire nuclear weapons, it is now clear that these Israeli suspicions were justified. But Israeli action was not to end the Iraqi programme, rather it delayed Iraqi efforts and increased the secrecy surrounding them. Supporters have argued that Israeli actions prevented Saddam Hussein from dominating the Middle East and that they established a new international norm. According to one such commentator:

> Since then, the use of brute military force against any form of major threat to the international community has become an accepted norm rather than the exception, not only by the United States but also by other leading powers, as well as by the international community as a whole ... To a large extent, the seeds of the present global campaign against the threat of nuclear terrorism were planted on June 7 1981

by eight daring pilots who in less than two minutes destroyed Iraq's ambitions to become a nuclear state.[10]

In fact, the international community has *not* accepted the legitimacy of preventive wars and, for the reasons outlined above, it would be extremely undesirable if it were to do so because it would make brute force the only arbiter of world politics.

Moreover, just as the Japanese attack on Pearl Harbor had achieved military advantage at the expense of earning the bitter hatred of the American people, so those who defend Israeli actions ignore the major political disadvantages which the Israelis reaped as a result of their military victories. They were increasingly seen as 'aggressors' and their isolation has grown steadily. By 2003, polls showed that Israel was regarded in Europe as the primary threat to world peace.[11] Israelis can argue that they have to follow preventative and pre-emptive strategies because they are loathed by most of their neighbours, who regard them as interlopers responsible for ethnically cleansing the Palestinians. Thus the Israelis would say that their country has to live with the opprobrium which their military strategy makes necessary. But their situation is *sui generis*; the adoption of similar strategies by other major states would be disastrous.

## The United States creeps toward pre-emptive and preventive strategies

The precedent of the Israeli strike against the Iraqi reactor in 1981 is just one of many factors encouraging the United States to adopt pre-emptive and preventive strategies. When the decline of the Soviet Union in the 1980s left the United States as the only superpower, it could afford to use its military forces without fear of becoming embroiled in a general war. Consequently it launched air strikes to punish enemies for past actions on a number of occasions in the 1980s and 1990s. On each occasion there followed a prolonged argument, particularly among Europeans, about the legitimacy and moral justification for such attacks, as well as about the intelligence on which they were based. But most of these strikes were in response to specific acts of aggression against US citizens. Even though they were intended to deter future attacks, they were not uniquely or primarily pre-emptive or preventive strikes. They may, however, have created the state of mind in which a doctrine of preventive and pre-emptive warfare could be adopted.

In April 1986, President Reagan ordered air strikes against Libya in retaliation for what he had learnt, from intercepted messages, was a

Libyan-backed terrorist attack on US servicemen in a Berlin disco-theque.[12] Subsequently Libya was involved in terrorist attacks against US citizens, including the destruction of a Pan American Boeing 747 over Scotland, although the frequency of such attacks declined and they eventually ceased altogether.[13] Libya has, indeed, now abandoned its effort to confront the West, support terrorism and develop WMD. In fact it is often held up as the best example of the success of the new US policy of threatening states that plan to develop such weapons.[14]

In August 1998, President Clinton ordered a cruise missile strike against terrorist bases in Afghanistan because intelligence reports suggested that Osama bin Laden was behind the attack on US embassies in East Africa which had killed 257 people. At the same time, the United States destroyed what it believed to be a chemical weapons plant in Khartoum because it understood that the building was linked to bin Laden.[15] Like the attack on Libya, the strike against Afghanistan could be seen as punitive and, in so far as the United States hoped to kill bin Laden and weaken al-Qaeda, perhaps also preventive.

When the al-Qaeda leader emerged unharmed, the United States increasingly isolated the Afghan government to force it to hand him over for trial.[16] Almost immediately a group called the International Islamic Front for Holy War against Jews and Crusaders announced that it was mobilizing to launch 'pitiless' attacks against the United States and Israel, and that it would try to destroy ships and aircraft, and force the closure of companies and banks.[17] The simultaneous attack by the United States on the alleged CW factory in Khartoum was preventive. However, almost immediately, doubts arose about whether the Sudanese plant was actually manufacturing nerve gas. US intelligence fears about the factory were apparently based on the presence of a nerve gas ingredient, the chemical EMPTA, but many analysts argued that this had peaceful uses and it is now generally accepted that the evidence for the attack on the plant was weak.[18]

Calls from within the United States to make preventive strikes to stop the proliferation of weapons of mass destruction grew throughout the 1990s. In 1994 the United States Air University Press published a pamphlet by Franklin Wolf on 'Air Power as a Non-Proliferation Tool'. While admitting that force should only be used as a last resort to prevent nuclear proliferation, Wolf nevertheless believed that 'military force offers much to the non-proliferation regime, representing much untapped potential'.

According to Wolf, the United States should launch preventive strikes on any country that is determined to ignore international pressure and advance its nuclear programme. However, he admitted that public support for such measures was fragile, that media criticism of civilian casualties would be considerable and that the intelligence, which would be needed to justify preventive attacks, was often inaccurate, while the threat of attack would encourage evasion by proliferators. If the attack did not entirely destroy the nuclear facilities targeted, he pointed out, then: '[O]pportunities for restrike are considerably fewer than they would be in time of war ... In short the reconnaissance and intelligence demands of counter-proliferation ... are considerable and need attention.'[19] In fact, the March 2003 attack on Iraq suggests that these demands often cannot be met and that each occasion when the intelligence proves false will greatly increase hostility to this sort of attack.

## The US decision to launch preventive war

The US military offensive against Afghanistan in October 2001 could be justified as a defensive measure in the face of 9/11. It was also both preventive and pre-emptive, as it was designed to eliminate al-Qaeda once and for all. Nevertheless, as we have pointed out elsewhere, it had UN sanction and very high levels of support across the world. About 70 per cent of the British population backed the attack and only between 10 and 20 per cent were critical. Most however did not believe it would prevent further attacks, indeed 59 per cent believed it made such attacks more likely. Evidently the idea that the United States should punish its attacker was more convincing than the instrumental notion that an attack would be tactically beneficial.[20] Certainly, the support for the war with Afghanistan was much higher than it was for the attack on Iraq eighteen months later.

Among the grounds given for that attack were that the Iraqis had defied the United Nations, were developing weapons of mass destruction, had supported terrorism and were ruled by a tyrannical regime. However the US Congressional debate about the authorization for the use of force against Iraq on October 10 2002 constantly reverted back to the question of pre-emptive and/or preventive war. Democratic Minority Leader Richard Gephardt voted for the authorization because of September 11 and 'the clear' evidence that terrorists wanted to use weapons of mass destruction against the United States. But he warned that the resolution was not, 'an endorsement or acceptance of the President's new policy of pre-emption. Iraq is unique and this resolution is a unique response. A full discussion of the President's new pre-emption policy must come at another time'.[21] Six days earlier Senator Robert Byrd had pointed out that he had asked repeatedly why the United States had to go to war at that time and had received no answer. In his view, there was no new evidence pointing to the need for precipitate war. In other words Congress was being asked to approve preventive strikes:

> We are voting on this new doctrine of preventive strikes – pre-emptive strikes. There is nothing in this Constitution about pre-emptive strikes. Yet in this rag here, this resolution, we are being asked to vote the imprimatur of the Congress on that doctrine ... That is a mistake. Are we going to present the face of America as a bully going out at high noon with both guns blazing or are we going to maintain the face of America as a country which believes in justice, the rule of law, freedom and liberty and the rights of all people to work out their ultimate destiny?[22]

In the event, the US attack was not sanctioned by the Security Council and Iraq did not have weapons of mass destruction, though its ruler Saddam Hussein would, no doubt, have liked to have developed these and the US and British governments believed that he might already have done so. A number of Iraqis had defected to the United States peddling bogus claims that their country was producing biological weapons. One such, Adnan Saeed al-Haideri, was quoted in July 2002 alleging that there was a biological weapons factory under Saddam Hussein Hospital in Baghdad, and at least seven other locations where biological or chemical weapons were being prepared. None of this was true.[23] Nor was the interpretation of aerial photographs accurate. They did not prove, as Colin Powell told the Security Council, that the Iraqis were making WMD. As a former Director of the CIA wrote, 'both electronic surveillance and photos can be deceived'.[24] Allegations that Iraq was involved in terrorism were made by, among others, by supporters of the 'Project for the New American Century', who wrote to George Bush on September 20 2001:

> It may be that the Iraqi government provided assistance in some form that the recent attack on the United States [9/11]. But even if evidence does not link Iraq directly to the attack, any strategy aiming at the eradication of terrorism and its sponsors must include a determined effort to remove Saddam Hussein from power in Iraq.

In fact, there was no foundation to suggestions that Iraq was involved in the attack on 9/11, although Donald Rumsfeld, the US Defense Secretary, asserted the contrary to NATO in September 2002.[25] Eventually the administration had to admit that many of the charges against Iraq were unfounded.[26] Unfortunately, however, the retraction received far less publicity in the United States than the original claims.

We now know from the official British investigation in 2004 that the intelligence organizations 'made clear that the al-Qaeda-linked facilities in the Kurdish Ansar al Islam area were involved in the production of chemical and biological agents, but that they were beyond the control of the Iraqi regime'. The intelligence sources went on to say that there was evidence of contacts between al-Qaeda and members of the Iraqi regime but that it was most unlikely the Iraqis would actually cooperate with the terrorists.[27] Thus, like the earlier attack on the Khartoum factory, the experience of the war on Iraq reinforces the argument that preventive or pre-emptive strikes could be based on false evidence, sometimes supplied by mendacious defectors and other agents, conjured up by politicians against the advice of their intelligence services or simply mistaken. Never in modern British history has the case for war been subsequently exposed as so deeply flawed because the facts on which it was based were incorrect. Prime Minister Blair gave the impression in a dossier released in September 2002 that the Iraqis were capable of using WMD within 45 minutes and failed to make clear that, even if this had been true, the government was talking of tactical weapons, not ones which could strike Britain.[28]

In the US case there was, however, a much earlier precedent. In 1898 the United States went to war with Spain in large part because the US warship *Maine* had blown up in Havana with the loss of 266 lives. The US believed that the Spanish blew up the ship. The Spanish insisted it was an accident and their view was eventually confirmed by British experts. Three-quarters of a century later, US Admiral Hyman Rickover commented:

> In the modern technological age, the battle cry: 'Remember the Maine!' should have a special meaning for us; with almost instant-aneous communications that can command weapons of unprecedented power, we can no longer approach technical problems with the casualness and confidence held by the Americans in 1898.

Rickover went on to warn that technical problems should be examined carefully by experts so that people in 'high places' do not exert US power 'without more careful consideration of the consequences' than they did in 1898.[29] Events leading up to the March 2003 war suggest that his warning has still not been heeded.

The decision to launch a preventive attack on Iraq in March 2003 also confirms the argument of allied statesmen in 1919 that military considerations should not be allowed to outweigh political, legal and ethical factors. It seems very likely that in March 2003 the UN inspections in Iraq were curtailed and war launched simply because it was considered militarily convenient to attack before the hot Iraqi summer. But it was precisely this sort of consideration which, as we pointed out above, most continental European governments rejected and, consequently, the issue divided the United States from its major European allies more deeply than at any time since 1945.

Some commentators, especially neoconservatives, would argue that European criticisms of pre-emptive and preventive strikes by the Israelis and the United States are a result of Europe's lack of military capacity. But the British and French are at least as capable of making pre-emptive strikes on states such as Iraq, as are the Israelis. Much more importantly, the Europeans have come to believe that war should only be fought as a last resort when all other courses have been exhausted. In contrast, many in the United States argue that, after the cold war, small wars can and should be politically instrumental. This approach was summarized in the famous phrase by the Prussian strategist Karl von Clausewitz that 'war is nothing but a continuation of politics with the admixture of other means', but Europeans would see the Iraq War as more than that and try to bind it within the confines of international law.[30]

## Fire discipline

Rightly or wrongly, many Europeans have become critical of the training and fire discipline of US forces. Older people remember the Vietnam War and the massacres at My Lai on March 16 1968 and elsewhere. They look back to the mission to rescue US embassy hostages in Iran when a US helicopter crashed into a transport, and the attempt ended in humiliating failure.[31] They recall the shooting down of an Iranian airliner on July 3 1988 by the *USS Vincennes* under the mistaken impression that it was a small fighter-bomber. They watched the films of the disastrous raid in October 1993 by US Rangers and Delta Force troops to capture two Somali clan leaders in Bakara market, Mogadishu. They recall the accidental killing of four Canadian soldiers in April 2002 and wounding of eight others because a US fighter pilot mistook them for Taliban troops. They saw the photographs of US Marines killing wounded Iraqis during the attack on Fallujah in November 2004 and they were shocked by the shooting of Nicola Calipari, the Italian intelligence agent, by US troops at a checkpoint in Iraq on March 4 2005.[32]

Calipari was accompanying an Italian journalist who had been freed by kidnappers. US forces had been warned that he was bringing the kidnapped journalist to Baghdad airport but those at the checkpoint had, presumably, not been alerted and sprayed his car with bullets.[33] Defenders of the American forces rightly pointed out that such terrible mistakes always happen in tense situations in warfare, that the US has been involved in far more wars than any other country and thus its forces are bound to have made more mistakes than those belonging to other powers, but the criticisms continue to circulate and, indeed, to grow. And this growth is important because it enhances fears of the US doctrines of preventive and pre-emptive war; the combination of a trigger-happy administration and trigger-happy armed forces seems particularly menacing.

Furthermore, history has made Europeans much more aware than Americans of the financial, physical and emotional costs of warfare and thus perhaps more determined that it should only be waged as a last resort; US military casualties in the First World War were only some 3% of the Allied total, and even more Europeans died afterwards from starvation and disease than were killed in the trenches. The devastation wrought by the Second World War was more widespread; it impoverished the whole of Europe for a generation. In contrast, the US economy grew dramatically during the Second World War until it was as powerful as all of the rest of the developed countries put together.[34] It is not surprising then that Europeans should view warfare as a last resort. And, if it is a last resort, it cannot be preventive, not least because a decision for war should be taken for legal, moral and political rather than military reasons.

Not only have Europeans suffered vastly more than Americans have from war; they also suffered from a particular form of warfare – bombing from the air. Americans have always been proponents of the use of air power because it is a supremely technical way of fighting and because it has kept wars away from their own shores. In 1945, when Gallup asked the US public which branch of the services they believed the government should fund most extensively so that the United States would remain a great power, 43.6 per cent wanted their taxes spent on air services, 22.1 per cent on the Navy and 8.4 per cent on the army.[35] The Europeans have always been much more cautious about this form of power, undoubtedly because they have been the victims of bomber attacks: Britain in the First World War, Germany, Britain, France and Italy in the Second. For them aircraft strikes mean not clean, surgical warfare but the sound of the air raid siren, the crash of bombs, the screams of the injured and, subsequently, the stink of putrefying bodies in smashed houses.[36] And though the immediate memories of bombs landing on their European homelands are dying with the wartime generation, the debate about the legitimacy and morality of such attacks is actually widening.[37] A writer who entitled his account of a bombing campaign *Lucrative Targets* would be regarded by many in Europe as a psychopath, even if he commended the US Air Force in the first Gulf War for making the greatest efforts to avoid civilian casualties.[38]

## Precision attacks

Recent technical innovations have encouraged the United States to attack terrorists and perhaps other menacing individuals or groups without declaring war on the country where they are lurking. Cruise missiles were used in the attacks on Afghanistan and Iraq in 1998, on Afghanistan in 2001 and on Iraq in 2003. These can be very precise, but they still depend on good and timely intelligence if they are to hit their targets. More recently the United States used an unmanned Predator aircraft to kill 'terrorists' in Yemen.

It is only too easy to see the quandary in which the United States was placed. It knows that al-Qaeda is determined to attack the United States and dedicated to destroying the Western way of life. It discovered that a group of al-Qaeda supporters was travelling in Yemen. It may have told the Yemeni government what was happening, but whether it did or not, the temptation to attack the car they were using proved irresistible. Their belief that they took the right decision may have been reinforced when Nasser Al-Bahr, who was involved in the al-Queda attack on the *USS Cole*, was caught but then released by the Yemeni government. He subsequently gave an interview with the London daily *Al-Quds Al-Arabi* explaining that the aim of the attack was to show that terrorists could damage the most powerful US warships and thus raise Muslim morale.[39]

The unwillingness or inability of other governments to deal with terrorists in their territory tempts Washington to take the law into its own hands. But such a US response is a slippery slope. Suppose that the al-Qaeda cell were somewhere in Europe and the government of the European country could not act against the cell for legal reasons. Should the United States kill the members of the cell, as the Israelis subsequently killed those terrorists who murdered eleven of their athletes at the Munich Olympics in 1972?[40] Democracies notoriously have difficulty controlling their own citizens' behaviour and bringing them to justice when they are suspected of being involved with terrorist organizations. US citizens were, for example, the primary source of funds and weapons for the IRA, which carried on a violent struggle against the British in Northern Ireland, a campaign that took the lives of more people than died on 9/11, yet the United States would hardly have condoned covert warfare inside their territory against the perpetrators.

Similarly Britain has been accused by India of allowing extremist movements, which are responsible for the uprising and killings in Kashmir, to operate from its territory. A number of those who volunteered to fight for the Taliban in Afghanistan also came from Britain. And the first wave of suicide bombers in London in July 2005 were British citizens. Moreover, around the world it has been very difficult to prove before courts that some of those suspected of being involved with September 11 itself were actually guilty. How would the British feel if the United States destroyed a house in Hampstead or Tipton that they suspected of harbouring terrorists? If it is only legitimate to use force against suspected terrorists in the Third World, then this says little about the equality of states and peoples.

Of course, it may be said, quite reasonably, that assassination is not the same as terrorism, but rather a preventive strike on a single person.[41] 9/11 deliberately targeted civilians, while an attempt to assassinate a tyrant such as Saddam Hussein, or a member of al-Qaeda, would be discriminatory, only targeting individuals responsible for violence. But the victims of such attacks will see the perpetrators as terrorists; the British certainly regarded the IRA's efforts to blow up the hotel where Mrs Thatcher was staying in Brighton or to mortar 10 Downing Street as terrorist attacks.[42] No doubt, the United States would feel the same about an attack on George W. Bush or other members of the administration whom considerable numbers of Afghans and Iraqis undoubtedly hold responsible for the deaths of their fellow citizens. Certainly there was outrage in the United States at the attempted assassination of George Bush Senior.

There is a relatively clear distinction between assassination and random terrorism but, though the first may sometimes be morally defensible and the second never, both are corrosive of international legal order. In any case, it is hard to think of many examples of assassination that have benefited the perpetrators politically in the long run – most have been utterly counter-productive. Acquiring a reputation for assassination means that a country or an organization can be held responsible for every unexpected death. The KGB was blamed for the death of the former Czech leader Alexander Dubcek in 1992; the South African intelligence services were said to have tried to kill Prince Charles in Zimbabwe in April 1980.[43] Mossad has been blamed variously for the attack on the *USS Cole* and for 9/11.[44] The British were accused of placing a bomb which destroyed the aircraft carrying UN Secretary General Dag Hammarskjöld in Northern Rhodesia in September 1961.[45]

There is certainly a strong temptation for Western governments to respond with force when they are under attack from terrorist groups. But they should weigh the arguments carefully before they weaken international and domestic law in this way. The intelligence on which their response is based may turn out to be false, their weapons may be less discriminating than they hoped, they may be seen to be operating in Third World states in ways which they would consider wholly unacceptable in the West, and they may gain a reputation for assassination which leads to accusations that they are complicit in cases where they are wholly innocent.

## Preventive war and the 'axis of evil'

If the preventive nature of the war on terrorism ties the United States in legal, moral and semantic knots, military action against regimes held to be assisting terrorists has also brought great practical difficulties. The United States overthrew the governments in Afghanistan and Iraq in 2001 and 2003 on the grounds, in part, that they supported terrorist movements. Destroying their governments was not, in fact, very difficult because of the strength of US air power. But each defeated government had to be replaced with another more sympathetic to the United States and that could only be done with the support of the local inhabitants because otherwise, as we shall see later, they might fight an unconventional war in their own country and gradually undermine the very reason for the US action in the first place. The patient, legal answer to terrorism is slow and frustrating but it will be the most successful in the long run.

The ancestors of most Americans fled Europe because they hated its quarrels and repressive governments, yet ironically it is precisely those quarrels and the suffering they caused which have encouraged Europeans to be more sceptical than their American counterparts of the use of military force. This is only too obvious in the discussions on the war on terrorism. President George W. Bush and his advisors have argued that 9/11 has placed the United States in the same sort of struggle for survival as the Israelis. The perpetrators of the 9/11 attack were different from other terrorists because they wanted to kill as many people as possible.[46] They would stop at nothing, including using weapons of mass destruction and destroying nuclear power stations, to advance their cause. As Vice President Richard Cheney put it in August 2002:

> Deliverable weapons of mass destruction in the hands of a terror network, or a murderous dictator, or the two working together, constitutes as grave a threat as can be imagined. The risks of inaction are far greater than the risks of action.[47]

The US administration has argued that it is 'at war with terrorism' and that democratic states have often launched preventive and pre-emptive attacks in wartime. President Bush argues, therefore, that he is following precedent by launching strikes against Iraq or other members of the 'axis of evil'. But administration spokesmen have sometimes admitted that this 'war' may last for decades and so, for the indefinite future, the strategy can be used to threaten any state which appears hostile to the United States and which is believed to be developing weapons of mass destruction.[48] Terrorism is a consequence of the politicization of the masses and it can be no more be eradicated than mass political involvement (see Chapter 7). Washington has thus, permanently, arrogated to itself the right to use force against and within any state where it believes terrorists are operating. The United States has absolute sovereignty; every other state's sovereignty is conditional on Washington's approval. Long before the United States acquired its present hegemonic position, the most astute Western analysts pointed out:

> that the balance of power is not something conjured up by Machiavellian statesmen, but is a permanent, a necessary, and, to a large extent, a healthy aspect of international politics; that dangers arise when it is absent.[49]

Many feel that Washington wants to attack states developing WMD not because they threaten the United States or its allies but because WMD are 'equalizers' to the great conventional military superiority of the US. Those who take this view could quote the CIA. Its spokesman told Senator Carl Levin on October 2 2002 that it believed the threat that Saddam Hussein might attack the United States using WMD was low unless the United States attacked first, in which case it would be high.[50] In other words, WMD were weapons of last resort against an over-mighty United States.

One is left with the conclusion that the United States practised deterrence during the cold war because it believed that its potential enemies thought the same way and followed the same military policies. Now that the United States no longer has to deter the Soviet Union it has not itself been deterred from attacking Iraq. However, while US officials claim that Pyongyang and Teheran cannot be trusted not to launch a primitive nuclear weapon against the United States or its allies, they completely ignore the fate which would overtake the two countries in such circumstances. Iran or North Korea might at some future date be able to damage an American city. In retaliation, the United States could turn such countries into radioactive deserts from which recovery would never be possible. For what possible reason would their governments even consider making a feeble attack on the United States except in retaliation against a preventive US war?

## Advantages and disadvantages of preventive war

Plainly the world is at a turning-point in the development of international relations, international law and security policy. We have to weigh the advantages which preventive and pre-emptive strikes against terrorist bases and rogue states give to the United States against the political disadvantages. In particular, Washington has coerced Libya into abandoning its support for terrorism and its attempts to produce WMD. It has destroyed the Taliban regime in Afghanistan which befriended Osama bin Laden and his colleagues. It has made it unlikely that any other government will support terrorism as directly as Libya, North Korea and Syria did in the past. On the other hand, consideration should be given to the problems caused by the policy of preventive war:

- The damage to international law and international institutions such as the United Nations.
- The growing perception in poorer countries that the lives of Western peoples are valued more highly than the lives of Muslims and others living in the Third World.
- The fear that pre-emptive and preventive strikes have evoked even among the United States' allies.
- The bitter anger among those unable to respond to US attacks and thus their growing willingness to support terrorist attacks.
- The encouragement given to other states to launch preventive wars.
- The consequent encouragement of arms races around the world to build up forces against a future attack.

Plainly Europeans believe that these disadvantages are too great and do not accept the claim that a new norm has been established under which brute force is accepted in international affairs. Their opinions are confirmed by the frequent failure of the intelligence on which preventive and pre-emptive strikes have allegedly been based:

- The Sudanese factory was probably not producing chemical weapons.
- The Iraqis were not developing weapons of mass destruction.
- The Iraqis were not involved in 9/11.

Much human Intelligence is based on bazaar gossip, as the investigations into the allegations about Iraqi weapons of mass destruction made all too clear. Despite the efforts to disparage them, international bodies such as the International Atomic Energy Agency are highly professional and must be involved when the assessment of nuclear, biological and chemical weapons programmes is concerned.[51]

Just as the traditional wisdom about the importance of maintaining a balance of power has been vindicated by the history of the last decade, so have the traditional concerns about preventive wars. Not a shred of evidence has been provided that contemporary 'rogue' states are somehow so irrational that they cannot be deterred as Stalin, Mao and their successors were through the decades of the cold war. The invasion of Iraq and the overthrow of Saddam Hussein are now facts, but the weakness of the arguments for preventive war need to be exposed before any future war is undertaken against the 'axis of evil' countries or others perceived to be hostile to the United States.

## Notes

1   *The Times*, 17 June 2002.
2   'US National Strategy to Combat WMD', 11 December 2002, The White House, http://www.acronym.org.uk/docs0212
3   Sifry, Micah and Cerf, Christopher, *The Iraq War Reader: History, Documents, Opinions* (New York: Touchstone Books, 2003), p. 385.
4   Lawrence Freedman, *The Evolution of Nuclear Strategy* (London: Macmillan, 1981); Norman Friedman, *Fifty Year War: Conflict and Strategy in the cold war* (Annapolis: Naval Institute Press, 2000), p. 290.
5   Arthur J. Marder (ed.), *Fear God and Dread Nought: The Correspondence of Admiral of the Fleet Lord Fisher*, vol. 11 (London: Jonathan Cape, 1956), p. 20.
6   Motti Golani, 'Chief of Staff in Quest of a War: Moshe Dayan Leads Israel into War', *Journal of Strategic Studies* (March 2001).
7   Moshe Dayan, *Story of My Life* (London: Weidenfeld & Nicolson, 1976), p. 147.
8   For Israeli justification of the 1967 attack see Chaim Herzog, *The Arab-Israeli Wars* (London: Arms and Armour, 1982), pp. 147–53; Abba Eban, *Personal Witness: Peace Through My Eyes* (London: Jonathan Cape, 1993), ch. 20.
9   Steve Weissman and Herbert Krosney, *The Islamic Bomb: The Nuclear Threat to Israel and the Middle East* (New York: Times Books, 1981), ch. 16.
10  Uri Bar-Joseph, 'Epilogue' in Amos Perlmutter, Michael Handel, Uri Bar-Joseph, *Two Minutes Over Baghdad* (London: Frank Cass, 2003), p. 174.
11  'EU Poll: US tied for Second Biggest Threat to World Peace', http://www.xent.com/pipermail/fork/week-of-Mon-20031103
12  George P. Schultz, *Turmoil and Triumph: Diplomacy, Power and the Victory of the American Idea* (New York: Scribner's, 1993), ch. 33.
13  IISS *Strategic Survey 1998/9*, p. 69.

14   *The Times*, 13 March 2004; *New York Times*, 25 March 2004.
15   *The Times*, 21 August 1998.
16   *The Hindu* (Madras), 31 October 1999; *The Times*, 5 February 2001.
17   *The Times*, 26 August 1998.
18   *The Times*, 25 and 28 August, and 3 and 22 September 1998.
19   Franklin R. Woolf, *Of Carrots and Sticks or Air Power as a Nonproliferation Tool* (Maxwell, AL: Air University Press, July 1994), p. 44.
20   'War on Afghanistan Poll', 11 October 2001, http://www.mori.com/polls/2001/granada
21   Sifry and Cerf, *The Iraq War Reader*, p. 366.
22   Sifry and Cerf, *The Iraq War Reader*, p. 376.
23   *The Times*, 12 July 2002.
24   Stansfield Turner, *Secrecy and Democracy: The CIA in Transition* (London: Sidgwick & Jackson, 1986), p. 211.
25   *Los Angeles Times*, 25 September 2002; *Guardian*, 4 September 2002; *Globe and Mail* (Toronto), 21 September 2002; *Los Angeles Times*, 21 September 2002.
26   Sifry and Cerf, *The Iraq War Reader*, pp. 223 and 267.
27   *Review of Intelligence on Weapons of Mass Destruction: Report of a Committee of Privy Councillors under the Rt Hon. Lord Butler* (London: Stationery Office, 2004).
28   *Review of Intelligence*, pp. 85–6.
29   David Woodward, *Sunk! How the Great Battleships Were Lost* (London: George Allen & Unwin, 1982), p. 37.
30   Michael Howard and Peter Paret (eds), *Clausewitz on War* (Princeton University Press, 1984).
31   Gary Sick, *All Fall Down: America's Fateful Encounter with Iran* (London: Tauris, 1985), p. 297.
32   *The Times*, 6 May 2005.
33   *The Times*, 27 April 2005.
34   Paul Kennedy, *The Rise and Fall of the Great Powers* (London: Unwin Hyman, 1988), p. 369.
35   *Public Opinion Quarterly* (Summer 1945).
36   For British reactions to 'the blitz' see Angus Calder, *The People's War: Britain 1939–45* (London: Jonathan Cape, 1969); Maureen Waller, *London 1945* (London: John Murray, 2005), ch. 1; for the targets of the British air offensive see John Terraine, *A Time for Courage: The Royal Air Force in the European War* (New York: Macmillan, 1985).
37   Nicholas Stargardt, 'Victims of Bombing and Retaliation', *German Historical Institute Bulletin* (November 2004), 57.
38   Perry D. Jamieson, *Lucrative Targets: The US Air Force in the Kuwaiti Theatre of Operations*, (Washington: Air Force History and Museums Program, 2001).
39   *Special Dispatch N. 766- Jihad and Terrorism*, Middle East Media Research Institute, 19 August 2004.
40   George Jonas, *Vengeance: The True Story of an Israeli Counter-Terrorist Mission* (London: Collins, 1984).
41   Edward Hyams, *Killing No Murder: A Study of Assassination as a Political Means* (London: Nelson, 1969).
42   Margaret Thatcher, *The Downing Street Years* (New York: HarperCollins, 1993), p. 382.
43   *The Times*, 12 November 1991 and 19 August 1998.

44   *Special Dispatch N. 766- Jihad and Terrorism*, The Middle East Media Research Institute, 19 August 2004.
45   *The Times*, 1 January 1992 and 20 August 1998.
46   *The 9/11 Commission Report: Final Report of the National Commission on Terrorist Attacks upon the United State* (New York: Norton, 2004), pp. 146–51.
47   Sifry and Serf, *The Iraq War Reader*, p. 298.
48   *The Times*, 31 August 2004.
49   Max Beloff, *The Balance of Power* (London: George Allen & Unwin, 1968), p. 3.
50   Sifry and Cerf, *The Iraq War Reader*, p. 368.
51   For criticism of the IAEA see Gary Milhollin, 'The Iraqi Bomb', *The New Yorker*, 1 February 1993, pp. 47ff.

# 7
# Misunderstanding Terrorism: The Sword

After 9/11, the Bush administration was tempted into adopting a strategy as old as war itself to avenge and protect America: the use of both the sword and the shield. But that choice was based on a serious misunderstanding of the terrorist threat, and consequently the government made grave mistakes in its foreign policy. The administration should have attempted to win over the terrorists' supporters in the wider community, and formed an international coalition against the threat and to isolate the extremists. Its bellicose policies had the reverse effects because terrorism cannot be curbed by military force.

An appropriate response to 9/11 depended on correctly appreciating the conditions that motivate such attacks, analysing the goals of the terrorists, and then subtly weighing the consequences of the various possible responses. Terrorists, by definition and necessity, employ asymmetrical warfare: the United States has vast sums of money and advanced weaponry while all the terrorists have is their commitment, their lives (which they can sacrifice in suicidal attacks) and small and relatively primitive weapons. Since US security policy has often involved the frequent use of armed force, and tends to deal with the symptoms not the causes of terrorism, it is important to consider whether military intervention itself is one of the causes of terrorism, not the consequence of or answer to it.

## The new face of conflict

After the horrific events in New York, Washington and Pennsylvania on September 11 2001, the question quickly became how the United States and its allies should react. The first temptation was to pulverize all enemies – to demolish the perpetrators of the violence. The administration and the US people agreed on a military response, and that was the option chosen. Clearly, the ideal response would rather have addressed the reasons for terrorism, brought the perpetrators to justice and avoided escalating the situation by provoking more revenge and fostering a new blood cycle. Certainly, it was not in its own interest for the United States to create the soil, seeds and nutrients for future terrorist activity.

The attacks on 9/11 were appalling. The number of deaths surpassed those at Pearl Harbor in 1941: 2,600 people died at the World Trade Centre, 125 at the Pentagon, and 256 on the four aircraft. It was clear that the attackers would provide inspiration for dissident groups around the world. Such terrorism is morally repugnant, whoever carries it out. But the scale was hardly unprecedented; the 1993–8 Rwanda massacres resulted in as many deaths of Tutsi and Hutu as took place in New York and Washington not just one day but every day – for one hundred days. A dispassionate comparison of the carnage was impossible because of the trauma that the United States had suffered, but the US administration needed to rise above the emotional fray and formulate a strategy which had a much greater chance of success than the one adopted.

What was unprecedented on September 11 was that the most powerful state in the world proved vulnerable at home to attack from outside its borders.[1] This was the worst terrorist attack on the United States ever instigated from outside, the culmination of an escalating Islamist offensive. The year before there had been an estimated 423 terrorist outrages around the world, almost half of which involved US interests or citizens.[2] Many of the threats and three major terrorist offensives against US interests over the previous decade had come from Islamist extremists. On February 1993, a group led by Ramzi Yousef tried to bring down the World Trade Centre; using a truck bomb his group killed six people and caused more than 1000 injuries. In August 1998, al-Qaeda terrorists drove truck bombs into US embassies in Kenya and Tanzania. And again in October 2000 al-Qaeda used explosives to blow a hole in the side of the destroyer *USS Cole*, killing 17 military personnel. President Bill Clinton responded to the second of these attacks with a cruise missile offensive against an al-Qaeda base in Afghanistan (from which bin Laden escaped) that clearly did nothing to end the offensive or deter further attacks. Subsequent plans for special forces operations to capture the terrorist leader were shelved without explanation.

Between February 1993 and April 1998 the Taleban government in Afghanistan declined several requests to hand bin Laden over to the United States. In the most explicit piece of public information available, on August 6 2001, President Bush received a Daily Brief warning entitled 'Bin Laden Determined to Strike in US', but the administration did not take the warning seriously enough to prepare any new emergency plans for homeland security.

In theory, there was an entire spectrum of possible responses to the terrorist events of 9/11, ranging from the annihilation of the terrorists' bases by nuclear or conventional bombing, through special-forces attempts to assassinate bin Laden, to trying to find out what the terrorists wanted, who their backers were and how their funds could be interdicted and their groups infiltrated. The Bush administration chose to respond with a global 'war on terrorism' – a war on 'evil' as the president called it. Immediately after 9/11 the US government announced that the initial goals of the war would be to:

- capture Osama bin Laden;
- capture Mullah Omar (the Taleban leader);
- close down al-Qaeda in Afghanistan and elsewhere; and
- release US prisoners in Afghanistan.

In formulating these specific tactical goals, the primary consideration should have been whether a 'war on terrorism' would work successfully and pragmatically. It needed to meet six strategic objectives:

1. Infiltrating and diminishing terrorist organizations, rather than increasing their attractions to potential recruits.
2. Avoiding damage to the United States, its citizens, its image in the world or its alliances.
3. Remaining cost-effective and avoiding a reduction of the ability of the US armed forces to perform other important functions, or undermining the US economy.
4. Ensuring it was generally seen to be 'just' because it did not cause excessive 'collateral' damage by killing or injuring too many civilians.
5. Reducing the prospects for conflict between the Muslim World and the West.
6. Making sure its objectives were, and were perceived to be, realistic.

As for the success of immediate tactical goals of the war on terrorism, US prisoners in Afghanistan were freed, but four years later Osama bin Laden and Mullar Omar are still, apparently, at large. Al-Qaeda has re-emerged in parts of Afghanistan and elsewhere. As for the six strategic objectives that should have been met: terrorist activity has not appreciably decreased around the world, while the intervention in Iraq has increased the attraction of asymmetrical warfare for many radical Muslims; serious damage has been done to the US image, alliances and economy; US forces are so strained that the US could not mount another ground war if there were a major challenge elsewhere; the failure to discover weapons of mass destruction in Iraq or any evidence that Baghdad was involved in 9/11, combined with massive civilian deaths there during the insurgency, have undermined the claim that intervention was a 'just war' and greatly exacerbated tensions between Muslims and the West, leading to the attacks on the Madrid railway, the London transportation system, and elsewhere.

The idea of conducting an interminable war on terrorism, or especially on evil, is widely regarded as ridiculous. One cannot go to war with terrorism any more than one can go to war against poverty, drugs, or crime – all of which have been tried without success in America. A war is a tactic, a method or a way of describing a major effort. Declaring a war on terrorism is tantamount to declaring that the United States will assassinate or bomb terrorism. Such a 'war' is unlimited in scope and one will never know if or when it has been terminated.

## Terrorism as a concept

The concept of terrorism must be clarified if any light is to be shed on the problem or tactics designed to counter it. The standard definition (there are at least 109 of them to choose from) is 'the systematic use of violence or threat of violence against civilians and/or states to obtain political concessions'. Recall that when the term '*La Terreur*' was first coined for Robespierre's Committee of Safety during the French Revolution it meant the indiscriminate murder of ordinary civilians by the government of the day.[3] In other words, the authorities used mass executions to terrorize their own people. It was *state* terrorism. Over the years, the term evolved from its initial conception to imply that non-state actors, not governments, were the main perpetrators of terrorism.

While the United Nations has grappled with this problem of definition it has not solved it.[4] A proposed UN convention on terrorism has been stalled since 1997 because some member states will not allow terrorism to be defined by the nature of the act but only by its purpose. A suicide bomber is not a terrorist, they say, if the act is carried out for a righteous reason such as liberation or to resist foreign occupation. The word terrorism implies, correctly enough, that all such acts are heinous. But it is true that the purposes might be noble, even if the methods are repugnant. Furthermore, the term is also often used by governments to anathematize all asymmetrical warfare, even if it targets soldiers. Yet, in one of his most inspiring speeches Winston Churchill promised in 1940 that the

British people would fight on the beaches and in the hills if the Nazis invaded. No doubt Hitler would have denounced attacks on Nazi troops as terrorism. Plainly, finding an agreed definition will never be easy.

## New and old terrorism

Today we are more familiar with hostage-taking and suicide bombing as terrorist weapons than the French guillotine, but the results are similar. Terror is used by individuals, groups or states in an attempt to force governments either to alter their policies in the direction the terrorists demand, or for revenge. Examples are legion: the Grand Hotel in Brighton where Mrs Thatcher was staying while attending the Conservative Party conference was blown up by the IRA in 1984; Pan American Flight 103 was blown out of the sky over Lockerbie in Scotland in 1988 by a concealed bomb placed aboard by Libyan and, possibly, Syrian terrorists; a US government building was blown up in Oklahoma City in 1995; American embassies were blown up in Tanzania and Kenya in 1998, and Sarin gas was used in 1995 to attack passengers in a Tokyo subway – thousands were affected and 12 died.

As these examples show, not only the definition but also the form of terrorism has altered. Sometimes the violence is not even used to demand specific concessions but rather is employed as a form of reprisal against the citizens of a state despised for its political activities or its very nature. The destruction of the Pan American airliner was just such an act, and the Tokyo subway bombers also had no concrete or realizable demands. On September 11 2001 when the terrorists hijacked commercial aircraft and flew them into the Twin Towers of the New York Trade Centre and the Pentagon, they made no demands. It is clear from such attacks that innocent bystanders may become targets of the hatred for the perceived wickedness of the civilization or country they represent.

There are thousands of volumes on terrorism, and research in this field is extremely diverse, and often contradictory. Studies of violence-prone groups compare disparate cases, providing categories or checklists concerning organization, leadership, demography, ideology, operations, communications, weapons, funding and external support.[5] Studies of group alienation show that historical experiences and values interact with a group's relative economic deprivation. Since many discontented groups do not become violent, even though they possess some, or all, of the required characteristics, how can one determine which of them are inclined to be strife-prone? The literature is conclusive that groups which both have the resources and seek an ideologically defined transformation of society are more likely to become violent than those that do not. Thus, it is not only the objective conditions of economic and social deprivation that pre-dispose individuals towards violence. As Peter C. Sederberg expresses it, discontent is a state of mind.[6] Or, as Ted Gurr put it, 'What we expect more than what we experience affects our feelings of discontent.'[7]

Thus, discontent, strife and eventually violence occur when an individual or group is affected by an ideology that identifies the group and increases its cohesion. 'Ideology' is an organized set of ideas and values that purport to explain and evaluate conditions and propose guidelines for action. 'Identification' is defined as the way individuals empathize with the political conditions affecting others.[8] Bin Laden's message, 'Hostility towards America is a religious duty, and we hope to be rewarded by God,' is precisely the type of maxim that builds on ideology and iden-tification.[9] A violent group must have both an ideology that can guide the actions of its members and the resources necessary for analysis, organ-ization and action. Ideology may aid terrorists in delegitimizing the state and its institutions but they also need a coherent organization, commit-ted leadership, adequate resources such as weapons and funding, and geographical proximity to external support if they are to be successful.

Sometimes, oppressed groups feel that only shocking and violent actions can gain them the respect and attention they deserve. If the government tries to repress the terrorists' actions with brutality, a retribution–revenge cycle begins in which the actions of each side are fuelled by escalating demands for vengeance. The original reasons for the terrorists' actions may become less significant than the desires for revenge, and their per-secution may widen their support among those who share their religion, nationality or political beliefs.[10]

Over time, terrorism has also come to mean both the 'threat' and 'use' of violence: 'Kill one; frighten ten thousand,' as a Chinese author described it. Terrorists use fear as a weapon. Fear of terrorism in the United States has been so great since 9/11 that there is no need for the terrorists to do anything. Intelligence reports that terrorists might act can be enough to reduce stock prices, stop flights of aircraft, disturb traffic patterns, and cause hospitals and schools to close. State and police actions follow, some-times legally, sometimes illegally, to meet public demands that 'some-thing must be done' and assuage the government's fear that it will be accused of complacency if action is not taken. Clearly, terrorism needs to be understood both in terms of the actual violence used and the violence implied or feared.

Alienated groups who use violence should not be viewed as mentally deranged or psychotic.[11] In fact, their behaviour is seldom, if ever, radically senseless or absurd.[12] Instead of dismissing manifestations of violence as being based on deviant personalities or primarily criminal behaviour, we should understand groups that behave this way in terms of their social psychology.[13] Cycles of violence in the Middle East, South Asia and elsewhere are not isolated incidents provoked by madmen and fanatics. They cannot be explained by inflammatory newspaper headlines about individuals and their fanaticisms. Such high levels of violence are the result of widespread anger, hatred and frustrations, emotions that are fomented over time through group suffering and often, but not always, accompanied by experiences, sometimes vicarious, of extreme economic or social deprivation and persecution.

In this regard we need to understand that realities may be constructed. The distinction between myths and realities is not simple. Violence-prone individuals have a unique understanding of reality, with strong perceptions and interpretations of what is of value to them. In their 'rational' understanding, all things may come together in a world-view of good versus evil. Their thinking provides an elaborate explanation of why they hate someone or something. Throughout history there have been such hostile groups who based their violent acts on feelings of injustice or hatred. Almost all religions, philosophies and ideologies have attracted adherents prepared to shed the blood of others or die for a cause themselves. In this particular case, their unique understanding of reality explains why the Islamist terrorists hate America – why, in their eyes, a jihad is reasonable, even necessary. Jessica Stern put it thus following her interviews with terrorists:

> What seems to happen is that they enter into a kind of trance, where the world is divided between good and evil, victim and oppressor. Uncertainty and ambivalence ... are banished. There is no room for the other side's point of view ... They persuade themselves that any action – even a heinous crime – is justified. They know they are right, not just politically, but morally. They believe that God is on their side.[14]

The increasing number and ferocity of religious terrorist groups may be difficult for secularists to comprehend because the norms, rules and organization of the West are to a large extent based on a separation of church and state. This is not the case for religious terrorists, whose influence derives from their strong beliefs in commitment and resistance to compromise. Their actions are buttressed by messianism – a belief in the imminent transformation of the world – that strengthens their conviction that the end of the world is about to take place anyway. When death for a cause is sacred there is little difficulty in threatening to destroy oneself and others in a suicide bombing.

Born of insecurity, terrorist organizations have, first of all, to ensure their survival. Thus, the terrorists are usually linked by a decentralized power structure that prioritizes secrecy, and allows the subunits considerable autonomy of action. Members receive all the benefits of the group – a cloak of anonymity, the likelihood of escaping blame in a large organization, support and justifications for their actions and perhaps the promise of salvation in a glorious afterlife.[15]

Terrorist organizations have a well-known ability to regenerate themselves if attacked by the forces of power and authority. Because of their deep sense of threat, exclusion and generational experiences of direct violence, they are always preparing for the worst. It is not just rational calculations that make a terrorist. Such groups require loyalty and devotion to a cause greater than themselves. It is the fanaticism, the excess of loyalty to a cause that provides the glue for a terrorist organization.

The evidence gathered about al-Qaeda since 9/11 indicates just how terrorism works. The organization, or movement as perhaps it should be called, has proven flexible, adaptive and durable. According to the annual *Strategic Survey* at least 18,000 individuals trained in al-Qaeda camps remain at large in 60 countries.[16] Despite US claims to have reduced his finances, bin Laden had billions of dollars stashed away before 9/11, of which he has apparently lost only some $120 million. In terms of its actions, since the United States wiped out its training bases in Afghanistan, al-Qaeda has mounted or been blamed for terrorist attacks in Tunisia, Pakistan, Indonesia, Yemen, Kuwait, Morocco, Turkey, Spain, Saudi Arabia, the United Kingdom[17] and, of course, Iraq. In the latter, it is clear that the so-called terrorists, consisting of former Baathists, radical Shiites and Sunnis, foreign fighters, and criminals, are only loosely linked together. One US marine described efforts to combat the insurgents in Iraq as like 'punching a balloon in the fog.'[18]

The movement is now so feared that a small coterie led by Osama bin Laden, Abu Musab al-Zarqawi and their followers do not even need to act to get attention. Because of fear alone, after 9/11 the United States curtailed civil liberties and began to create the rudiments of a security state.

## Al-Qaeda, affiliates, regional jihadists and copycats

Recognizing that terrorists are not insane is the first step in understanding them. But what are they and in particular what is al-Qaeda?[19] Of the many types of terrorists, including nationalist, religious and revolutionary, al-Qaeda is clearly of the religious variety.[20] True believers are fully committed and immune from compromise. Messianism is the cornerstone of their beliefs. Dying for their cause and eliminating enemies is believed to be not only rational but sacred, hence the propensity for martyrdom and suicide bombers. Perhaps the psychology of the religious terrorist is closest to Serge Stepniak-Kravchinski's well-known description:

> The terrorist is noble, terrible, irresistibly fascinating, for he combines in himself the two sublimities of human grandeur: the martyr and the hero. From the day he swears in the depths of his heart to free the people and the country, he knows he is consecrated to death. He goes forth to meet it fearlessly, and can die without flinching, not like a Christian of old, but like a warrior accustomed to look death in the face.[21]

As we point out elsewhere, Muslim militants in general and al-Qaeda in particular are powered by their disgust with the moral degeneracy of the West. The movement is based on a radical internationalist ideology which combines theological justifications with political demands. It is a quarter of a century old. The issue of whether or not there is a worldwide al-Qaeda network that has 'franchised' is irrelevant. Clearly, there is a vast global audience for its exploits and those of its affiliates, with the internet acting as a multiplier. Around the world there are many thousands of unemployed, underemployed, mal employed, disaffected and dislocated Muslims and others who already embrace violently antiwestern doctrines or who can easily be encouraged to do so. This phenomenon is not new. Radical youngsters willing to devote their lives to the pursuit of universal goals in groups such as the German Baader–Meinhof Gang or the Italian Red Brigades or French Maoists have been prevalent over recent decades. Indeed they are an unfortunate, but inevitable, facet of the modern democratic age. What is new is that there are now large Muslim diasporas born in or living throughout Europe, especially in countries with colonial histories such as Britain and France. Hundreds or perhaps thousands of them have turned to radical Islam.

Looking for a universal truth, uprooted from their culture, frustrated by Western society, dejected and not integrated in their new societies, they are a receptive audience for al-Qaeda and its ideology. They come in many forms: members and converts to al-Qaeda, regional jihad organizations, disaffected youth with various levels of loyalty and commitment to the jihadist causes and simply angry and disoriented youth. There is no one type.

Because of their inchoate and ever-changing nature the least-organized of these impromptu groups or 'groupuscles' are difficult to penetrate and to keep under surveillance, as they may have no connections to a broader terrorist network and only minimal or no outside assistance for their attacks. Often merely embryonic in nature, they may even be without any defined organization. They can never be eliminated entirely in any free and democratic society as they are linked by their perceptions of injustice and Muslim suffering, especially in Iraq and Palestine. In a confirmed statement from one of the second wave of terrorists in London in July 2005, the suspect denied any connection with al-Qaeda and claimed that the attack was inspired by the Iraq War.[22] One British Muslim reportedly pointed to his head and said of the underground bombers in London that 'al-Qaeda is inside'.[23]

Porous borders, fake documents and world-wide sympathizers provide global mobility to the more organized groupings of jihadist militants around the world. They mix with the local diasporas in Western countries, nourishing and being nourished by them. In other words, mobile immigrants and frustrated members of diasporas combine, providing recruits and habitats for the terrorist causes. They therefore offer no easy or obvious target for governments to attack, as they may have no headquarters or training camps, or even leadership. Many are undoubtedly linked to criminal elements in the target countries. Some seem well educated and are from middle class homes, others are poor and dejected youths.

This may explain why the British Joint Terrorism Analysis Centre advised the government to lower the threat level on terrorism about three weeks before the July 7 2005 attack in London. The Centre, like George Bush, was focused on the global organized terrorist menace and not on the local diaspora or its allies. Yet the terrorists can be home-grown or from another country. In the case of the 7 July attacks in London, three of the perpetrators were ethnic Pakistanis born in Britain, and the fourth was a British citizen born in Jamaica and converted to Islam. In the abortive attack that followed two weeks later, the attackers included a British resident born in Somalia, an Ethiopian who posed as a Somali refugee to obtain residency, a British citizen born in Eritrea and radicalized in prison, and a fourth unknown person. Little is known yet about their training but so far it appears that this did not take place in the al-Qaeda camps in Afghanistan. In the Spanish train bombing, most were Moroccans but there also were Spanish natives with no connection to international jidhaism. All the leaders have not been found, but among those arrested the leader appears to be from Tunisia, and there were radical Muslims and petty criminals in the group.

The habitats of these criminals are ethnic/religious ghettos where displaced immigrants and their children are cut off from the culture of their homeland – 'internal colonies' as the *Economist* calls them.[24] In Britain, for example, there are approximately 1.3 million Muslims, about 3 percent of the total population. In order to understand terrorists from such areas there is a need to identify the roots of their violence and rebellion and how they are recruited to the jihadist cause. Deep hatreds arise from fundamental grievances caused by humiliation, poverty and exclusion. Until we come to grips with this primary attraction for the disaffected in our communities' efforts at creating homeland security and attacking foreign lands will be pointless.[25] But while individuals may be disaffected through poverty and isolation they also require a justification for violence before they will act. Globalization and Western intervention in the Third World provide these justifications, and there is no doubt that Britain's war in Iraq has helped to radicalize a section of the Muslim youth. Even Prime Minister Blair gave credence to this idea when after 7/7 he admitted, 'I'm not saying these things don't affect their warped reasoning and warped logic as to what they do, or they don't use these things to try and recruit people.'[26]

Islamist terrorism, then, is the unwanted and unforeseen consequence of the steady march of globalization, modernity and Western interventionism. Some, perhaps all, religions are under attack from modernity. Its effects on alienated people cannot be vanquished by war and occupation. In fact, the continued occupation of Muslim countries by those of other religious persuasions will only compound the problems, not diminish them.

A war cannot eliminate such groups. Calling them international terrorists unwittingly encourages the emergence of other groups to engage in copycat acts of horror. Engaging in a war on terrorism dignifies them as leaders and heroes of their people or faith while in fact they act like murderers and criminals. In a liberal democracy there will always be chances for disaffected groups to do stupid things. We need to delegitimize them and their actions. What we must not do is lose our own values in pursuit of something that is not possible. We need to be resilient but reasonable.

In 1998, bin Laden explained his specific political complaints and grievances:

> For over seven years the United States has been occupying the lands of Islam in the holiest of places, the Arabian Peninsula, plundering its riches, dictating to its rulers, humiliating its people, terrorizing its

neighbours, and turning its bases in the Peninsula into a spearhead through which to fight the neighboring Muslim peoples.[27]

He went on to cite US pro-Israeli policies and its oppression and lack of recognition of the Palestine people.

Al-Qaeda and its affiliates combine religious beliefs about American wrong-doing with the duty to act under disciplined leadership and organization. They impose a state of collective alarm among their enemies. Thus, the four threats to be countered by the West are:

1. the terrorist organizations,
2. the ideas and ideology encouraging support for the organizations,
3. the Western policies which provide fuel for the development of these ideas, and
4. our own peoples' fear of the terrorist actions.

## Anti-terrorist strategies

How well has the United States in particular and the West in general responded to the terrorist threat? In evaluating the responses one must look beyond simply how well they have prevented terrorist acts and managed their consequences. We also need to bear in mind how the strategies have affected our own public; how our allies have responded; and whether our actions have created a new crop of dedicated terrorists. We need a clear vision of what we were, and are, trying to achieve, and an accurate assessment of how well we have done in the primary task of reducing terrorism. It is quite possible that the war on Iraq and the consequent division that it has created will sustain the very myths the terrorists wish to convey – namely that the United States is supremely self-centred and evil. By attacking Iraq the United States may have helped to perpetuate the very myths that terrorist leaders need, helping them to regenerate the arguments that perpetuate the use of violence for political ends.

As well as the official statements of President Bush defining the enemy, the administration has published three documents that structure the US response, namely the *National Security Strategy of the United States*, the *US National Strategy for Combating Terrorism* and the *US National Strategy to Combat Weapons of Mass Destruction*.

The paper on combating terrorism defines terrorism as 'premeditated, politically motivated violence perpetrated against non-combatant targets by subnational groups or clandestine agents'.[28] But elsewhere President

Bush has used a wider conception of terrorism. As he put it on September 14, 2001, 'Our responsibility to history is already clear: to answer these attacks and rid the world of evil.'[29] This broad and vague goal has created an overly wide net in the search for terrorists. Included as evil enemies of the civilized world are the al-Qaeda network, other terrorist organizations of a global, regional or local scope, rogue states – including Iraq, Iran and North Korea and other unnamed countries – as well as, in a general way, terrorism as a phenomenon, and weapons of mass destruction.[30]

All of these individual topics have been subsumed and spoken about at one time or another as an undifferentiated threat to the United States – an evil, like communism, which must be totally eliminated. This approach could be excused as mere rhetoric and political propaganda, but unfortunately it has had a direct effect on foreign policy and, in particular, on putting the Iraq issue on the anti-terrorist agenda. President Bush made the most direct connection between these two types of terrorism when he declared, 'You can't distinguish between al-Qaeda and Saddam when you talk about the war on terrorism. They're both equally bad, and equally as evil, and equally as destructive.'[31]

Moreover, as we pointed out in Chapter 6, this comprehensive approach to terrorism was accompanied in the National Security Strategy by a switch to a preventive strike strategy from the older strategy of containment and deterrence. The new policy found its first expression in the attack on Iraq. The anti-terrorism policy and the belief that Iraq possessed WMD were both used to justify the preventive war.

President Bush has declared that the US successes include: the seizure of $200 million of terrorists' funds, the incapacitation of 3000 al-Qaeda operatives world-wide and the conviction of more than 140 terrorists in the United States.[32] At other times the administration has claimed that some three-quarters of al-Qaeda's leadership have been captured or killed. Such counter-terrorism successes were fostered by good intelligence and overt and covert police action, with the military in a supporting role. But has the United States crushed the use of terrorism as a weapon? The answer is so massively negative that the question appears naïve. Both terrorism and the war on it continue unabated.

Clearly, a war on terrorism writ large should never have been part of US policy. The world requires policies that make terrorist actions less frequent and less attractive to the disaffected. Otherwise, we inadvertently fulfil terrorist prophecies and provide them with leaders, martyrs and justifications for violence into the future. We need to destroy the myths that perpetuate violence, not their people. We need to set our policies in the context of how historical grievances impact on terrorism.

## Bush's moment: war without purpose

The American government's response to the terrorist events in New York and Washington on September 11 2001, then, was inadequate. In its haste to lash out at the perpetrators of 9/11 it interpreted terrorism too broadly and consequently made serious mistakes in its foreign policies – in particular its conflation of terrorism with war in Iraq. Its contention that terrorism can be stopped by a military response – attacking and forcing democracy on other lands – is self-defeating.[33]

The 'war on terrorism' has not been, and cannot be, won. Neither the US government's goals nor the basic criteria we formulated at the beginning of the chapter have been met. 'Micro-surgery' to capture terrorist leaders and to infiltrate terrorist groups would have been more appropriate than all-out war on an ill-defined target in the contest with terrorism. It would have provided a more measured, calibrated approach – one that would have dealt with the problem, as far as possible without encouraging insurgency and revenge. But Bush chose war.

The United States has been under attack by Islamic fundamentalists since at least the Teheran embassy siege of 1979. In order to resolve its current problems with international terrorism, it must accept that its own policies particularly, but not exclusively, in the Middle East are provocative, and that terrorism is a consequence of globalization, politicization and modernization, not primarily of a lack of democracy or civil rights in the Muslim world. The United States should have reconsidered its assumptions when it learned that the UN Security Council would not join in an attack on Iraq. Far from crushing terrorism with its military war, the United States has created a human abattoir in Iraq.

Military attacks on terrorists will not resolve either the basic social, economic, political and religious issues behind the 9/11 attacks or the causes that give rise to terrorism in the first place. Nor can absolute security ever be achieved in an open and democratic country. The search for invulnerability is naïve. Success should be defined in terms of reducing the threats rather than absolutely eliminating them. Perhaps a new kind of containment policy is needed, since terrorism will never be totally eliminated. The wars on poverty, drugs, crime and illiteracy have not worked, and neither will a war on terrorism. What we need is a 'war of ideas' – a campaign based on a positive image of US interest in a democratic and just world. If US leaders have faith in their soft power, they should not blench from such a contest.

We make a modest plea. The United States spends more on defence than the next nine richest countries of the world combined, but on foreign aid it ranks last on a per capita basis when compared with European states. Rather than spending ever more money on the sword and the shield – the military war on terrorism and homeland defense – why not invest more in other strategies that would limit the number of terrorists? This could be done by redefining and limiting the war on terrorism, and by spending more money to try to influence people to support American policies. Such strategies would have a better chance of success than a 'war' on terrorism in reducing the scourge of terrorism in the twenty-first century.

## Notes

1  The second-worst terrorist attack on the United States was the 1995 bombing of the Oklahoma City Federal Building by an American, Timothy McVeigh, which killed 168 people.
2  Each year the state department reports to Congress on terrorism. See the annual *Patterns of Global Terrorism*. Of course, they may make mistakes in their assessment; see Alan B. Krueger and David D. Laitin, 'Misunderstanding Terrorism', *Foreign Affairs* ( September/October 2004), 8–13.
3  Another scholar has traced the history of terrorism back to the Sicarii sect of Zealots in AD 66–73. See Grant Wardlaw, *Political Terrorism* (Cambridge: Cambridge University Press, 1989), p. 18.
4  The 'High Level Panel on Threats, Challenges and Change' made limited progress in outlining the definitional components of terrorism; see *A More Secure World: Our Shared Responsibility*, p. 45; found at www.un.org/secureworld
5  Bonnie Cordes, Brian M. Jenkins and Konrad Kellen, *A Conceptual Framework for Analyzing Terrorist Groups* (Santa Monica, CA: Rand, 1985).
6  Ibid, p. 85.
7  James C. Davies, 'Toward a Theory of Revolution', in Robert J. Jackson and Michael Stein (eds), *Issues in Comparative Politics* (New York: St Martin's Press, 1971), pp. 370–84.
8  Sederberg, *Terrorist Myths*, p. 85.
9  Philip Jenkins, *Images of Terror: What We Can and Can't Know about Terrorism* (New York: Aldine de Gruyter, 2003); and Walter Laqueur, *No End to War: Terrorism in the Twenty-First Century* (New York: Continuum, 2003).
10 Suicide bombers perhaps best represent these broad characteristics of terrorists. The fear that can be produced by an opponent whose desire to kill someone is greater than his own will to live is not difficult to understand. Moreover, the large supply of individuals prepared to engage in suicide terrorism has made this the choice method of modern terrorism. Robert Pape has shown that suicide bombing has increased dramatically in the past two decades and that while these actions account for only 3 per cent of all incidents they produce 48 per cent of all the deaths caused by terrorism; Robert A. Pape, *Dying to Win: The Strategic Logic of Suicide Terrorism* (New York: Random House, 2005).
11 Michael Stohl (ed.), *The Politics of Terrorism*, 3rd edn (New York: Marcel Dekker, 1988), pp. 8–11.

12  Ibid. p. 77.
13  See, for example, Richard E. Rubenstein, *Alchemists of Revolution* (New York: Basic Books, 1989).
14  Jessica Stern, *Terror in the Name of God* (New York: HarperCollins, 2003) p. 282.
15  Jonathan L. Freedman, J. Merrill Carlsmith and David O. Sears, *Social Psychology* (Englewood Cliffs, NJ: Prentice-Hall, 1970).
16  Cited in Bruce Hoffman, 'Al Qaeda and the War on Terrorism: An Update', *Current History* (December 2004), 423–6; *Strategic Survey 2003/4*, p. 6.
17  Prime Minister Tony Blair finds parallels between the July incidents in London and the actions of the IRA invidious. In the 36 years of the IRA's war, over 3600 people were killed in the name of national self-determination. The last bombs were set off in 1995 and the IRA said it would end its war in July 2005. In 1998 Sinn Fein, the political wing of the movement, signed the Good Friday peace accord and began to contest elections. Mr Blair maintains that the IRA philosophy and methods are entirely different from those of the jihadist terrorists as these have illegitimate demands and provide a different level of threat, especially in the use of suicide bombers. This distinction between freedom fighter and terrorist is one that many scholars would contest.
18  *New York Times*, 17 September 2005.
19  Jonathan Randal, *Osama: The Making of a Terrorist* (New York: Alfred A. Knopf 2004); Jason Burke. *Al-Qaeda: Casting a Shadow of Terror* (London: Tauris, 2004).
20  Charles Townshend, *Terrorism: A Very Short Introduction* (Oxford University Press, 2002), p. 98.
21  Cited in Townshend, *Terrorism*, p. 31.
22  *Globe and Mail* (Toronto), 1 August 2005.
23  *New York Times*, 31 July 2005.
24  *Economist*, 16 July 2005.
25  Robert S. Leiken, 'Europe's Angry Muslims', *Foreign Affairs* (July/August 2005), 120–35.
26  *Globe and Mail* (Toronto), 27 July 2005. MI5 has also accepted the link between Iraq and terrorist attacks on the West; see *The Times*, 28 July 2005.
27  Fatwah urging jihad against Americans.
28  *The U.S. National Strategy for Combating Terrorism*, p. 1.
29  *The National Security Strategy of the United States*, p. 5.
30  Many terrorist groups pose no threat to the United States and, are clearly not anti-American – examples include the Basque separatist ETA, the Provisional wing of the Irish Republican Army (IRA) and the Tamil Tigers in Sri Lanka.
31  *Washington Post*, 26 September 2002.
32  Speech to FBI Academy, September 2003.
33  For a strong argument that democracy will not reduce terrorism see F. Gregory Gause III, 'Can Democracy Stop Terrorism?', *Foreign Affairs* (September/October 2005), 62–76.

# 8
# Homeland (In)Security: The Shield

There are times when people believe the story of their lives or their country breaks into two periods: the before and the after. Following such an irreparable break people discover that they have changed and will never be the same again; some become stronger and others more vulnerable. Deep-seated fear and apprehension sweep away the insignificant and force them to focus on fundamentals such as security and liberty. Such were the events of 9/11 and their unintended consequences. American political leaders referred to the event as having 'changed everything' and, while they brandished their sword, they set about insulating the homeland by shielding it from the world.

This chapter assesses the impact of the 'war on terrorism' on the home front, analysing its benefits in terms of security and its costs in terms of democracy, human rights and the economy. As we discussed earlier, governments do have the right in international law to defend themselves against international terrorism; the danger is that their actions may seriously damage the democratic freedoms of their citizens. The issue comes down to whether democratic states can subdue virulent terrorism without surrendering their own freedoms. What costs are acceptable in this struggle? A second crucial factor is how to prioritize where limited resources should be directed. Should more funds be spent on border protection or against the threat of nuclear terrorism?

This is not the first time in the United States that political leaders have tried to insulate the country from outside pressures. Its historical patterns of understanding the world have stabilized into fixed positions. When wrong occurs, its past experiences and learned patterns of response prevent America from fresh, clear-eyed approaches and new directions. Immediately after the United States became an independent country it tried to avoid any entanglements in Europe. Its ensuing, much-celebrated isolationism flowed from this idea, as did the Monroe Doctrine in which the United States declared the Western Hemisphere to be within its sphere of interest and that other powers should keep out.

Americans have a passion for comfort and security, searching for protection behind oceans, avoiding entangling alliances, building missile defence systems and enlarging homeland security. Recent efforts to set themselves apart from the rest of the world include decisions not to participate in: the Kyoto Agreement, the Comprehensive Test Ban Treaty (which bans all nuclear testing), the Small-Arms Control Pact to limit the spread of rifles across the world, the Anti-Land Mines Agreement, the Biological Weapons Agreement, and the International Criminal Court. These negative positions, like the disdain the United States shows for UN decisions it does not like, have decreased stability and harmony in the world without increasing American security. Neither have the wars in Afghanistan and Iraq immunized Americans, Britons, Spaniards or others from terrorist attacks at home. But from the American government's point of view its opposition to these international treaties and its involvement in these wars have been in the national interest, and that is enough to justify them.

We have noted that the unprecedented attacks of September 11 demonstrated to Americans that they were not safe on their home ground and created a collective sense of insecurity. Used to the notion of playing and fighting on the lands of other peoples, they suddenly found themselves also vulnerable to external attack. A national panic arose – even within the halls of government itself. The fragile state of American psychology was evident during the anthrax attacks on government establishments that occurred shortly after 9/11. Although only five lives were lost and the actions were probably not carried out by a terrorist at all (mostly likely by a disgruntled US laboratory worker), the country succumbed to mass hysteria.

Shortly after the United States administration began its war on terrorism, it formulated broad but somewhat rudimentary ideas about how to defend the homeland. In the aftermath of 9/11 it was easy to convince Congress and the American people that more than a sword was required to vanquish the enemy. The United States also needed a shield: borders had to be sealed against terrorist penetration, enemy combatants jailed, possible collaborators detained or sent abroad to foreign prisons, intelligence agencies reinforced and a new Department of Homeland Security created. Enemies would have to be held captive without charge and sometimes tortured in Guantanamo and elsewhere.[1] In times of war or perceived national dangers, even liberal democracies can be tempted to adopt such measures, infringing human rights in ways that contradict their own principles and may be inappropriate to the problem or crisis. Neither the justice of the proposals nor the financial costs were important considerations to the US government. What mattered was to make the country safe from attack. As Mark Danner put it:

> America tends to respond to such attacks, or the threat of them, in predictably paranoid ways. Notably, by 'rounding up the usual suspects' and by dividing the world, dramatically and hysterically, in a good part and an evil part. September 11 was no exception – we have seen this American tendency in its purest form.[2]

There are many reasons to confront the dilemmas involved in the American approach to preventing terrorism in the homeland – especially to clarify the contrasting relations between concepts such as freedom and security, intelligence and privacy, and open borders and keeping the 'bad guys' out. Democracy requires a free and open society and rests on a high degree of trust among people and civic participation. The efficient flow of people, goods, capital and ideas across borders is crucial to the health of the country's economy. But free citizens can also be terrorists, and borders can be channels for the flow of illegal immigrants, drugs, terrorists and weapons of mass destruction.

It was mandatory for the government to focus on homeland security, but unfortunately a miasma of political odors quickly began to emanate from some of the specific programmes. The United States did not need to set up a parallel criminal justice system, adopt military tribunals, hold deportation hearings in secret, send subjects to foreign countries or torture prisoners. As Philip B. Heyman put it, the extra-legal approaches taken by the Bush administration do 'not warrant their cost in lost values of a democratic society'.[3]

Since 9/11 most developed countries have taken defensive measures to protect their homelands. They have adopted new anti-terrorist laws, set up new military command structures, created new transportation security administrations, adopted emergency preparedness measures, developed co-ordinating institutions such as the Office of Homeland Security in the United States, and signed border security and anti-terrorist agreements with other countries. In the United States a colour-coded warning system informs Americans that they are at the yellow stage of heightened alert if, for example, one of Bin Laden's jailed officials says that maybe there will be an attack on American financial interests. Then again, maybe there won't be. But the warning system serves to frighten Americans nevertheless.

The United States has developed new coordination policies with most countries around the world including those in the European Union and Canada. Within North America, new structures and procedures sprout almost daily. A 30-point plan between Canada and the United States calls for Canadians to be integrated into the US foreign terrorist-tracking taskforce; new visitor visa policies; joint units to assess information on travellers; more immigration control officers overseas; new biometric identifiers for documents; safe third-country agreement; expanding border-enforcement teams; and enhancing Project North Star – that is improving communication and cooperation between Canadian and US law enforcement personnel. The protocol with the European Union is less exhaustive but covers such topics as asset-freezing, designating terrorist groups, extradition agreements, and the implementation of US–EUROPOL agreements on the exchange of personal data on terrorists. Bilateral agreements have been signed with individual European states about shipping and trade.

The desire to have both prosperity and security is as old as history. Peter Ackroyd's book *London the Biography* surveys the entire history of the ebb and flow of prosperity and security in England.[4] Naturally there never was total security in London; solutions had to be reinvented over and over again for over 2000 years. The combination of security with prosperity, though vital, was always elusive. The bombings of July 2005 were just the most recent violent attacks that London has endured throughout its history. It is difficult for writers to think in terms of paired oxymorons like security and freedom, or security and open borders because traditionally intellectuals have been either students of conflict and security, hanging their assumptions on notions of sovereignty and military force, or students of humanitarian causes such as economic development and aid, basing their premises on freedom, human rights and human dignity. There has been an ideological divide, with the much of the 'left' studying development and poverty, and much of the 'right' examining security and the military. The two groups even differ in their conceptions of terms such as security and terrorism. And yet understanding international terrorism requires knowledge of both perspectives.

Public servants and politicians too find it problematic to think about open borders and security because they are a product of the administrative roles they play. The management of security has been a black hole in Western democracies. Politicians want to be re-elected and need to pander to the public's short-term opinions. Department of Defense officers provide military solutions, while police and judges have their own ideas of criminal justice. One is reminded of George Bernard Shaw's play *The Doctors' Dilemma* in which each physician has his own favorite remedy that he employs in every case, regardless of what illness he is treating.

## Civil liberties

The war on terrorism made it imperative for Americans to reconsider the level of their security at home. This was not the first time that US leaders have been tempted to use their power to control people inside the homeland. During the Second World War the United States interned German and Japanese Americans, and it curtailed free speech in the McCarthy era during the cold war. As governments pursue more and more security for citizens at home, civil liberties are, to an ever larger degree, reduced. What balance should be aimed for?

In the rush to defend itself against terrorism, the United States began to reshape itself into a high-security state, giving up freedoms for security, smothering reason and legal traditions with emotion and patriotism. In their fear, many Americans came to believe that protecting themselves against the unknown was more important than their freedoms or privacy. The government's appeal to patriotism countered all efforts to defend civil liberties against resulting intrusions. Samuel Johnson once observed that 'patriotism is the last refuge of a scoundrel', but it is more often the first response to fear and outrage.

Terrorists use unconventional methods to attack vulnerable targets in free and open societies, creating a siege mentality – invoking a nervousness about unusual and suspicious behaviour. The dilemma for democrats is that their society may respond by turning against itself, destroying the freedom and openness it admires. A free and democratic country needs to conduct itself by its own principles, not those of its adversaries.

The 9/11 terrorism made Americans aware that they are as vulnerable as people elsewhere and will need to learn to deal with terrorism as other countries have done by patience, cunning and good management. But they have overreacted. The phrase 'war on terrorism' provides no definition of what constitutes victory or even gives notice about when the war will be over. At the same time it is evident that there can be no final or complete victory over terrorism because it is part of the social fabric itself; it emerges from the nature of society and cannot be fully eliminated any more than conflict can. Much like a chronic disease it cannot be completely eradicated, but it can be managed and lived with. However no politician or political party can afford to be seen as soft on terrorism. The flame of freedom and liberty seems to burn less brightly when one is under terrorist attack.

Since 9/11 many changes have been made to American domestic laws, regulations and structures in the name of fighting terrorism. So far there has been no attack on free speech or the right of assembly in the United States. But a parallel justice system was put in place: people now can be held for indefinite periods without trial, there are new forms of warrantless wiretaps, and detainees can be tried by secret military tribunals. In this balance of security and freedom, the essential question is how long these draconian measures will continue, given that once it has begun, a war on terrorism may never end.

## The Patriot Act

Within weeks of 9/11, in the name of national security and in a pervasive atmosphere of siege, Congress overwhelmingly passed the Patriot Act that had been drafted by the Department of Justice. In the atmosphere of frenzy that had overcome the nation, the Act was rushed through Congress in six weeks in closed-door negotiations, with no committee reports, and no final hearings. It passed in the House of Representatives by 357 to 66, and by 98 to 1 in the Senate. The Act 'Uniting and Strengthening America by Providing Appropriate Tools Required to Intercept and Obstruct Terrorism' was signed into law on October 26 2001 to the applause of a large proportion of Americans. Unfortunately few politicians had read, and even fewer seem to have understood, the 342-page document that would be used to reduce the rights of United States citizens. The fact that the Patriot Act conflicts in several respects with American civil liberties was certainly not discussed publicly to any significant extent. While it poses problems for both the Fifth Amendment to the US Constitution (protection of due process) and the Fourth Amendment (safeguard against unreasonable searches and seizures), public analysis of the murky Act remains derisory even today.

In order to understand the Patriot Act, one must first appreciate that much earlier former President Jimmy Carter's Democratic administration passed a Foreign Intelligence Surveillance Act (FISA) that allowed the federal government to use electronic methods in the surveillance of citizens and resident aliens alleged to have been acting on behalf of foreign governments. The Patriot Act goes much further to give federal law enforcement officers more tools to track down and prosecute terrorists by increasing the government's capacities for law enforcement and collection of intelligence. Under the new Act the government has only to claim that persons are being investigated as part of a foreign intelligence operation in order to legally infringe their civil liberties.

The Patriot Act makes surveillance of everyone easier than it was under the FISA. Section 206 permits roving wiretaps and section 215 allows the business records and computer activities of citizens to be searched in terrorist cases. It allows the government to subpoena library records, medical records, insurance and university student records. It also provides a new regulatory framework for preventing money-laundering.

Critics claim that the Act gives the government an opportunity to violate civil liberties, allowing the FBI, CIA and even the White House to spy on Americans and suppress political dissent. The law permits the government to obtain search warrants even when there is no evidence that a crime may have been committed. Section 213 allows the government to search people's homes and delay notifying them about it – so-called 'sneak and peek' searches. Section 215 permits the government to obtain library, medical and other records, but makes it a crime for the record-holders to reveal to the individual in question that such a request has been made or carried out. Moreover, the government can obtain the complete database from which an individual's file is extracted, thus gaining the ability to access information on everyone else in that database as well. Section 216 expands this right of access to the internet. While surveillance of internet content is prohibited, extracting information about transactions is not.

Despite the rapid passage of the Act, Congress implicitly recognized the inherent dangers of many portions of it by appending a sunset clause of December 31 2005 to sixteen of its clauses. In the spring of 2005 Attorney General Alberto R. Gonzales argued that to fail to pass the Act again would be tantamount to declaring 'unilateral disarmament' toward terrorism. Gonzales told Congress that the so-called 'sneak and peek' clause had been used 155 times for cases including terrorism, drug dealing and murder – but that this was less than 1 per cent of all search warrants issued. According to Gonzales, section 215 was used on 35 occasions to obtain information on driver's licences, apartment dwellers and telephone subscribers – but never on libraries.[5] He claimed that the disputed sections of the law had been used dozens of times to prosecute terrorism and other illegal acts.[6]

Under the rules of FISA, the National Security Agency (NSA) has been allowed to intercept faxes, emails, and phone conversations with foreigners, but the President also insists on wiretaps without court order. He bases this right on article 2 of the constitution that describes his executive power as commander in chief and the September 14 2001 resolution of Congress authorizing the President to 'use all necessary and appropriate force' against those responsible for 9/11. Congressional leaders had been told about the program of wiretapping without a court order. During his December 17 2005 radio talk President Bush admitted that in the weeks after 9/11 he authorized the NSA 'to intercept the international communications of people with known links to Al Qaeda and related terrorist organizations'. As he put it, these activities are reviewed every 45 days and 'I have re-authorized the program more than 30 times and I intend to continue, using the law and my constitutional authority.' As the Supreme Court has not ruled on this topic the issue remains moot as to whether the President's actions were legal. The Justice department has so far failed to provide specific legal authority for the surveillance program although it has cited the constitution, the Federalist papers, the writings of former Presidents, scholarly papers and court cases in defence of these actions.

Also draconian are the Patriot Act rules which allow the government to detain non-citizens suspected of terrorism. Under section 412 of the Act, non-citizens can be held for seven days before deportation proceedings have to commence or criminal charges be filed. Moreover, the government has found ways to circumvent even these rules by simply charging the detainees with technical immigration violations or small crimes. A suspect who cannot be deported can still be detained if the attorney general certifies that national security is at stake. By late 2004, 515 individuals had been deported in connection with September 11 investigations, mostly men of Middle Eastern and South Asian descent.[7]

According to the Homeland Security website the Act has been important in finding and dismantling terror cells in Portland, Oregon, in Lackawanna, New York, and in northern Virginia.[8] However, despite the government's claims, there have been no major successful prosecutions based on the Patriot Act and parts of it have been struck down by courts on appeals from the American Civil Liberties Union. While several hundred suspected terrorists have been detained, and many charges have been laid, most of these non-citizens were charged with immigration violations or petty crimes such as obtaining illegal commercial drivers' licences.[9] 90 per cent of all the cases against terrorists in the United States have failed. Only 39 persons have been convicted – and of those, few were found to have any connections to al-Qaeda. Most crimes were connected to the Columbian drug cartels, Rwanda's civil war or Palestinian causes.[10]

It should be borne in mind that there are about 20 million non-citizens in the United States and under this law their rights could be weakened, and for very meagre results. In March 2006, Congress made most clauses of the Patriot Act permanent and approved the two most controversial provisions for four more years.

## Enemy combatants

The administration created a further legal black hole in the name of the war on terrorism with its decision to act against what it called enemy or illegal combatants. A classified presidential document, signed on November 13 2001 and entitled 'Detention, Treatment, and Trial of Certain Noncitizens in the War against Terrorism', granted the president the power to incarcerate any non-citizens the government had reason to believe had engaged in terrorist planning, execution or harbouring individuals associated with terrorist acts, or simply if it was in the interest of the United States to do so.[11] Such alleged enemies were not 'prisoners of war' and thus did not come under the Geneva protocols on the protection of individuals captured in war.

Under the four Geneva Conventions of 1949 every person in enemy hands must have some status under international law – one is either a prisoner of war or a civilian. To get around this, the United States therefore invented a new category called 'illegal combatants'. Human-rights activists, however, claim that even if the prisoners did not fit all the conditions for POW status they still should be accorded it. The Bush administration argued that these prisoners were not POWs because they bore none of the trappings of regular soldiers such as uniforms and insignia, but it promised to abide by the Geneva Conventions regardless of the captives' status. The American military argued persuasively against the harsh interrogation techniques that might flow from the lack of protection offered enemy combatants but were advised by the Justice Department that military personnel would be immune from charges of torture under federal and international law because of the fight against terrorism.[12] And, as far as we know, Congress was not consulted on any aspects of the directive.

This presidential directive for enemy combatants went well beyond the Patriot Act, which requires the government to lay immigration or terrorist charges against non-citizens within seven days of their arrest. Alleged unlawful combatants can be kept indefinitely without trial or be tried by a military commission, with no access to a lawyer or other due-process rights. Moreover, this is not the first time that the United States has violated such rights: it suspended habeas corpus during the Civil War and the Palmer raids in 1920; notoriously, it also interned some foreign-born American citizens during the Second World War.

Even before 9/11 the CIA had been authorized to carry out renditions – that is to send non-citizens to other countries for interrogation even if they might be tortured there – but after 9/11 this right was expanded by presidential directive to include secret programmes allowing the CIA to transfer suspected terrorists to be imprisoned and interrogated in foreign countries rather than kept in American prisons. Despite the strict confidentiality of information on this topic, journalists have interviewed suspected terrorists, who have been sent to Egypt, Jordan, Pakistan, Saudi Arabia, and Syria. Some held in Egypt and elsewhere claim to have been tortured. One well-documented example concerned Maher Arar, a Syrian-born Canadian, who was detained at Kennedy airport two weeks after 9/11 and then transported to Syria, where he maintains he was beaten. A year later he was released without being charged with a crime.[13]

After the war in Afghanistan, the United States encouraged the imprisonment of those whom the administration termed 'unlawful enemy combatants' in selected prisons and military bases around the world. The best-known of these prisons, and the only ones on which we have significant information, are in Guantanamo Bay in Cuba, Bagram Airbase in Afghanistan, Belmarsh, London, in the United Kingdom and Abu Ghraib in Iraq, but other secret prisons are believed to exist. Initially, some 700 suspects from over 40 countries were held, of whom most were captured in Afghanistan. As of 2005, approximately 520 detainees from 40 countries were still being held at Camp X-Ray on the Cuban base. 232 detainees had been allowed to leave the prison, 149 of whom were released outright and 83 transferred to other governments.

President Bush established military commissions to try these enemy belligerents. The rules were harsh and one-sided: defendants were barred from seeing evidence against them, they had no appeal to the US court system, and guilty verdicts from only two-thirds of the members of the military commission were required for a conviction. The president's lawyer, Attorney General Alberto R. Gonzales, claimed that the president would refer to these courts only non-citizens who were members or active supporters of al-Qaeda or other international terrorist organizations targeting the United States. The detainees would have to be chargeable with offences against the international laws of war, such as targeting civilians, hiding among civilians or refusing to bear arms openly. Anyone charged would be able to challenge the commission's jurisdiction through a habeas corpus procedure in a federal court. But the prisoners would not have full access to the United States judicial system as they were not on US territory and therefore domestic laws would not apply.

Holding these prisoners in this way and without charge poses serious questions of legitimacy. In June 2004 the US Supreme Court ruled that its jurisdiction extended to Guantanamo and that detainees had a right to contest their detentions in the courts. This decision raised the prospect that the prisoners might have their status resolved in the regular court system in the United States.[14] In response, military Combatant Status Review Tribunals were set up to determine the status of each prisoner. However, they were suspended in response to the criticism that they were unconstitutional.

On July 15 2005 a federal appeals court (the US Court of Appeals for the District of Columbia) ruled unanimously that the military could resume the war crime trials of Guantanamo suspects. The three judges reversed a lower court decision that had halted the trials. The ruling on Salim Ahmed Hamdan – a driver for Osama bin Laden charged with conspiracy to commit attacks on civilians, murder and terrorism – concluded that such trials did not violate the Constitution, international law or American military law. The court said it was well established in the United States that the Geneva Conventions 'do not create judicially enforceable rights' – that is accusations based on them cannot be brought forward in lawsuits in the United States. It based its reasoning on the fact that Congress had given the president authority 'to use all necessary and appropriate force' against anyone involved in 9/11 and to stop international terrorism.[15]

The question of how US citizens should be treated in these cases reached a new level on September 9 2005 when a three-judge federal appeals court ruled unanimously that American citizens *as well as* foreigners could be held as 'enemy combatants.' The court ruled that the president was authorized to detain even American citizens under the powers granted to him by Congress. American Jose Padilla has now been held for several years for his alleged activity fighting US forces in Afghanistan alongside al-Qaeda forces. While he lost his challenge against being held in prison, he has not lost his right to further hearings on his case. His lawyer said they would appeal the decision as it was a 'sad day for the nation when a federal court finds the president has the power to detain indefinitely and without criminal charge any American citizen whom he deems is an enemy combatant.'[16] In late November 2005 the administration reversed its policy and indicted American citizen Padilla in a civilian court. The final outcome of the case is still in doubt.

As of early 2006 Hamdan is one of only 4 prisoners to have been charged with war crimes, while 12 others have been designated as eligible for trial. There are at present three types of tribunals:

1. Combatant status review panels. These determine if a prisoner belongs there. So far, they have found only 33 who do not belong.
2. Administrative review boards. They determine if detainees are still a threat to the United States – and whether they could be released.
3. Separately, about 200 prisoners are represented in lawsuits in US federal courts. These situations were made possible by the Supreme Court ruling of June 2004 that said detainees could use the civilian court system to challenge their incarceration.

In the spring of 2006 it is uncertain whether these tribunals will be continued, whether different court mechanisms will be used, or whether these prisoners simply will be held indefinitely without charge. While the Supreme Court upheld the right of the government to detain foreign combatants, it also said the prisoners had a right to lawyers, to ask for the rules of habeas corpus to apply, and that even in a war the detention of suspected enemy combatants still had to be subject to review by a neutral tribunal.[17] The president's dubious use of the term 'unlawful enemy combatants' remains a major part of the problem. There are no legal definitions of detainees, no legal rules for their internment, and there is no way to determine their rights under the Geneva Convention or American law. Even the number of prisoners the United States holds in some military bases around the world is unknown.

However, the Bush administration's claim that 9/11 justifies such actions has finally come under severe attack. Not only has the Supreme Court acted as mentioned to temper the presidential directive, but prominent figures such as former president Bill Clinton, many Democrats and some Republicans have said publicly that Guantanamo Prison should be closed down or conditions there improved. In February 2006 the United Nations joined the chorus of complaints about Guantanamo. A Human Rights Report concluded that the prison should be shut down because it allowed torture and placed prisoners in a legal 'no-man's' land without recourse to standard court proceedings.

Recognition is growing that the prisoners should either be released or charged with an offence. Criticisms have increased dramatically since the reports of prisoner abuse in Abu Ghraib in Iraq. The abuse and the lack of civil rights accorded to prisoners have tarnished America's reputation for justice throughout the world and increased the probability of further terrorist attacks. The justification for keeping the system according to one senior official is that '[t]he intelligence obtained by those rendered, detained and interrogated has disrupted terrorist operations ... It has saved lives in the United States and abroad, and it has resulted in the capture of other terrorists'.[18]

If they had been called POWs the prisoners would have come under the Geneva rules and been sent home at the end of the war if they had not committed war crimes – but this is difficult when the war is a never-ending one. As 'illegal' combatants, they should have been charged with an international crime. But charges are problematical because most of the prisoners were arrested in either Afghanistan or Iraq for defending countries that they claim had been attacked by the United States. The holding and treatment of prisoners remains a highly contentious aspect of the war on terrorism.

## Prison abuses

The abuses in Abu Ghraib and Guantanamo prisons have been well documented by official reports and journalist accounts.[19] Clearly, the prisoners have not been accorded the rights to be expected under international treaties or constitutional principles, as many have been subject to abuse and torture. Amnesty International called Guantanamo Prison 'the gulag of our times'.[20] The pictures of a handful of smirking male and female soldiers abusing and sexually humiliating hooded and naked prisoners at Abu Ghraib were only the tip of the iceberg. Official US interrogation policy allows such extreme measures as the use of so-called stress positions during interrogation procedures, threats from dogs, yelling, loud music, light control, and isolation.[21] Beyond these methods, the alleged and proven abuses include mistreatments of the Koran, sexual and physical abuse. Very young people have been kept in solitary confinement. Several soldiers have been punished for mistreating detainees, but the problem appears not to have been random, but rather systemic – that is emerging from rules set down from above. The Red Cross concluded: 'These methods of physical and psychological coercion were used by the military intelligence in a systematic way to gain confessions and extract information or other forms of cooperation ...'[22] The incidents have shown the United States not as liberators but as occupiers and tormentors – they have destroyed much faith in the American military.

The prisoner abuse at Abu Ghraib has been widely condemned, not least by half a dozen military inquiries and a high-ranking panel led by

James R. Schlesinger. The highest levels of the military and civilian leadership have been accused of not exercising sufficient oversight at the camp, of using a confusing array of policies and interrogation practices, and of not paying close attention to worsening conditions. One of the accused, General Jane Karpinski, a reserve officer, who ran the military prisons in Iraq, was suspended from command and Colonel Thomas M. Papas was reprimanded and fined because he had not ensured that the interrogators were properly trained and supervised. At the lowest end of the spectrum, a handful of junior guards were court-martialled.

Determining the guilt of more senior officials has been difficult. Torture, for example, was defined so rigidly by the government that in many cases what the soldiers were charged with doing to the prisoners was not considered to be torture as it was excluded by the definition. President Bush's point man for the White House on the topic of prison defined torture as giving excruciating pain 'equivalent to the pain that would be associated with serious physical injury so severe that death, organ failure, or permanent damage resulting in a loss of significant body function will likely result'.[23] Anything less than that, it seems, was permissible.

## Justice or security?

There are two competing schools of thought about how to assess the holding of prisoners at military bases. First, opponents of the detentions argue for a criminal justice approach based on the idea that prisoners are either guilty or they are not. They should be tried and if found innocent released, or if found guilty punished. Advocates of this position condemn the imprisonments from a legal or ethical viewpoint. They want to defend the innocent and are outraged by the American government's decision to hold prisoners for long periods without trial.

The second school of thought gives priority to obtaining intelligence and ensuring security. It argues that the issue is not simply one of guilt or lack of it, but of preventing 'illegal combatants' from carrying out future terrorist actions. Although the justifications for such an approach have not been made explicit by the administration, we can assume that the intelligence/security community believes the following:

1. The prisoners may provide useful information.
2. If new information comes to light from outside the prison about people, issues or events, the prisoners might be able to provide further information based on this which could be beneficial.

3. Were the prisoners to be released, they might give information to others about how they had been treated or what they had disclosed about the group's future plans, and thus could in effect warn terrorists about what the military knows about their intentions.

Each of these schools claims the high moral ground in its concern for justice. The first bases its outrage on philosophical or ethical notions about the just treatment of prisoners, the unfair holding of innocents, the maltreatment of prisoners, and the disallowance of the rights adopted by the Geneva rules. The second school claims moral ground on the basis that if it can prevent a future terrorist act then the 'minimal' harm done to prisoners will be worthwhile. Its proponents claim, for example, that information gleaned from these prisoners could prevent another 9/11 and thus save many innocent lives. They believe this trade-off is legitimate and justifiable. This is much the same argument as the military makes when it declares that civilian casualties should be prevented if possible, but that in war there will always be some innocents hurt. This second school of thought claims that the ethical position of the critics of incarceration is unsound because it is naïve about the tactics, methods and conspiratorial nature of terrorist organizations.

The conflict between these two schools of thought is a recurring theme in history. In times of war, armed conflict or terrorist events, even democratic societies have been tempted to adopt measures which infringe human rights. The argument is whether such actions are proportionate or disproportionate to the crisis at hand. It is always difficult to achieve the right balance between privacy and security. But in this particular case, two other major factors should be taken into account. First, the incarcerations have helped to recruit candidates for the terrorist cause, and second, the treatment of prisoners issue has fuelled propaganda that the United States is evil and has damaged the credibility of its call for American-style liberty and democracy around the world. When the United States says it wants to bring democracy and freedom to the Middle East, supporters of prisoners' rights ask: what standards do American leaders and troops require of themselves?

The secrecy surrounding the detainees continues, fuelling suspicions of abuse. According to the *Washington Post*, the Department of Justice refuses requests for information regarding the 1017 people it has detained.[24] It declines to provide answers about how many people were taken into custody, what charges have been filed, the status of the cases, and whether and how they are still being held. The *Post* contends that the Department of Justice not only refuses to provide the answers, but will not explain why it refuses. Are these the standards of an open and free society? The situation is considered so serious that in October 2005 the US Senate voted 90–9 to back a proposal prohibiting 'cruel, inhuman or degrading treatment or punishment' against anyone in government custody, regardless of where they are held.[25]

## The Department of Homeland Security

9/11 inspired the development of several new government institutions. Perhaps the most important of them was the Department of Homeland Security, with a budget of about 50 billion dollars in 2005. The new institution consolidates in one department 22 agencies, including immigration, coastguard, customs, emergency preparedness, and the Secret Service. Its 180,000 employees were initially directed by Tom Ridge and are currently led by Secretary Michael Chertoff, who has toned down some of the rhetoric of his predecessor.[26]

Other parts of the government were also reorganized. A North Command was added to the military to coordinate homeland defence. The intelligence community was thoroughly revamped and a national intelligence director appointed to be the principal advisor to the president and brief him daily on security issues. A National Counterterrorism Centre (NCTC) was set up to analyse information collected on domestic and international terrorism and a Terrorist Screening Centre (TSC) was inaugurated to consolidate terrorist watch lists from the various agencies. Steps have been taken to protect critical infrastructure, to provide vaccines and other medicines in the event of biological, chemical and radiological attacks, and to increase funds and training for first-responders.

The most visible successes of the new Department of Homeland Security have been in airline security. With almost 2 million passengers a day the industry is a prime target for crime or terrorism – as 9/11 showed. Under the department's directions airlines have reinforced their airplane cockpits, and incognito US marshals are aboard many flights, especially those going overseas. The department has taken over airport security, hiring, training and now controlling more than 45,000 federal security screeners. However, the government has not provided the same level of security to other forms of transportation. For example, by mid 2005 the United States had spent about $18 billion on upgrading airline security but only $250 million on passenger rail security. Even more problematic perhaps is the rail transportation system for goods. Daily, toxic chemicals are shipped unsecured into large cities where a terrorist attack could kill thousands, and there are more than a hundred chemical plants spread around the country where an attack would risk the lives of a million or more people. The department also directs the US Border and Protection Agency, which consolidates all border activities, and the US Coast Guard. Both have intensified their surveillance procedures.

Efforts to starve the terrorists of funding were enhanced by new rules in the Patriot Act. On September 23 2001 President Bush issued an executive order requiring officials to target terrorist assets and funding, an order that has allowed the blocking of terrorist assets, seizure of cash, and the arrest of leaders of companies, charities and banks implicated in laundering funds. Some would argue that aside from airline security this has been the most successful accomplishment in the anti-terrorism campaign to date.

The department's weakest initiative appears to be the colour-coded threat advisory system. Although the system may help first-line responders such as the police and immigration officers, it is of little use to the public, since the changes in colour are not accompanied by information about how people should respond – except for the nebulous suggestion that they should be more vigilant. Moreover, almost all studies of the various agencies related to homeland security in the United States have concluded that they lack sufficient funds. This is especially true of the front-line institutions that have to respond to a terrorist attack. Firefighters, police and hospitals continue to lack adequate financing and are unprepared to handle massive emergencies of the sort which hurricanes Katrina and Rita caused in the American South in August 2005, or which terrorists might produce. To indicate the extent of the problem, the Federal Emergency Management Agency (FEMA) had its staff and budget cut shortly before the hurricanes took place. But the essential problem is that there is a virtually limitless supply of terrorist targets – including transportation, energy, financial, chemical, food and cybernet networks, and none of their vulnerabilities have been substantially reduced by the creation of the Department of Homeland Security.

## Border controls

Providing absolute security to the US territory would require being able to locate all people and goods at all times. Travellers coming through airports and crossing borders would have to be screened, sorted and followed. As one critic facetiously put it, they would have to be shepherded through 'large filtration plants' to ensure only clean people and sanitized luggage and goods get through. Containers and even mail which moves on planes, ships, trucks and trains would have to be checked, and then equipped with locks or seals. Electronic tags and GSP transponders would need to be affixed inside the boxes to provide computers with information about where they are at all times. As stringent and futuristic as such ideas may be, the search for absolute security is exactly what the United States says it is striving for and demanding of others.

The American Container Security Initiative, which was designed to prevent terrorists from putting explosive devices in containerized cargo, must now be adhered to by every country that wishes to trade with the United States. The Initiative aims to identify suspicious cargo before it enters US ports. Agents are stationed in foreign ports, a manifest is required before a ship enters a US port, and containers must be identified and equipped with electronic, tamper-proof container seals.

But the massive problems to be surmounted in order to achieve absolute security can be indicated with just a few examples. One expert has shown that in 2000, 489 million people and 127 million passenger cars entered the United States.[27] There also were 11.6 million maritime containers, 11.5 million trucks, 2.2 million railroad cars, 829,000 aircraft and 211,000 vessels that passed routine US inspection points. In the case of the containers alone, it takes about three hours to search just one 40-ft shipping container adequately. By 2006 only about 5 per cent of cargo containers coming to the United States are thoroughly inspected; to screen all the containers and other cargo that enter the country would require hiring large numbers of new inspectors.

Difficult as screening every incoming container would be, screening people is even more problematic. The many issues concerning immigration and airport and aircraft security are by now quite familiar. However it is worth noting that even with refined techniques and intensive surveillance in place, thousands still stream illegally from Mexico into the southern United States every year. In fact, the number is so great that, despite their illegality, state governments are obliged to find ways to supply these immigrants with social policies, education, health care, and even driver's licences. It is clear that desperate people will go to great lengths to devise ingenious ways to cross borders; long coastlines and land borders will always be vulnerable. Home-grown terrorists, such as those who attacked London on 7/7 2005, would, of course, be unaffected by improvements in border controls.

In short, North American borders cannot be made completely invulnerable to attack without adopting draconian measures such as requiring that all goods and services pass US-approved inspections on foreign territory before entering the United States. Such inspection points might take the form of fortresses on other people's lands as in the colonial empires of the past. The current American policy of forcing other countries to adhere to strict standards for shipping is well-intentioned, but one doubts the ability or will of all countries to comply. The UN announcement in January 2004 that fewer than half (93) of the members of the United Nations had submitted reports on their measures to implement UN guidelines on freezing assets, banning travel and embargoing arms of al-Qaeda and the Taliban may be indicative either of the inability of countries to conform to the regulations or of their rejection of the American-led 'war or terrorism'.

## The Intelligence agencies

President Bush asked for and got comprehensive examinations of the events of 9/11, the first and most inclusive of which was carried out by ten members of a bipartisan September 11 Commission. It took almost two years to produce its report, but rather than pointing out who was culpable, the report dealt mostly with history and process, concentrating on what the authors called 'getting the system right'. On July 22 2004 it concluded: 'The combination of an overwhelming number of priorities, flat budgets, an out-moded structure, and bureaucratic rivalries resulted in an insufficient response to this new challenge.'[28] The report faulted both operational failures and coordination issues for making 9/11 possible and went on to conclude that all agencies, including the FBI and CIA, should come under one powerful intelligence director who would report directly to the president. Since the commission reported, even more information about the lack of unified collection and dissemination of intelligence has come to light. We now know that the Federal Aviation Agency (FAA) produced reports as early as 1998 and 1999 indicating that bin Laden and al-Qaeda posed a hijacking threat, and indeed the State Department claims that it warned about such terrorist threats even earlier.[29]

On March 31 2005 a second Commission on the Intelligence Capabilities of the United States, led by Lawrence H. Silberman and Charles S. Robb, concluded that the US intelligence system had been wrong in almost all of its judgments about Iraq's weapons of mass destruction and called for wholesale reorganization of the country's spy agencies.[30] A Senate report on Intelligence the same month said the CIA and other agencies had 'a lack of information-sharing, poor management, and inadequate intelligence collection'.[31] The general thrust of all three reports was that intelligence should be streamlined and centralized.

Following these reports, President Bush appointed John D. Negroponte to be the new director of intelligence and gave him responsibility for providing the presidential daily briefing, instead of the CIA director. This allowed Porter J. Goss, head of the CIA, to concentrate on running the agency. Despite this administrative change the CIA continues to be pre-eminent in covert action and human intelligence. Under the law, however, covert activities can be carried out only with presidential authorization and congressional notification, and these operations are devised so that American government involvement is disguised and meant never to be acknowledged.[32]

In mid December 2004 a bill based on these recommendations was passed by Congress and signed by the president. It provided the most important restructuring of the country's system for gathering and sharing intelligence since the creation of the CIA in 1947 and also approved the new National Counterterrorism Center to co-ordinate information ('connect the dots') and a new independent civil liberties body to review government privacy policies.

During the cold war, intelligence agencies had one principal target – the Soviet Union and it allies – and a finite, though increasing, amount of information to cope with. Today, the 15 intelligence agencies spend about $40 billion annually, have many targets, complex missions and a massive amount of information to deal with in many languages.[33] The assumption of all the commissions was that these issues could be reduced by unifying intelligence and streamlining the process for gathering and analysing information, before sending it to the president.

Despite this massive restructuring, the ability of US intelligence agencies to cope effectively with the new tasks and required methods is still questionable. The new, more coordinated and centralized system could mean that even fewer voices are heard in the White House, as information is now channelled through only one person, the new director of intelligence. Instead of receiving countervailing advice, the president may now hear only one set of opinions. Such administrative changes often turn out to be window-dressing, providing only an illusion of progress, but may prove overly centralized, misguided and even dangerous.

The CIA lacks trained, specialized Americans to carry out vital tasks in foreign, poorer countries. Few Americans with the requisite language and educational skills wish to live in those parts of the world that are most prone to harbouring terrorists, but hiring foreigners can cause other problems concerning discipline and control. For example, foreign informants fed bogus information about weapons of mass destruction to US intelligence agencies throughout Saddam Hussein's last years in power. Until the recruitment problem is overcome, intelligence agencies will be limited in what they can accomplish, particularly given the secrecy and regenerational nature of terrorist groups. In mid February 2005, Porter J. Goss, the new director of the CIA, recognized this fact when he asked for a 50 per cent budget increase for human Intelligence.

More generally, from a democratic and civil-libertarian view, American intelligence agencies and security forces still lack accountability and transparency. The extensive use of such organizations always raises the classic political chestnut of who will guard the guardians. This problem is compounded because President Bush and other politicians, who claim to have been defending freedom around the world, have also been strong supporters of ideas, measures and organizations that have reduced liberty at home. We see this today, for example, in laws such as the Patriot Act and the rules governing the military tribunals that were set up for foreign prisoners in Iraq and Cuba.

## Nuclear terrorism

Instead of focusing time and money on comparatively ineffective 'homeland security' programs, the US administration could have focused more attention on minimizing one of the most dangerous transnational threats to its people. As Graham Allison demonstrated in his important volume, nuclear terrorism is just such a menace.[34] After September 11, the President had an historic opportunity to unite and mobilize the international community to deal with this problem. The Islamist terrorists had proven that they were determined to kill as many people as possible and thus they might be willing to use WMD.

While developing a nuclear weapons program is still very expensive and time-consuming because it involves the acquisition of fissile material, the manufacture of a working bomb and the construction of a delivery system, information about how to do it has become more widespread. In short, the public dissemination of information about nuclear technology has made the production of nuclear weapons much easier. In order to test this, the US military recently asked two physics graduates to attempt to produce a nuclear weapon without the aid of any secret information. The graduates had no experience in atomic energy, yet they showed how the project could, in theory, be completed within thirty months, if the fissile material were available.[35] If potential proliferators had access to any classified weapons schematics and one or two experienced scientists, production of nuclear weapons could be completed even faster.[36]

Another scenario for the spread of nuclear weapons to hostile entities, either state actors or terrorists, would be for them to buy or steal a tactical nuclear weapon. At the conclusion of the cold war, the nuclear stockpile of the Soviet Union was dispersed throughout the former communist states. In order to prevent nuclear weapons from getting into the hands of hostile ethnic groups or volatile states, Presidents George H.W. Bush and Mikhail Gorbachev both recalled their nuclear weapons from deployment.[37] The American Congress passed the Nunn–Lugar Soviet Nuclear Threat Reduction Act of 1991 to aid the Russian government in dismantling its numerous nuclear weapons. It allowed the US government to fund the secure removal and transportation of Soviet nuclear weapons.[38] The enormous number of nuclear weapons in these states prompted the then secretary of defense Dick Cheney to give this conservative estimate: 'If the Soviets do an excellent job at retaining control over their stockpile of nuclear weapons – let's assume they've got 25,000 to 30,000; that's a ballpark figure – and they are 99 per cent successful, that would mean you could still have as many as 250 that they were not able to control.'[39]

While he later retracted it, Russian President Boris Yeltsin's national security adviser, Alexander Lebed, stated in one interview that the Russian government could not account for 84 one-kilotonne nuclear weapons.[40] This problem was compounded by the fact that the Nunn–Lugar Act came at a time of massive social and political upheaval against the new post-Soviet states and within their militaries. These relatively 'small' nuclear weapons apparently had no security system to prevent accidental or unauthorized use, could be set up in thirty minutes, and could allegedly fit into a suitcase or backpack.

In addition to the threat posed by loose nuclear weapons, the United States also faces nuclear risks related to the use of fissile materials in nuclear power plants. It is easier to make a radiological weapon out of such material than an atomic bomb. Radiological weapons consist of conventional explosives surrounded by radioactive material which could be scattered across a town. Such material has been spirited out of Russian and East European nuclear power stations and research centres since the collapse of the Soviet Union. About a hundred attempts to sell such material were reported in 1992 alone. One attempt led to the interception of smugglers in Bavaria who were trying to sell 2.2 kilograms of enriched uranium brought from Eastern Europe for £294,000.[41] Many of these incidents were simply confidence tricks involving 'red mercury' and, in most cases where uranium was involved, it was not enriched to the level necessary for making an atomic bomb.[42]

In other cases the level of enrichment was unclear from press reports; in April 1993 Slovak police arrested two businessmen trying to sell 3 kilograms of enriched uranium-235 and in December of the following year Czech authorities claimed they had intercepted weapons-grade material.[43] In December 2001 seven alleged mobsters were arrested outside Moscow trying to sell a kilo of uranium-235 for £20,000.[44] Police in Greece, Turkey and Georgia all intercepted such fissile material during the course of the same year. For example, Georgian police arrested three men who were trying to sell 1.5 kilos of enriched uranium from a nuclear submarine. Even more alarming was the discovery in 2004 that a Soviet scientist living in Siberia had been hiding 400 grams of plutonium-238 in his garage. The scientist kept the material for six years in case it fell into the 'wrong hands'.[45] The distinction between the various types of fissile material is vital because much of it would be suitable for radiological, but not nuclear, weapons.

There are about 430 fission reactors in the world, producing an estimated 345 gigawatts of electrical power.[46] For fuel, these power plants use enriched uranium, which is a necessary ingredient in nuclear weapons. The byproduct of nuclear power is radioactive fuel rods and materials that can be refined into Pl-239, a very potent fissile material. Thus, with every use of a nuclear power plant, the amount of fissile material grows world-wide. At the end of 2003, there were an estimated 3402 tonnes of highly enriched Uranium and 350 tonnes of plutonium produced by civilian nuclear power plants. This would provide enough radioactive material to create large numbers of nuclear weapons.[47]

After the collapse of the Soviet Union, nuclear fuel was left without any safeguards in the various former Soviet states. For example, after Russia withdrew from Kazakhstan, a warehouse was discovered there that housed enough highly enriched uranium for the production of twenty crude nuclear weapons. The warehouse had been left guarded by nothing more than a padlock since the late 1980s.[48] Even today, Russia and the former Soviet states continue to lack adequate security measures to deal with existing nuclear fuel in the region. As reported by German officials, over 700 nuclear sales were attempted within the first three years of the collapse of the Soviet Union.[49]

One might expect the former Soviet Union to have been inadequately prepared to deal with loose nuclear material, but North America is also insecure. In order to test the security of American nuclear facilities, the United States military sent an outmanned special forces team to breach the Los Alamos National Laboratory. The unit incapacitated the guards and stole enough highly enriched uranium to produce several nuclear weapons. The only problem faced by the team was that the fissile material was too heavy for them to carry; they stole a cart from a local Home Depot store and were able to move the weapons material.[50]

Weak storage security at nuclear power plants poses additional threats to the United States. Nuclear waste, in the form of spent fuel cells, is cooled by being immersed in water for roughly ten years, and then moved to dry lockers. These fuel rods can produce weapons-grade plutonium to be used in high-yield nuclear devices. Russian nuclear power plants produce over one tonne of plutonium every year as a byproduct of heating and powering Russian communities. There is an estimated 52,000 tonnes of waste that is not securely stored, providing a virtual shopping mall for theft by potential nuclear terrorists.[51]

The impact of a nuclear explosion in a city can hardly be exaggerated. For example, if a nuclear weapon were detonated in an isolated attack in Manhattan, assuming no warning and clear weather, all major structures would be destroyed, including the Empire State Building, Madison Square Garden, Penn Station and the New York Public Library. Within one second, at least 75,000 people would die. Within four seconds, roughly 300,000 people – everyone within direct line of sight of the blast – would be dead. Those outside the direct line of sight would receive lung and eardrum injuries. By the end, there would be roughly 800,000 dead, 900,000 injured, and 20 square miles of property destroyed. There are not enough hospital beds in all of New York and New Jersey, so many of the injured would eventually die from lack of medical care.[52]

Given the massive impact of the threat of a nuclear attack on the United States, the US administration would be well advised to make a concerted effort at curtailing the spread of nuclear weapons into the hands of terrorists. There are a few obvious steps that it could take in this regard:

1. It should secure existing nuclear sources by increasing cooperation with international institutions, such as the International Atomic Energy Agency (IAEA) to safeguard existing nuclear weapons, production facilities, and civilian power plants.
2. It should increase funding to the Nunn–Lugar program in order to secure loose Russian nuclear weapons.
3. It should focus more on preventing proliferation than on developing new weapons technologies. By investing in national missile defense systems, the United States is encouraging the Russian and Chinese governments to develop weapons that can evade the American shield.[53] US approval of the study and development of new tactical and low-yield nuclear weapons ('mini-nukes') can only have the same impact.
4. It could make it a priority to remove high enriched uranium (HEU) and plutonium from nuclear reactors. There is enough American HEU in 43 countries for the theoretical development of 1000 nuclear

weapons, and enough American HEU in each of Iran, Pakistan, Israel and South Africa for at least one.[54] The United States should expedite the conversion of nuclear reactors to low enriched uranium, and the Nunn–Lugar program should be expanded in order to focus energy on dismantling weapons in Eastern Europe.

5. Lastly, the United States should petition international organizations to aid in the disposal of radioactive nuclear waste. A multilateral team should have the responsibility of establishing and maintaining secure holding facilities in nuclear countries. To keep highly radioactive materials out of unsafe storage facilities, Graham Allison suggests fuel-cycling, a process by which Middle Eastern states would receive processed fuel rods as long as the material would be returned and the enrichment facilities dismantled.

The risk to security from the use of nuclear weapons by terrorists should be a top American foreign policy concern. A significantly increased investment backed by a multilateral approach would allow the United States to reduce the risk posed by nuclear terrorism. This is an area where the United States could take positive steps to increase its homeland security at less cost and with more return on its money than expensive and dangerous wars overseas.

## Financial costs

The costs of war in Iraq have already deflected the United States from its primary anti-terrorist goal of eradicating the al-Qaeda network. Most of the financial burden is falling on the United States alone. According to some calculations the cost of maintaining the US forces in Iraq is $4–5 billion a month. Bush's first budget request to cover military and recon-struction costs in Afghanistan and Iraq was for $87 billion, but this was just the beginning. Unless Iraq stabilizes, this will need to be repeated for years to come. The cost of the war to the end of 2005 is now pre-dicted at $300 billion. One economist has calculated that if the war con-tinues for five more years this will increase by another $460 billion, not including an estimated $315 billion for long-term veterans' costs.[55] This large financial outlay needs to be added to the dramatic sums that the United States already spends to maintain about 370,000 active and reserve troops overseas from South Korea to the Balkans.

When these figures are placed in the context of economists' forecasts of a deficit of $480 billion for fiscal year 2004, and a predicted total cumula-tive deficit of $1.4 trillion for the decade 2003–13, one can surmise that eventually the policy will have to change. Government spending on education and transportation has also increased dramatically since 2000. Recent legislation in the United States including massive tax cuts, other tax revisions and the medicare prescription drug benefits plan will also impact on the budgetary deficit and may make tradeoffs necessary. The public is becoming increasing worried about the financial stability of the US to wage the war in Iraq. A poll taken on September 9–13 2005 by the *New York Times* and CBS News showed that 53 per cent of Americans were concerned that the war was absorbing resources needed in the United States. The administration may yet be forced to change its tax proposals or to cut overseas military expenditures.

In the short run, the financial issues are gaining prominence – can this war on terrorism be cost-efficient?

## Homeland insecurities

If such large-scale organizational, technical and personnel changes are needed to deter al-Qaeda and other terrorist organizations from new attacks, then what is wrong with the overall policy thrust behind the attempt to enhance homeland security? There are many answers to this question, but three are vital:

1. Trying to provide perfect security against the outside world by border controls is an unattainable, dangerous and futile goal. It will result in an endless and hopeless search for answers that can never be obtained. It is too all-encompassing with no objective or measurable goals to be achieved. It sets priorities and spends money on the wrong things.
2. The attack on the World Trade Center and the Pentagon increased the responsibilities of immigration, customs and security services. American intelligence agencies have been in serious need of reform for over a decade; September 11 showed just how powerful this require-ment was. But the reforms have led to abuses of civil rights that are not acceptable in a democratic society. The aim should be to enhance surveillance without compromising the fundamental principles of law and civil liberty.
3. The financial costs of waging wars in Afghanistan and Iraq at the same time as providing the type of absolute security suggested by administration officials is too high for even the American economy to sustain in the long term. The threats should be prioritized so that sufficient funds and expertise are available for the most serious threats such as nuclear terrorism.

## Security or insecurity?

Perhaps what is actually accomplished in the critical issue of homeland security will come down to how much Americans, Europeans (in particular the British) and others feel they need and want to change their daily lives – how they travel; how they ship goods; whether they agree to report to the local police when they move from one location to the next; whether they are willing to submit to electronic surveillance; and whether they are ready to finance such invasive new policies. Will they be willing to withstand the inconveniences, loss of privacy and expenses required to pragmatically reduce their states' vulnerability to future attacks – especially when there is no end in sight to either the restrictions or the terrorism?

It is not sufficient to live in a fortress, keeping out the underprivileged and their goods. In this age of globalization, countries have little choice but to engage with the world – preferably multilaterally. Walls never keep out enemies for long, as the history of Hadrian's Wall and the Great Wall of China attest. Rather than building security walls, America and its allies would be better off to invest funds, energy and diplomacy to build bridges, reaching out and improving other peoples' lives and futures. Security is vital but not at the cost of isolation, xenophobia and the loss of values characterized by an open and free society at home, and an internationally minded foreign policy abroad. In politics, judgments and predictions are not irrefutable truths, only more or less probable conjectures, but we can be fairly certain that the United States will never again be free of all forms of terrorist attack.

Despite good intentions, administrative reforms and the astronomical costs of the war on terrorism the United States remains vulnerable. The attacks on Afghanistan and Iraq have increased terrorist threats and, despite the massive efforts at homeland security, critical infrastructures, global networks and public venues continue to be soft targets for the next group of terrorists. There can never be a permanent victory in the war on terrorism, nor perfect homeland security. America and its allies will need to learn to live with the risks of terrorism just as they do with some diseases and traffic accidents. The sooner the administration focuses on the economic, cultural and political roots of terrorism and stops using new terrorist events to ratchet up more restrictions on democratic freedoms the better off we all will be.

The United States will have to learn to focus on the probable, not the impossible. Its leaders can never build a perfect shield against terrorism. The illusion that they can do so only feeds the temptations of power.

# Notes

1   In Mark Danner, 'What Are You Going to Do with That?', *New York Review of Books*, 23 June 2005, p. 53.
2   Ibid.
3   Cited in Ethan Bronner's review in *New York Times Book Review*, 22 February 2004, of Philip B. Heymann, *Terrorism, Freedom and Security: Winning Without War* (Cambridge, MA: MIT Press, 2003).
4   Peter Ackroyd, *London The Biography* (London: Chatto & Windus, 2000).
5   While this may have been true at the time, the FBI did demand the library records under the Patriot Act from a Connecticut institution in August 2005; see *New York Times*, 26 August 2005.
6   *New York Times*, 10 April 2005.
7   Nancy Soderberg, *The Superpower Myth: The Use and Misuse of American Might* (Hoboken, NJ: Wiley, 2005), p. 318, citing Department of Justice, www.lifeandliberty.org/ (accessed 23 February 2004).
8   http://www.whitehouse.gov/homeland/ (accessed 21 June 2005).
9   Nancy Soderberg, *The Superpower Myth*, pp. 313–26.
10  *The Guardian*, 13 June 2005.
11  The president's directive is cited in Nancy Soderberg, *The Superpower Myth*, p. 320.
12  *New York Times*, 29 July 2005.
13  By the fall of 2005 there was growing evidence that the Canadian security organizations may have been implicated in this and other similar cases. A judicial enquiry is underway.
14  *New York Times*, 29 June 2004.
15  *New York Times*, 16 July 2005.
16  *New York Times*, 10 September 2005.
17  This difficult set of legal cases is discussed in Ronald Dworkin, 'What the Court Really Said', *New York Review of Books*, 12 August 2004; also compare Anthony Lewis, 'Making Torture Legal', *New York Review of Books*, 15 July 2004.
18  *New York Times*, 6 March, 2005.
19  See Seymour M. Hersh, *Chain of Command: The Road from 9/11 to Abu Ghraib* (New York: HarperCollins, 2003); Mark Danner, *Torture and Truth: America, Abu Ghraib and the War on Terror* (New York: New York Review of Books, Inc., 2004); Chris Mackey and Greg Miller, *The Interrogators* (New York: Little, Brown, 2004); Sanford Levinson (ed.), *Torture* (Oxford University Press, 2004); Meron Benvenisti *et al.*, *Abu Ghraib: The Politics of Torture* (Berkeley, CA: North Atlantic, 2004); James R. Schlesinger *et al.*, *Final Report of the Independent Panel to Review DOD Detention Operations* (August 2004).
20  *International Herald Tribune*, 6 June 2005.
21  *New York Times*, 27 August, 2004.
22  Danner, 'What are you going to do with that?', p. 53.
23  Quoted in Sanford Levinson's review of Mark Danner's *Torture and Truth* in *Los Angeles Book Review*, 11 November 2004.
24  Editorial, *Washington Post*, 31 October 2004.
25  *The Guardian*, 7 October 2005.
26  See a summary of recent changes in direction in Rebecca Cox, 'Six-Point Agenda for Change in the US Department of Security', *RUSI Newsbrief*, vol. 25, no. 9 (September 2005).

27 Stephen E. Flynn, 'America the Vulnerable', *Foreign Affairs*, vol. 81, no. 1 (February 2002), 60–74.

28 *The 9/11 Commission Report* (New York: Norton, 2003), p. xcvi; for an excellent overview see Richard A. Falkenrath, 'The 9/11 Commission Report', *International Security*, vol. 29, no. 3 (Winter 2004/5), 170–190.

29 *New York Times*, 17 August and 14 September 2005.

30 *New York Times*, 1 April 2005.

31 *Economist*, 19 March 2005.

32 *New York Times*, 28 June 2005.

33 Amy B. Zegart, 'September 11 and the Adaptation Failure of US Intelligence Agencies', *International Security*, vol. 29, no. 4 (Spring 2005), 78–111.

34 Allison, Graham, *Nuclear Terrorism: The Ultimate Preventable Catastrophe* (New York: Henry Holt, 2005).

35 *Guardian Unlimited*, 24 June 2003: 'How Two Students Built an A-Bomb', available from http://www.guardian.co.uk/nuclear/article/0,2763,983714,00.html

36 Various guides on nuclear issues, including 'An Encyclopedia for the Preparation of Nuclear Weapons' have appeared on Islamist websites. They are made available and translated from Arabic on www.emritv.org

37 Allison, *Nuclear Terrorism*, p. 69.

38 Ibid.

39 Interview on *Meet the Press*, 15 December 1991.

40 Allison, *Nuclear Terrorism*, p. 43.

41 *The Times*, 17 October 1992.

42 *The Times*, 25 January 1992.

43 *The Times*, 1 April 1993 and 21 December 1994.

44 *The Times*, 8 December 2001.

45 *The Times*, 3 November 2004.

46 Dennis Wingo, *Moonrush: Improving Life on Earth with the Moon's Resources* (Burlington: Apogee Books, 2004), p. 65.

47 David Albright, and Kimberly Kramer. 'Fissile Material: Stockpiles Still Growing', *Bulletin of the Atomic Scientists* (November/December 2004). Available from http://www.thebulletin.org/article.php?art_ofn=nd04albright_016 (accessed 1 October 2005).

48 Allison, *Nuclear Terrorism*, p. 64.

49 Allison, *Nuclear Terrorism*, p. 72.

50 Allison, *Nuclear Terrorism*, p. 83.

51 Michael Long, 'Half Life: The Lethal Legacy of America's Nuclear Waste,' *National Geographic* (July 2002) 14.

52 Atomicarchive.com 'New York City Example', Atomic Archive [home page on-line]; available from http://www.atomicarchive.com/Example/Example1.shtml (accessed 1 October 2005).

53 Allison, *Nuclear Terrorism*, p. 191.

54 Allison, *Nuclear Terrorism*, p. 154.

55 See Linda Bilmes, 'The Trillion-Dollar War', *New York Times*, 20 August 2005.

# 9
# Creating Quagmires: Winning the Wars, Losing the Peace

The 'war on terrorism' is a classic illustration of the dangers inherent in succumbing to the temptation to use military power. The consequences of recent unleashed American military power will be with us for decades. A month after September 11 2001 the United States launched Operation Enduring Freedom against the government of Afghanistan, to be followed by Operation Iraqi Freedom in Iraq on March 19 2003. The names for the operations were, no doubt, chosen to advertise their benevolent objectives, but in each case the question has become not just whether the United States and its allies were justified but whether they have created quagmires: winning the conventional wars but losing the 'peace'.

Viewed from afar and history, the grand dramas of war and the grief that they entail appear inevitable and necessary. The actors struggle on some great winds of change, pulled along by forces mightier than themselves. The protagonists and victims are insignificant, if they are seen at all. What matters are abstract principles of democracy, freedom, justice and national security. Viewed up close, these same events appear to be determined by volition, human choice and error. Personalities, relationships and happenchance seem to be the propelling characteristics of war and peace. At such close proximity the river of time gives way to personality traits of wisdom and stupidity, bravery and cowardice.

In this chapter we examine the consequences and justice of the wars in Afghanistan and Iraq. We look at the situation from both far away and up close, paralleling the two cases and also comparing them with some counter-insurgency efforts during the twentieth century. In so doing we give both historical perspective and immediacy to questions about the consequences of these wars. Bearing in mind the apology of the former United States Defence Secretary Robert McNamara for the errors of the American war in Vietnam, and particularly the failure to win the 'hearts and minds of people',[1] we ask if the US administration approached the problem of regime change in Afghanistan and Iraq in the most effective way to serve its objectives, or whether it launched its armed forces into permanent quagmires of insurgency. Will the countries achieve permanent stability and democracy? Or will they join the ranks of failed states with the potential to do great harm to American and Western interests in the long run? In short, are the consequences of these wars justifiable?

As we have pointed out, after 9/11, instantly and not surprisingly, Americans wanted vengeance. Since al-Qaeda was an organization and not a country, the US government set out to wreak vengeance on those countries that harboured it. This of course meant basically Afghanistan, the staging point for the attack on 9/11, but it also implied the possibility of a US attack on any other countries that the administration considered to be aiding anti-American terrorists. For some in the Bush administration this meant that the United States might attack Iraq or other countries in the 'axis of evil', namely Iran and North Korea, but Iraq was the immediate target.

## Context and war in Afghanistan

For centuries Afghanistan was a buffer state between the British and Tsarist empires because of its inhospitable terrain, the reputation of its people for being formidable warriors, and the jealousy between St Petersburg and London.[2] After the Russian revolution in 1917 and the end of British power in South Asia in 1947, Soviet influence in Afghanistan increased until eventually in 1978 radical army officers took over the government, forming a coalition with the Marxist People's Democratic Party. The efforts of the pro-Soviet government to centralize and modernize the country gave rise to an Islamic insurgency. Not surprisingly, tribal and sectarian violence broke out, as Afghanistan was and is riven with divisions. The Pashtuns have approximately 38 per cent of the population followed by the Tajiks with 25 per cent, the Hazara with 19 per cent and the Uzbeks with 8 per cent. As we will see below, Pashtuns formed the majority of the fundamentalist Taliban while the other three groups were most prevalent in the fight against them.

In 1979 the Soviet Union intervened massively to help the radical government and in so doing provoked one of the defining moments of the cold war. By the mid 1980s several Afghan factions – most to varying degrees Islamic fundamentalist – joined in overt opposition to the Russian troops. With an estimated 80,000 troops the Afghan partisans, or mujahidin, resisted Soviet occupation, aided by generous American technical and financial support. Resistance bases formed in and around Peshawar, Pakistan. As many as 35,000 Muslim radicals were recruited from 40 countries to fight the Russians, and Ahmad Rashid claims that before the Russians left Afghanistan more than 100,000 foreign Muslims had joined the cause.[3]

With congressional approval the US administration supplied advisers and even American-made Stinger anti-aircraft missiles to shoot down Soviet helicopter gunships.[4] With enormous sums of US and Saudi money funnelled through Pakistan, the CIA aided the various Afghan factions, and helped to recruit the figure who later became America's Enemy Number One – Osama bin Laden. This protégé from a wealthy and well-connected Saudi family aided the Islamist Taliban with weapons and money. He helped to set up al-Qaeda (which means military base) as a centre for Arab Afghans and their families. But eventually he was also allowed to establish terrorist training camps in Afghanistan.

In April 1988, the United Nations brokered a ceasefire agreement that required the withdrawal of Soviet forces from Afghanistan. Although the Soviet Union and United States were to be co-guarantors of the accord, both had to agree not to interfere in the internal affairs of the country. However, stability did not ensue. In 1989 when the Russians accepted defeat and the last soldiers left the country, the various factions of the mujahidin divided regionally (north and south), linguistically (Farsi and Pushto), and doctrinally (Shia and Sunni). Rather than come together to forge a new unified regime, they fought each other viciously across the land. Out of a population of 20 million people, as many as 1 million died in the fighting, 1.5 million were injured, and approximately 5 million became refugees.[5]

Amidst regional disputes and continual violence, a new Afghan government run by the Taliban was set up. Pakistan supported the new regime economically, militarily and diplomatically, but with Russia out of the war, American interest in Afghanistan quickly evaporated. Even when the Islamists took over the country the Americans showed little concern.

The Taliban core was based on an Afghan Islamic and Pashtun tribal movement that originated in Pakistan during the Soviet occupation. The word *Talib* means student and referred to the student movement cultivated in the madrasas (Islamic schools) that had been nourished by the brutality of the cold war. By the time of the 9/11 attacks the Taliban controlled about 90 per cent of Afghanistan. They had rejuvenated Islamic ideology in all aspects of society – politics, law, economy and foreign policy – and implemented a radical interpretation of Muslim Sharia law. They banned women from public life, opposed television, films and singing, and outlawed games with balls and most music.[6] It was in this setting in 1998 that Osama bin Laden declared jihad or holy war 'against Jews and Crusaders'.

The 9/11 terrorist attacks revived the dormant US strategic interest in Afghanistan. Almost immediately al-Qaeda was identified as responsible for the atrocities and its host, the Taliban regime, was marked as the first target for reprisals. A month later the war on Afghanistan began. US military strength, especially air power, was harnessed to the hardened soldiers of the Northern Alliance forces, since US bombs alone would not have been decisive. The Taliban forces were organized in dispersed groups of less than 200 fighters, so the US needed the mujahidin and the support of anti-Taliban figures such as Hamid Karzai, who managed to rally some Pashtun elements against the Taliban. After their defeat the al-Qaeda network dispersed, not only through Afghanistan and Pakistan, but also around the world. Even four years later, after the first elections in Afghanistan, there is still no clear trail to bin Laden. He and his movement appear to be working on a much longer time-frame than the US government.[7]

## Context and war in Iraq

In the First World War the Ottoman empire, the Islamic heartland, fought alongside Austria and Germany against Britain, Russia and France. When it was defeated, Britain and France divided the former Turkish colonies in the Middle East between themselves. Britain received a League of Nations mandate to control Mesopotamia, or Iraq, which combined the old Ottoman provinces centred in Mosul, Baghdad and Basra. Emir Faisal became the first king of Iraq and over the next two decades the country achieved independence, a constitutional monarchy, and wealth as it benefited from its oil-rich territories which were earning £74 million a year, a considerable sum in those days.[8] Already, however, the Iraqi army had given evidence of the brutality for which it was to be famed by carrying out the mass-murder of Assyrian Christians who had worked for the British.[9] The 1937 Treaty of Saadabad reconciled the Sunnis of Iraq with the Shiites of Iran, and Britain tried constantly to mediate the various interests in the region in order to keep secure access to Middle Eastern oil.

King Faisal I died in 1933 and the army installed a new government in 1936, although the king's son remained nominally head of state. During the Second World War the army would have supported the Axis powers, but the British forces remaining in the country installed a sympathetic regime, though at the cost of making the king once again a Western puppet. The system did not last long. In 1958 Faisal II and his advisers were murdered by a Baghdad mob and the dismembered body of his powerful uncle Abd al-Ilah was paraded in triumph through the city.[10] Internal instability and factional fighting led to a military coup in July 1968 that, in turn, allowed the Baathist party and Saddam Hussein to take control of government. Saddam became president in 1979 after destroying all opposition. The next two and a half decades of Saddam's history were bloody both inside and outside the country.

In 1980 Iraq attacked neighbouring Iran in an effort to gain control of its oilfields and the Shatt al Arab waterway. Iran was recovering from the deposal of the Shah by Ayatollah Khomeini and other religious leaders and Saddam obviously believed that the instability of the Iranian regime would allow him a quick victory. But it was not to be. Patriotism and Shiite fervour prevailed as the Iranians pulled together.[11] The war dragged on for eight years with no clear winner and over a million dead, followed by an unsteady peace.

A decade later Iraq invaded Kuwait in an attempt to void the debt which it had built up during the war with Iran and enable it to obtain control of Kuwaiti oil. But with UN Security Council support, many Arab states on side, and almost no opposition, the United States mobilized a large coalition to free Kuwait. In four days the allies smashed the Iraqi army and freed Kuwait, but did not occupy Iraq or even advance into the heartland of the country.[12] Ensuing revolts by the Shiites in the south and Kurds in the north were not supported by the West, although Britain and the United States established 'no fly zones' to prevent Baghdad using fixed-wing aircraft over these regions. As a consequence the Kurds were able to achieve effective autonomy, although otherwise Saddam Hussein kept his authoritarian control intact.

International efforts to control Iraq's weapons development began with the end of the Gulf War. The Iraqis promised the United Nations that they would disclose and destroy all weapons of mass destruction, but the various UN efforts to enforce this agreement were incomplete and the inspectors left with their work unfinished. Richard Butler, the head of the UN inspection teams, reported at the end of 1998 that, in the 'absence of full co-operation by Iraq, the mission is not able to conduct the disarmament mandated by the Security Council'.[13] Finally, in 2002 the UN Security Council unanimously passed Resolution 1441 criticizing Iraq's non-compliance with the treaty that had ended the fighting more than a decade earlier, and demanded that the UN weapons inspectors be allowed to return.

In early 2003 the United States and Britain proposed a Security Council resolution authorizing military force against Iraq for non-compliance with earlier resolutions, but it was withdrawn when France threatened to veto it and Germany, Russia, and China strongly opposed the idea.[14] For the American administration the situation in Iraq could not be tolerated. Despite the fact that the Security Council could not be persuaded to support the United States, Britain, Australia and a handful of other countries joined the United States in going to war with Iraq in March, 2003 as a so-called 'coalition of the willing'.[15]

The war ended quickly with few American or coalition casualties, but after the fall of Baghdad, insurgent activities – mortar attacks and suicide bombings – escalated. The conventional military assault on Iraq, like its predecessors, had been a clear victory but the insurgency continued and intensified, threatening to break out into a civil war.

## Justifications and denunciations of the wars

Throughout the prewar and war periods the United States stressed three justifications for going to war: that there were WMD in Iraq (unconfirmed by UN weapons inspectors and disproved by later investigations); that Iraq was linked to the al-Qaeda terrorist organization and perhaps the 9/11 attacks (proven to be false by later official investigations); and that the brutal dictatorship of Saddam Hussein had to be destroyed.

The United States backed up its position with arguments linked by neoconservative ideology. As Paul Wolfowitz, Undersecretary of Defence, put it in New York when he addressed the Council of Foreign Relations:

> Iraq's weapons of mass terror and the terror networks to which the Iraqi regime are linked are not two separate themes – not two separate threats. They are part of the same threat. Disarming Iraq and the War on Terror are not merely related. Disarming Iraq of its chemical and biological weapons and dismantling its nuclear weapons program is a crucial part of winning the War on Terror.[16]

Or as President Bush proffered on June 17 2004, 'The reason I keep insisting that there was a relationship between Iraq and Saddam and al-Qaeda is that there was a relationship between Iraq and al-Qaeda.'[17]

The fundamental theme of opponents of the Iraq War, although not of the Afghanistan war, was based on the ethical question – 'Was it a just war?' This theme has a long history and has been summarized brilliantly by Michael Walzer.[18] The theory of just war is based on the premises that war should be fought only for a good or just cause, by a legitimate authority, as a last resort, and if it is likely to succeed. The argument is often evoked by Christian leaders. Bob Elgar, general secretary of the National Council of Churches, representing 50 million American Christians, used it to denounce the war in Iraq when he declared, 'Before we justify going to war, we need to see that Iraq poses a clear and present danger, and I just don't see it.'[19] The war was also denounced by the leaders of the Roman Catholic and Anglican Churches on similar bases.[20]

Just war theory is used to examine and judge violent conflicts under three headings: the cause of war – *jus ad bellum*; the conduct of war – *jus in bello*; the consequences of war – *jus post bellum*. Below we will examine the conduct and consequences of the wars to show how and why the dangerous quagmires developed. But the American administration's original justification for the wars concerns us first.

The credibility of the US justification for the Iraq War was challenged immediately and tirelessly. In their early work, the UN inspectors were unsure whether or not Iraq possessed WMD. Their inspections revealed that many weapons had been destroyed and the nuclear programme ended. When the inspectors later returned, the United States ridiculed the credibility of their reports as well as the actions of the new director of the UN inspection commission (UNMOVIC), Hans Blix. Despite the derision, Blix insisted in 2003 that the inspectors needed more time to evaluate Iraqi claims that no weapons existed. In his book he subsequently pointed out that virtually every claim made by the American administration proved wrong – all the information about weapons programmes proved false, including the reports of aluminum tubes, yellowcake and mobile labs.[21]

The United States and its allies searched for other reasons to go to war that would justify the use of preventive war – that is, a declaration of war when a threat is not imminent. When their proposed link between the 9/11 terrorists and the Iraqi regime did not hold up to scrutiny, the US administration started to justify war by the nature of the Iraqi regime itself. It was easy to argue that Saddam Hussein's regime was undemocratic, wicked and engaged in human rights violations. Those who make this charge did not lack moral discernment; there was a humanitarian justification for the war. Saddam was a harsh dictator who used violence, fear, torture, executions and ethnic cleansing. His was clearly an evil regime. But the logical problem with this as a justification for the war was that the major human-rights violations against the Kurds and the bombing of citizens and Iranians had occurred many years earlier. A war based on these facts could only be seen as delayed revenge or punishment of Iraq for its earlier actions.

In short, there was no justifiable *casus belli*.[22] Many other governments throughout the world were just as bad as the one in Iraq, but there was no plan to attack them. It was not a necessary war but a war of choice, and therefore unjust. The United States, Britain and the other coalition members relieved the world of a monster who had killed untold numbers, but their justifications for the war were nothing short of official dissembling carried out with brazen ebullience. After three years the key question still remains – why did we go to war?

The United Nations has recently set out the conditions it believes would make war acceptable today.[23] The UN guidelines for deciding when to use force are as follows:

1. Seriousness of the threat. Is the threat serious enough to justify *prima facie* the use of force?
2. Proper purpose. Is the primary purpose of the use of force to halt or avert the threat in question?
3. Last resort. Has every non-military option been explored and exhausted?
4. Proportional means. Is the force proposed the minimum necessary to meet the threat?
5. Balance of consequences. Is it clear that the consequences of action will not be worse than the consequences of inaction?

Had a link between the 9/11 terrorists and Iraq been established, there would have been an argument for war based on the internationally recognized right of self-defence. But there was no way to link the war with the defeat of terrorism and so the first and second criteria were undermined.[24] The third principle was also inadequate, as the war was not the last resort. The UN inspectors had not completed their work and they were hopeful that increased Iraqi cooperation would facilitate their operations. The fourth criterion calls for a distinction to be made between combatants and noncombatants, with the latter harmed as little as possible. During the initial, conventional operations, the US and the 'coalition of the willing' made great efforts to ensure that civilians were not targeted, but the ensuing urban insurgency and counter-insurgency were much more destructive, and many commentators would argue that minimum force was not always used.

It is true that inaction would have left Saddam Hussein in power together with his horrific regime. But this has to be weighed against the thousands of civilian casualties and the property damage caused by the invasion, the threatened civil war between Kurds, Sunnis and Shiites, the massive wastage of US resources, the damage to Washington's reputation as its justifications for the war were exposed and the increased Muslim anger against the West in general. Finally, there had to be an exit strategy that did not rely on Iraqis welcoming the invaders with open arms and settling down in democratic peace and harmony. Nothing in Iraqi history justified such naiveté – not relations between the constituent parts of the country, the appalling end of its monarchical government, or the nature of Saddam Hussein's government. Even after Iraq's elections, the United States and its allies are still there. Colin Powell was clearly off the mark when he promised that the United States would not stay in Iraq after the war and the toppling of Saddam: '[W]e are not hanging on for the sake of hanging on ... We are not occupiers. We have come under a legal term having to do with international law, but we came as liberators.'[25]

In other words, there is a strong case against the US government's commencement and conduct of the wars, particularly in Iraq. The United States attacked Afghanistan because it could not attack al-Qaeda in any other way. The war in Iraq lacks even this type of legitimacy and certainly does not meet the standard of justification offered for the 1991 invasion of Iraq after its assault on Kuwait. In short, the attack on Iraq does not meet UN criteria. So, what can be concluded about the consequences of these ill-conceived wars, as in the final analysis the issue may not be so much whether the war was legitimate but what its results are.

## Consequences of the wars

In attacking Afghanistan the US government listed its four goals as capturing Osama bin Laden, capturing Mullah Omar, closing down al-Qaeda in Afghanistan and elsewhere, and releasing US prisoners in Afghanistan. On September 17 2001, Bush declared 'I want justice ... there's an old poster out West, that I recall, that said "Wanted, Dead or Alive".'[26] More than four years later, and at great cost, only the last of these four objectives has been accomplished. If the first and primary objective of the US was to stop al-Qaeda, it has managed the opposite. The Islamists have continued the war on 'Jews and Crusaders' and international terrorism has grown – witness the train bombings in Madrid, the hotel bombings in Bali, the London underground bombings and other major violent events throughout the world.

The US administration continues to find Islamic countries opaque. Bin Laden's prophecy seems to be working – Islam and the West seem more and more to be on a collision path. President Bush apparently declared after 9/11 that there would not be one great victory but rather 'the patient accumulation of successes'. Today, however, the situation bears more resemblance to the *Economist* magazine's description of it as 'the hapless accumulation of failures'.[27] Normally the military prepares its invasions and occupations on a worst-case scenario. In the case of Iraq that seems to have been true only of the invasion. The occupation appears to have been based on a best-case scenario.

## Afghanistan since the war

Thanks to the US bombing campaign and ferocious fighting by the Northern Alliance, the authoritarian Taliban regime was eliminated. Hamid Karzai, a Pashtun royalist from the south, was chosen to head the interim government, and in December 2001 the United Nations convened a variety of Afghan factions in Bonn to develop a power-sharing arrangement and plan the future of Afghanistan. The Bonn Agreement established the legitimacy of the interim government and paved the way for Hamid Karzai to take office. Karzai was officially elected president in October 2005 and elections for the 249-seat Wolesi Jirga (lower house of parliament) and 34 provincial councils took place in relative peace on September 18 2005. It is this legislature that determines the nature of the 'Status of Force' agreements with the United States and the United Nations. But the election concluded the international agreement signed in Bonn in 2001.

Much of Afghanistan remains insecure: a constitution exists but is unenforceable in most of the country, and women still face severe legal and social discrimination. Warlords control much of the country and insurgents linked to the former Taliban have made a strong revival and continue to operate and kill along the Pakistan border.[28] One estimate is that the number of attacks by insurgents increased by 20 per cent in 2005. As of the spring of 2006 about 18,000 US troops and 14,000 other foreign troops remain in Afghanistan. Effective international peace-keeping is confined to Kabul, but NATO is beginning to set up units in other parts of the country, particularly in the volatile Kandahar region. Sporadic violence continues throughout the country and some of the fighting has been as severe as any in Iraq, while US army officers complain that 'it's like a hydra – you cut off one snake's head and it grows back again'.[29] Inside neighbouring Pakistan, which is vital to the future of Afghanistan, General Musharraf governs as an autocrat with the support of the United States in a sort of Faustian bargain, and terrorist bases remain in the regions along its borders.

The fate of Afghanistan as a stable state remains in question. Considerable violence continues in the rural areas of the south and east and opium production is running high. Roads and power plants are in drastic need of repair. Only 6 per cent of Afghanis have electricity. The country lacks the funds to run an effective civil service and cannot pay for its own military or police. With no significant democratic tradition and a resurgence of sporadic violence the situation in Afghanistan remains perilous.

## Iraq since the war

Three years after the initial invasion, and despite the presence of 140,000 US troops in the country, the United States cannot end the insurgency. Former Baathists, imported jihad fighters and newly minted nationalists keep up the pressure. The situation is extremely dangerous. Each day brings more carnage from bombs and mortars; the autumn of 2005 brought single days when more than 200 Iraqis and Americans died. The insurgents are primarily Sunni Iraqis and foreign fighters, principally from Saudi Arabia and elsewhere in the Middle East. Although the Shiites are the largest grouping in Iraq and Iran, they make up less than 15 per cent of the 1.3 billion Muslims in the world. In other words, there are many foreign Sunni Muslims to support those who lost power and influence in Iraq. Inside the country, the militant Sunni community, which dominated the country for years under Saddam and even before, is both anti-Shiite and anti-American. It wants to derail Iraq's transition to a US-dominated regime and set off a civil war to restore its power. It is supported by those Sunnis who were dismissed by the US government, by the 3 million former members of the Baath Party and by the former 700,000 strong army and security forces – a large pool from which the insurgents can continue to draw new recruits.[30]

Even pragmatic optimists claim that the United States will be in Iraq for 10 to 20 years. They base their argument on the fact that the United States has been in Korea and Germany for a half century. Pessimists claim that only a miracle will prevent Iraq from breaking up or falling into a prolonged civil war. Perhaps the United States can prevent this but, in many ways, its presence is itself now part of the problem. Much of the Arab world thinks the United States is biased against Islam, semi-colonial in its attitude and reliant on raw military power. The occupation has set off waves of anger and opprobrium that mobilize and embolden radical Islamists everywhere. The Iraqi government forces are not strong enough to hold off the insurgents and will require outside help for a generation or more. But the intellectual mountain that the

United States has to climb to keep its forces in Iraq, supporting the new Iraqi government while avoiding being cast as invaders, may simply prove too steep, as it has in many other insurgencies.

The dangers in post-war Iraq are driving the educated elite into exile. While many feared Saddam Hussein and his sons, they are even more concerned today about their lack of security. Apart from Kurdistan, which has achieved a good deal of stability, one of the few reasonably secure areas is the Green Zone, the area named for the green of trees, grass and river but which is, in fact, a maze of concrete blocks, barbed wire and bunkers. It is a giant fortress for politicians, troops, foreign contractors, and diplomats, having a population of some ten thousand people who run the government offices and the US and other embassies. Few can safely leave the compound without being escorted by heavily armed guards or taken by armoured buses to the airport. Everyone wants to abolish the Green Zone as it is symbolic of Iraqi insecurity but, like the policies towards the Iraqi occupation generally, no one knows how to replace it.

All Iraqis and foreigners in the country fear violence. Women are less free than under Saddam's regime; they fear abduction, rape and murder. As one woman told a *New York Times* reporter, 'Under Saddam we could drive, we could walk down the street until two in the morning. Who would have thought the Americans could have made it worse for women? This is liberation?'[31] In parts of Afghanistan many women have taken off their burkas, but in Iraq the number of veils has increased and some women are hiding at home.

Most Iraqis are living in dangerous circumstances and many have little hope of significant employment. Perhaps up to 70 per cent of the workforce is unemployed, with perhaps 12 million unemployed before the war and 13 million after. The United States has tried to help out by providing temporary jobs, for street cleaners for example, but the situation cannot be rectified by short-term solutions. Poverty, armed dissidents, crime and violence all afflict the civilian population. Attacks on coalition troops, Red Cross and UN personnel, and Iraqi supporters of the United States have been continual. The coalition has been forced to reply with violent reprisals and new ways to restrict the movement and freedom of Iraqis, from imprisonment to requiring all residents to have identity cards to move about the country.

While violence in Iraq continues unabated, ordinary Americans are told little about day-to-day difficulties in the country.[32] The occupiers and reporters see only part of the picture. Daily reports on US television are cursory or non-existent – the result of 'hotel journalism', since reporters have little choice but to be 'embedded' in military units or stay safe inside hotels in or outside the Green Zone in Baghdad. US reporters know that American policy has failed in Iraq, but they hesitate to say so because they might be accused of anti-American bias and lack of patriotism and perhaps lose their jobs. They are left to 'scatter their observations and bury the counterpoints deep within their columns, trusting readers to move beyond the headlines and pick up the hints.'[33]

Americans have been led to believe that this is a necessary war being carried out in a reasonable fashion – that it will protect them and their freedoms from terrorism. But they have been shielded from the sheer brutality of the war, getting only a rare glimpse of what is behind the masks and pretences. War is ugly, hence the need to keep it as a last resort.[34] War is also highly alluring to a powerful state such as the United States, especially high-tech warfare in which the military often do not see beyond their targets to the human suffering behind them. Air warfare is particularly vicious in this regard. Only when airmen are separated from their high-tech shields do they experience the full brutality of the war. In high-tech wars enemies and innocents are dehumanized.

In 2006, President Bush declared that 30,000 Iraqis have died as a result of the initial incursion and ongoing violence. Yet another survey from Britain concluded that about 100,000 Iraqis have died in the war.[35] As for American casualties (which now number about 2,500), they, too, are often downplayed in the Western media. US soldiers are being killed, wounded in action, and left with psychiatric problems, often without due recognition for their services. Americans are not allowed to see pictures of the grizzly deaths and injuries of their military in the slaughterhouse of war in Iraq. Rather, the US government minimizes the negative aspects of the war by painting it in idealized images. Instead of deaths and injuries it talks about collateral damage and makes dubious claims about the protection and promotion of democracy in the greater Middle East.

On occasion American leaders have hinted that there will be a Marshall Plan for the reconstruction of Afghanistan and Iraq. Both President Bush and L. Paul Bremer, the US civil administrator in Iraq until June 2004, have used the analogy. But it was misleading. George Marshall himself argued in 1947 that 'It would be neither fitting nor efficacious for this government to undertake to draw up unilaterally a program designed to place Europe on its feet economically. This is the business of the Europeans. The initiative, I think, must come from Europe.'[36] In other words, for the plan to work, the Europeans had to design it – not the Americans. But in Iraq, no acceptable plan has been put forward by the Sunnis, Shiites and Kurds. Moreover, the Marshall Plan was finite in costs and duration, taking the form of both loans and grants, and with the US Congress appropriating the reconstruction money each year after an evaluation. However in the Iraq War, despite its best efforts to explain the costs, the US administration found it difficult to justify even the request for the initial funding. Unlike the Marshall Plan in which the European enemies had to match contributions (and even then much of it was made up of loans), the Iraq reconstruction plan so far consists of several billion dollars, all in grants. Reconstruction in Iraq has also been hindered by reliance on American defence contractors and inattention to Iraqi expertise. Kidnappings and severe insecurity plague most projects. Promised funds have been slow to materialize and most of what has been spent has come out of Iraq's own oil revenues. After three years, electricity and clean water are still unavailable on a regular basis to much of the population.

## Constitutional developments in Iraq

Iraqi history and social structures make the country an unlikely candidate for a permanent constitutional system. Previous attempts have failed. Iraqi politics are particularly brutal and since the fall of Saddam there has been no time for the evolution of democratic culture or mores. Indeed paradoxically it is the very unpromising nature of the situation which encourages Washington to keep military forces there. If the United States had simply left the Iraqis to find an alternative to Saddam Hussein the country would probably have broken into three parts: Kurdistan, a rump Sunni state and a Shiite state around Basra. Alternatively, as the army had been dominated by the Sunnis, they might have reimposed control from Baghdad and resumed the traditional Iraqi system of government by brute force and military coup. In any case, Washington was determined not to allow this. It expected Iraqis to welcome US forces as liberators and, with America's guidance, to establish a democratic constitutional form of government. Its first disappointment came when the liberated Iraqis proceeded to sack Baghdad and destroy their cultural heritage and centres of government. The second was when it discovered that a fully fledged insurgency against US presence was spreading, particularly in the Sunni region.

Not unexpectedly, given the lack of post-war preparation, stability and security in Iraq after the war have not progressed well. No durable regime was put in place following the preliminary elections of January 2005 and violence continued unabated – even in the relatively peaceful Basra area controlled by the British.[37] In this election 8.5 million Iraqis voted (a turnout of 58 per cent) but very few Sunnis participated, and the government found it impossible to construct a coalition that adequately represented all factions. The impasse was caused by both hardline Sunnis who wanted their share of government positions and spoils and hardline Shiites who wanted to impose their will on Sunni Arabs, Kurds and secular Shiites.

Despite these issues, the goal of Iraqi governments and the US administration continues to be democratic advancement in the country, and some progress has been made. In May 2003 Iraq was fully occupied, by July 2004 it had an interim government, and in January 2005 the country successfully elected a transitional assembly. This assembly appointed 71 Iraqis to draft a constitution which was ratified by referendum on October 15 2005 and further elections followed in December 2005.

Drafting the constitution proved very difficult. The drafters were in mortal danger every day, and 13 Sunni members walked out after two of their colleagues were assassinated. According to a proclamation of the so-called al-Qaeda court in August 2005, 'We will kill anyone who ... drafts a constitution.'[38] But despite these threats, long delays, and even missing the final deadline, the members did come up with a draft. The draft used vague language to cover the fissures between the rival groups, particularly over the essential constitutional question about how Iraq could be both a democracy and an Islamic state at the same time. Nevertheless, the assembly voted to accept the document and sent the country forward towards the decisive referendum. Then after constant demands from the Sunnis the assembly again amended the constitution. The constitution is, in essence, a Shia–Kurd compromise. Sunnis remained violently opposed to it, arguing that it will drive the country further apart, not unite it. As one Sunni member of the Assembly put it: 'We have reached a point where this constitution contains the seeds of the division of Iraq.'[39]

The preamble to the constitution attempts to unite the country behind a symbolic call to Iraqi greatness. It begins 'We, the sons of Mesopotamia, land of the prophets, resting place of the holy imams, the leaders of civilization, and the creators of the alphabet, cradle of arithmetic ...' and then goes on to gloss over the divisions that occur along the many sectarian and religious fault-lines with vague language and leaving unresolved issues for future legislatures. The major issues concern:

1. Centralization versus regional autonomy and federalism. Essentially this issue comes down to how much scope should be allotted for Kurdish and perhaps Shiite autonomy. The Sunnis and Kurds are far

apart on the question. Even the Shiites are divided, as some maintain that federalism will lead to a divided state and that the idea of divided authority goes against the concept of central Islamic rule. No subject received more contradictory opinions than this one in the drafting process.

2. What institutions, federal or local, should have power over oil resources? The Kurds want this power decentralized and they also want to control the rich oil fields of Kirkuk. (The latter issue is particularly sensitive because tens of thousands of Kurds were expelled from there by Saddam's government and replaced by Arab migrants.) In the end, much of the early text on federalism and resources was deleted because of Sunni opposition. The constitution puts the federal government in charge of administering current oil and gas fields but provides no formula for dividing oil profits among the new legal entities. This will be decided by future legislatures.

3. The role of Islam, particularly the question of civil rights for women. The wording is vague, as the constitution says that 'Islam is the basic source of law' and no law should contradict its 'principles of jurisprudence'. But under article 30 Iraqis are given the choice of defining their own 'personal status' according to their own beliefs. This would seem to mean that Iraqis will be able to use religious law or civil law governing marriage, divorce and inheritance. In short, it is not clear whether Shariah, (Koranic) law will pertain or not on all social issues. If it does, secularists argue, Iraqi women will be put back fifty years in terms of their basic rights.

4. The role of former Baathists in the country. Under clause 132, the constitution bans ex-members of the 'Saddham Baath Party' from government positions, but leaves open the possibility that they may be allowed to disown their affiliation and restore their opportunities in the future. If the impact of this clause is not diluted further, many Sunnis will continue to feel that they are forced to fight on against the new regime and constitution.

Voting in the referendum proved relatively peaceful and the constitution was passed by large numbers. Had the people voted no in the referendum (this would have occurred had there been a two-thirds majority of no votes in any 3 Iraqi provinces out of 18) elections would still have been held for a second transitional assembly in December. The Sunnis constitute only 20 per cent of the 27 million Iraqis, but they have sizeable majorities in four provinces and could have negated the constitutional development of the country. Elections for a new assembly were held on

December 15 2005 and a new government followed. But the new assembly was so divided by hostile Shiite, Sunni and Kurdish parties that the first appointed Prime Minister has found it difficult and perhaps impossible to put in place a stable national coalition.

The constitution is of major importance, but the underlying political order is even more important than the legal document. The document itself is no more than a piece of paper and no better than the degree of consensus, or lack of it, in the country. The German Weimar constitution was excellent but it still coincided with a highly divided and ideologically riven country which gave rise to Adolf Hitler. The new Iraqi constitution may actually do more harm than good, as it reflects profound splits among the ethnic and religious groups and could lead to an eventual division of the country. Moreover, democratic government in Iraq is still far from a certainty and may never be realized. The elections were significant events, but whether the country has developed the necessary identity and national cohesion to remain a single state is still very questionable. Distrust and savage violence reigns in the country and solutions or mechanisms to overcome the fault-lines are visible only in the far distance, and are seen only with rose-coloured glasses. The question remains whether the construction of an Iraqi constitution will win the loyalty of millions of Iraqis and provide some form of shared vision of a future country.

The US administration has argued that democracy in Iraq would solve other problems in the Middle East. But the so-called 'road-map' for Israeli-Palestinian relations has made limited progress and the rest of the region remains highly unstable. The 'terrorist' organization Hamas has captured Palestine, and nine Middle East countries now have increasingly difficult relations between their Shiite and Sunni populations. Paul Bremer, Bush's point man in Iraq, has said that there are three rules for crisis handling – adapt, adapt and adapt. But that is not the same as running to catch up with events. The United States plan for the war on Iraq went no further than the removal of Saddam Hussein. The violent consequences of the war were not foreseen.

## Staying power and counter-insurgency

The central issue has become whether the United States can convince enough Iraqis, some of the Arab world and its own people that the presence of US forces in Iraq will build a stable society there. By July 2005, 47 per cent of the American population had concluded that the war in Iraq was hindering the war on terrorism.[40] 45 per cent felt it had increased the chances of a terrorist attack in the United States, against 22 per cent who believed it had reduced such chances. However, a majority of 52 per cent to 43 per cent still felt that the US forces should remain in Iraq until the situation there is stabilized. This is a confused and continuing message. The omens for the US people supporting a long-term occupation of the country do not seem good, and all options now look bleak.

The West's historic experience with counter-insurgency is very mixed, largely because foreign occupiers have difficulty sifting their enemies from their friends. France failed to put down rebellions in both Algeria and Vietnam. Britain failed in Israel, Cyprus and Aden, Israel pulled out of Lebanon, the United States failed in Vietnam, Lebanon and Somalia. In all these cases the occupiers finally decided that the price of staying was not worthwhile and just took their troops home.

The present case of Iraq resembles the 1983 Lebanese one, where the United States and its allies found themselves caught up in a maelstrom of religious, ethnic and political rivalries. If the Iraqi government and the occupiers cannot come up with a shared vision of the future, especially for the Sunnis, eventually there will be no point in staying. But does that mean the United States will cut and run as it finally did in Vietnam, Lebanon and Somalia? The answer is not clear, because despite the fact that no linkage was found between Iraq and 9/11, the US public was eager to punish someone for the attacks. Moreover, the situation does not quite parallel the Vietnam War because today's military is not like the one the United States sent to Vietnam with its unwilling and deprived conscripts, but rather a paid professional army. One way or another, the soldiers have chosen to join the army, even if the reserves and guards had no idea that they would see active service overseas. However the crucial issue is not the nature of the army but how it sees its role in states suffering from insurgencies and whether it has a suitable doctrine to win over the people there to the democratic path.

## Ending insurgencies

Britain has been the most successful of all the democracies at ending insurgencies. In the interwar years, Sir Charles Gwynn's *Imperial Policing* was the basic reference text. Its principal argument regarding guerrilla warfare went as follows:

> The admixture of rebels with a neutral or loyal element of the population adds to the difficulties of the task. Excessive severity may antagonize this element, add to the number of rebels, and leave a lasting

feeling of resentment and bitterness. On the other hand, the power and resolution of the Government forces must be displayed ... Mistakes of judgement may have far-reaching results. Military failure can be retrieved, but where a population is antagonized or the authority of the Government seriously upset, a long period may elapse before confidence is restored.[41]

Thus Gwynn emphasized that winning over potential supporters of the insurgents was the key to victory. Politics, not military operations, were the vital elements.

Gwynn's successor as guru of anti-guerrilla operations was Sir Robert Thompson, who was involved in British operations in Malaya in the 1950s. His 1974 book *Defeating Communist Insurgency* was studied closely by generations of British army officers for staff college examinations. Unfortunately its prescriptions have not been remembered or adopted in the war on terrorism; indeed almost every one of the errors that he identified has been made in Iraq.

Thompson's first principle is that the government must have a clear political aim. The United States has confused the political aims of its campaign against terrorism by boasting that it would do something about the so-called 'axis of evil' – North Korea, Iran and Iraq – as part of its objectives. Furthermore, Thompson argued that, if the political aim were not clear and kept in mind, short term and ad-hoc measures would be adopted which would undermine the long-term objectives.[42] In so far as the multiplicity of US targets split Washington's Western supporters, and its military operations in Iraq alienated most Muslims, the campaign has shown the dangers of ignoring Thompson's advice.

More specifically, the United States intended to depose Saddam Hussein and to establish a democratic Iraqi government. But military factors have frequently been allowed to trump the political agenda; American soldiers who lurk in fortified positions such as the Green Zone are useless in an insurgency: they simply provide targets. Faced with an insurgency, the military's task is to win over the people and persuade them that they have a common goal in setting up a democratic state. The military have to be approachable. They have to be seen by the local people and communicate with them. Military force protection, as it is called – the laudable concern with one's own forces' casualties – has to be sacrificed to these goals, otherwise the struggle is lost from the beginning.

Thompson's second principle is that the government should operate within the law despite the temptations to behave otherwise: 'the excuses being that the processes of law are too cumbersome, that the normal safeguards in the law for the individual are not designed for an insurgency and that a terrorist deserves to be treated as an outlaw anyway'.[43] The mistreatment of prisoners in Abu Ghraib and Camp Breadbasket, and the upsurge of anger that it has caused across the Arab world, are a perfect illustration of the point he was making. The US willingness to hold prisoners without trial and to employ torture will from now onwards be taken as proof positive of the hypocrisy of its criticisms of human rights abuses in the Muslim world (see Chapter 8). Some Muslim writers have long argued that the West in general and the United States in particular are decadent, and now the improper behaviour of US soldiers has given them concrete evidence of this.

Thompson's third principle is that the government must have a plan coordinating all aspects of its effort against the insurgents; 'otherwise a situation will arise in which military operations produce no lasting results because they are unsupported by civil follow-up action'. This is an accurate description of what has happened in Afghanistan and Iraq. The existing governments were overthrown, but insufficient plans were made to replace them and the resulting insurgencies and chaos gave al-Qaeda more rather than less room to manoeuvre and attack the United States in Iraq and elsewhere.

Thompson's fourth principle is that the defeat of political subversion was more important than attacking the insurgents themselves. For the United States, winning the sympathy of the Muslim world is far more important than capturing terrorists because if it does not then more will always be recruited. It is no good devastating a city like Fallujah to destroy the insurgents hiding there if this simply creates more insurgents and more hatred of the Iraqi government and its American backers. On the other hand, Washington's difficulties are compounded by the fact that even its minor defeats or signs of weakness encourage the terrorists. Bin Laden and others repeatedly cite Vietnam, Lebanon and Somalia to rally their supporters and show that the United States can be cowed and defeated. In Vietnam a small and backward Asian country (with aid from the USSR and China) forced Washington to abandon its South Vietnamese allies, withdraw its forces and sign a humiliating peace treaty. In Lebanon the destruction of the US marine barracks persuaded Washington to pull out its peacekeeping force; and in Somalia the death of a handful of soldiers had the same effect.

US handling of the struggle in Iraq since the invasion, and particularly the early withdrawal from Fallujah in 2004, paradoxically reinforced this image of both US brutality and US weakness in the face of constant guerrilla activity. Once more Gwynn and Thompson underline the central dilemma. If the government uses 'excessive' repression against insurgents this will encourage those who are neutral to join their ranks. But 'the power and resolution of the government must be displayed. Anything that can be interpreted as weakness encourages those who are sitting on the fence to keep on good terms with the rebels.'[44]

In a counterinsurgency the most important goal is to determine the motivation behind the violence and then respond in a way that is proportionate to the action and likely to give a solution. Terrorists learn from their experiences, discovering in particular how not to repeat their mistakes. In Iraq they have adapted continually – moving from one type of attack to another depending on the weakness of their opposition. The dilemma is simple: the United States and the Iraqi government need *both* to protect the peaceful citizens *and* to eliminate the terrorists. In other words, the terrorists must be isolated from their support and delegitimated. As Rand Corporation analyst Bruce Hoffman summarizes the lessons of counter-insurgency:

> First, always remember that the struggle is not primarily military, but political, social, economic and ideological. Second, learn to recognize the signs of a budding insurgency, and never let it develop momentum. Third, study and understand the enemy in advance. And fourth, put a strong emphasis on gathering up-to-the-minute local intelligence.[45]

If history is any clue we can normally expect the insurgents to outlast the invaders. Shaping states and nations is never easy, especially for foreigners. Afghanistan and Iraq are practically textbook cases of countries riven by ethnicity, religion, conflicts and memories of hatred, past and present. Building states that will last in these two lands is far from a foregone conclusion. The greatest error (but not the only one) of the war in both of these countries was the inability of the United States and its allies to plan for a viable endgame.

## Quagmires

The debate continues about whether the United States and its allies have been sucked into quagmires that will last for years in Afghanistan and Iraq. The US government and its allies say that political stability is about to descend on these countries and that they can soon reduce their troops. Even the UN Security Council acts as if it believes this. On June 8 2005 it voted unanimously for a US resolution authorizing the use of 'all necessary measures' by the occupation forces in partnership with the Iraqi government to bring peace to the country. These and similar acts appear to have given belated UN blessing to the invasion.

There is no doubt about where we stand on this issue. In Northern Ireland it took 36 years of internal warfare before the IRA declared an end to war, and the British government still had 10,500 soldiers and 3500 civilians there when the IRA agreed to lay down its weapons in the summer of 2005. The British were prepared to stay the course for over three decades and to use the required number of soldiers to end the violence. In Vietnam, the United States was not prepared to use enough troops or engage in an effective counter-insurgency strategy. It lost because it never earned the support of the local people and wasted its energy hunting down Vietcong guerillas.

Now the United States is making the same mistakes in Iraq. Despite a new constitution, an Iraqi government and elections, insecurity, murders and car-bombings continue. Do the insurgents have the same broad appeal as the Vietcong did among their population? It is uncertain how far their appeal reaches outside the Sunnis. But even if it is limited, in Vietnam over half a million US soldiers spent years combating the insurgency only to disengage from the country in shame. There are only approximately 140,000 US troops in Iraq for a population of about 25 million, or about half the population of Vietnam during the war. Over time, the American military personnel have been getting safer but the Iraqi security forces and general population have not.

The cases of Iraq and Vietnam are reasonably parallel – and the resemblance continues to increase. The main difference between Vietnam and Iraq is that the death of 2500 US servicemen and women has not yet turned a vast majority of Americans against the war. But in both cases the US had:

1. Difficulty building a strong, viable state.
2. Difficulty obtaining information about what was going on in the country. Policymakers were bewildered by the intelligence failures in Vietnam, as they are again today in Iraq.
3. Difficulty in understanding why the number of insurgents continues to grow, despite significant American battle victories.
4. Difficulty in accepting that the battle for the hearts and minds of people is/was failing and that nationalism continues to count.
5. Difficulty in understanding why the reconstruction plans did not work to reduce the number of insurgents as it did in other war-torn countries.

The spectres hanging over the occupation of Iraq are dangerous and unambiguous. The United States has not been able to penetrate the insurgents' organization in order to discover their plans. Despite the capture and trial of Saddam Hussein, the insurgents appear to be getting stronger. The country is riven by division and suspicion over religion, ethnicity and the constitution.[46] Sunnis, Shiites and Kurds fight for power, believers and secularists contest Islamic law, and they all have their own contending militias. The Sunni minority is now dispossessed of power, unable to profit from Saddam Hussein's rule as it did for decades. The Shiites are their main victims, with Abu Musab al-Zarqawi even boasting about his murders on his websites. The new Iraqi army and police are disproportionately composed of Shiites and Kurds. As of the spring of 2006, sectarian violence continues, with Sunni suicide bombings of Shiites and Kurds, and Shiite death-squads killing Sunnis. A senior military officer told the *New York Times* 'We are capturing or killing a lot of insurgents. But they're being replaced quicker than we can interdict their operations. There is always another insurgent ready to step up and take charge.'[47]

Suspicion and distrust of their government and of all foreigners by ordinary Iraqis is at an all-time high. The sectarian violence and constant reprisals illustrate that there is not enough political trust and willingness to compromise for the establishment of a viable democracy. The insurgency is about beliefs, perceptions, expectations and legitimacy. It can only be defeated if the insurgents lose the psychological war. It is a contest of wills between the insurgents and the counter-insurgents, and so far the insurgents are holding their own. In discussing the possibility of civil war, the US Ambassador to Iraq, Zalmay Khalilzad, told journalists in 2005: 'Iraq is poised at the crossroads between two starkly different visions. The foreign terrorists and hardline Baathists want Iraq to fall into a civil war.'[48] The International Institute for Strategic Studies reported that the Iraqi Police Service was almost up to the required strength, but the National Guard and the armed forces were far below the numbers required.[49] Even when mobilized and trained, these forces will be woefully inadequate to control such a fissiparous and violent country. While some indicators are positive, such as the 400 trained judges, the estimated size of the insurgency at 18,000 has hardly changed over the years and only 18 per cent of Iraqis believe the 'country is headed in the right directions'.[50] At any rate there is a relatively poor prospect of success or improvement in the situation.

One or a combination of the following four possibilities is theoretically possible in Iraq:

1. A stable liberal democracy with federal institutions.
2. A shaky liberal democracy with confederal institutions.
3. Fragmentation and inertia with extreme religious and sectarian violence.
4. Civil war.

The first two possibilities are based on the optimistic idea that the opponents are finite in number and destructible and that security can be established along with satisfactory post-war reconstruction, allowing the process of democratization to continue smoothly and satisfactorily. The third relies on the argument that the ethnic and religious groupings will decide that there is not enough national identity and consensus for the continuation of one country. The last and most pessimistic scenario is that religious differences will lead to a war among the groups, with the United States being one of the prime targets of all of them. In our opinion, the third and perhaps fourth scenarios are the most likely because if the United States pulls out Iraq will probably sink into turmoil with private militias and terrorists ruling vast parts of the country.[51] For political reasons the United States may attempt to reduce its troops in Iraq during 2006 to about 100,000 but it cannot reduce them more without further weakening the government there.

As discussion of the possibility of a US withdrawal from Iraq intensified in the autumn of 2005, the Bush administration published the *National Strategy for Victory in Iraq*. This stressed the administration's determination to persevere, the advances already made in Iraq and the disadvantages of a withdrawal: '[c]eding ground to terrorists in one of the world's most strategic regions will threaten the world's economy and America's security, growth, and prosperity, for decades to come.' The paper went on to argue that withdrawal would turn Iraq into a failed state and would embolden the terrorists who would become convinced that the United States 'cannot stand and fight'. The administration argued that this strategy meant that territory should be held once cleared of insurgents. Certainly, if this is so, it shows a much clearer understanding of the problem of guerrilla warfare than earlier operations which, as in Vietnam, stressed offensive warfare and destruction of the government's enemies. The paper claimed that 212,000 members of Iraqi security forces had been trained and of them 40 battalions were able to take the lead in the fight against the insurgents. The paper concluded: '[w]e are organized for victory to an extent not seen since the end of the cold war,' and quoted President Bush that, 'in Iraq, there is no peace without victory'.[52]

Plainly, from the administration's point of view, every discussion in the media about the possibility of withdrawal emboldens the insurgents and anti-American terrorists everywhere. Equally plainly, the US armed forces have learned from the insurgency in Iraq. The question is whether it is too late: the insurgents too entrenched, too many Iraqis alienated, the American people disillusioned and the operation taking too long. At the political level, the policy statement took some of the strength out of the opposition's claim that Bush had no endgame. Indeed the policy emerged from research done by academic pollsters which indicated that the American people would continue to accept military casualties as long as they were assured that there would be a final victory and not another drawn-out and failed war such as had occurred in Vietnam.

Nevertheless, the United States was unprepared for the massive post-war challenges of occupying a defeated Iraq – counterinsurgency, political transformation and reconstruction. In the early stages several tactical mistakes were made. Neither vital ammunition dumps, nor government documents, nor historic museums were guarded. But the major strategic error once again was that the US and its allies failed to understand the force of indigenous nationalism. Most of the insurgents were Iraqis steeped in an ideology based on a fusion of nationalist and religious sentiment. Insurgents can only operate with the tacit support of ordinary Iraqis. In order to stop an insurgency, invaders need to convince the local population to back efforts to eradicate violence and that they intend to leave the country as soon as it is stable. In these objectives the Americans failed and the 22 February 2006 destruction of the Golden Mosque in Samarra – the holist Shia Shrine In Iraq – continued the steady sectarian march towards civil war ... if it has not happened already. The US military may be preparing for a 'long war' in Iraq, but so are its opponents.

The situation remains perilous because once the die was cast and the United States and its allies declared war on Iraq, decisions have been like the proverbial ones 'between the plague and cholera'. As Machiavelli put it, men are shortsighted and cannot easily change their nature or behaviour. The proponents of these wars are confounded by their own alternatives. Chance or fortune may have played a role, but the United States and its allies chose to go to war. There was nothing inevitable about that. Bismarck had it right: 'Woe to the statesman whose reasoning for entering a war does not appear so plausible at its end as at its beginning.'

# Notes

1 Expressed completely in Robert McNamara, *In Retrospect: The Tragedy and Lessons of Vietnam* (New York: Times Books, 1995); also in the film *Fog of War*.

2 James Lunt, *Bokhara Burns* (New York: Barnes and Noble, 1969); Dorothy Woodman, *Himalayan Frontiers* (London: Cresset Press, 1969); Charles Miller, *Khyber: the Story of the North West Frontier* (London: Macdonald & Jane's, 1977).

3 Ahmed Rashid, 'The Taliban: Exporting Extremism', *Foreign Affairs*, vol. 78, no. 6 (December 1999), 22–36.

4 Philip Towle, *Pilots and Rebels: The Use of Aircraft in Unconventional Warfare* (London: Brassey's, 1989), pp. 190ff.

5 As of 2004, 1.5 million are still refugees in Pakistan, 1 million are in Iran and small numbers are scattered elsewhere. *Military Balance 2004–2005* (London: IISS/Oxford University Press, 2004), p. 31.

6 For details see Ahmed Rashid, *Militant Islam, Oil and Fundamentalism in Central Asia.* (New Haven, CT: Yale University Press). Also John K. Cooley, *Unholy Wars: Afghanistan, America and International Terrorism* (London: Pluto Press).

7 For an overview of the country after the defeat of the Taliban see Pankaj Mishra, 'The Real Afghanistan', *New York Review of Books*, 10 March 2005, 44–8.

8 Peter Slugett, *Britain in Iraq 1914–1932* (London: Ithaca Press, 1976); Michael Adams, *The Middle East: A Handbook* (London: Anthony Blond, 1971), p. 204.

9 Paul P.J. Hemphil, 'The Formation of the Iraqi Army', in Abbas Kelidar, *The Integration of Modern Iraq* (London: Croom Helm, 1979).

10 Elie Kedourie, 'Arab Political Memoirs', *Encounter* (November 1972); Archie Roosevelt, *For Lust of Knowing: Memoirs of an Intelligence Officer* (London: Weidenfeld & Nicolson, 1988), p. 138.

11 Revolutions tend to increase the military power of the state where they occur; see Jonathan R. Adelman, *Revolution, Armies and War* (Boulder, CO: Lynne Rienner, 1985).

12 Colin L. Powell, *My American Journey* (New York: Ballantine, 1995), p. 508.

13 Richard Butler, *Saddam Defiant* (London: Weidenfeld & Nicolson, 2000), p. 222.

14 Hans Blix, *Disarming Iraq* (New York: Pantheon, 2004), p. 248.

15 A strong case for the war can be found in Kenneth M. Pollack, *The Threatening Storm: the Case for Invading Iraq* (New York: Random House, 2002); A further defence of US actions after the war is found in Noah Feldman, *What We Owe Iraq: War and The Ethics of Nation Building* (Princeton University Press, 2004).

16 Quoted in the *New York Review of Books*, 21 October 2004.

17 White House, 'President Discusses Economy, Iraq in Cabinet Meeting', White House Press Release, 17 June 2004.

18 Michael Walzer, *Arguing About War* (New Haven, CT: Yale University Press).

19 David Masci and Kenneth Lukas, 'Ethics of War', *Global Issues* (Washington: CQ Press, 2005), p. 275.

20 *The Times*, 6 August and 5 September 2002, 15 October 2003.

21 Hans Blix, *Disarming Iraq*, pp. 232–4.

22 Well after the attack, the 9/11 Commission concluded there were no WMD in Iraq. *The 9/11 Commission Report: Final Report of the National Commission on*

*Terrorist Attacks on the US* (New York: Norton, 2004); see also Anonymous (Michael Scheurer), *Imperial Hubris: Why the West is Losing the War on Terror* (London: Brassey's, 2004) and Richard A. Clarke, *Against All Enemies: Inside America's War on Terror* (New York: Free Press, 2004).

23  See the UN report on providing a secure world at www.un.org/secureworld

24  Clarke, *Against All Enemies* p. 56.

25  *New York Times*, 15 September 2003.

26  White House, 'Guard and Reserves "Define Spirit of America"', White House Press Release, 17 September 2005.

27  *Economist*, 13 September 2003.

28  Admed Rashid, 'The Mess in Afghanistan', *New York Review of Books*, 12 February 2004, 24–7.

29  Catherine Philip, 'They Expected an Easy Ride', *The Times*, 30 July 2005.

30  Suicide bombers dominate the resistance and are perhaps the most difficult militants for westerners to understand. But much is known about them. Robert A. Pape's study of 315 suicide bombers world-wide during the past two years suggests that suicide terrorism is more a product of foreign occupation than of Islamic fundamentalism, but in Iraq it is almost certainly caused by both of these variables; Robert A. Pape, *Dying to Win: The Strategic Logic of Suicide Terrorism* (New York: Random House, 2005).

31  *New York Times*, 16 September 2003.

32  According to news reports, Iraqi civilians and police were still suffering 800 deaths a month as of July 2005; *New York Times*, 14 July 2005.

33  William Langewiesche, 'Hotel Baghdad', *Atlantic Monthly*, May 2005, 105–8.

34  See Chris Hedges, *War is a Force that Gives Us Meaning* (New York: Public Affairs, 2002).

35  *Washington Post*, 29 October 2004.

36  Quoted by Susan E. Rice in *Herald Tribune*, 25–26 October 2003.

37  *New York Times*, 22 September 2005.

38  'Al-Qaeda in Iraq Calls for Killing the Drafters of the Iraqi Constitution', Middle East Media Research Institute, 18 August 2005.

39  Mahmoud al Mashadani to the *New York Times*, 29 August 2005.

40  Pew Research Centre, 21 July 2005.

41  Sir Charles Gwynn, *Imperial Policing* (London: Macmillan, 1934), p. 7.

42  Robert Thompson, *Defeating Communist Insurgency: Experiences from Malaya and Vietnam* (London: Chatto & Windus, 1974) p. 51.

43  Thompson, *Defeating Communist Insurgency*, p. 52.

44  Gwynn, *Imperial Policing*, p. 5.

45  Bruce Hoffman, in *Atlantic Monthly* (July/August 2004), p. 42.

46  Larry Diamond, *Squandered Victory: The American Occupation and the Bungled Effort to Bring Democracy to Iraq* (New York: Times Books, 2005); and David L. Phillips, *Losing Iraq: Inside the Post-war Reconstruction Fiasco* (New York: Westview, 2005).

47  *New York Times*, 24 July 2005.

48  Ibid.

49  *The Military Balance 2004–2005* (London: IISS/Oxford University Press, 2004), p. 126.

50  Nina Kamp, *et al.*, 'The State of Iraq: An Update', *New York Times*, 9 September 2005.

51 For further discussions of each option (staying or getting out of Iraq soon) see James Dobbin, 'Winning the Unwinnable War', *Foreign Affairs*, vol. 84, no. 1 (January/February 2005), 16–25; Edward N. Luttwak, 'Iraq: The Logic of Disengagement', *Foreign Affairs*, vol. 84, no. 1 (January/ February 2005), 26–36; and Ahmed S. Hashim, *Insurgency and Counter-Insurgency in Iraq* (New York: Cornell, 2006).

52 National Strategy for Victory in Iraq, National Security Council, 2005, www.whitehouse.gov/infocus/iraq/iraq_national_strategy_1130.pdf

# 10
# The Burden of Power

The 9/11 attacks occurred only a dozen years after the fall of the Berlin Wall and the demise of the Soviet Union. As the sole remaining superpower, the United States faced a violent multipolar world and became the target of growing threats from terrorist extremists. Insecurity was ubiquitous. The US became involved in ugly, still unfinished wars in Afghanistan and Iraq, and bore the extreme financial costs associated with them, burdens compounded in 2005 by devastating hurricanes in the American South.

At the end of the cold war, US leaders still talked about the 'Vietnam Syndrome' – the alleged reluctance of its people to allow their armed forces to suffer casualties in foreign conflicts. But by 9/11 Washington believed it had discovered a way of dominating the ground from the air that minimized this problem. Thus it appeared to have immense power to retaliate against terrorist attacks. Moreover, it was not outraged by 9/11 alone; the US people and successive administrations had seen their diplomats murdered, individual Americans killed and US civilian aircraft hijacked or blown up by terrorist groups. Their pent-up anger against the ubiquitous threats was unleashed in the 'global war on terror'. But international terrorism presents a kind of threat different from the state-to-state confrontations of the past and requires a different response.

The temptation to use American military power was too great. It is not easy to resist such enticements, and George W. Bush succumbed. His war on Iraq actually increased the threat of international terrorism, as Americans increasingly realized: by July 2005, 45% believed it made the threat worse and only 22% believed it had the reverse effect.[1] Al-Qaeda has not been eliminated. Guerrilla warfare continues in Afghanistan and especially Iraq, and both governments depend upon the presence of thousands of foreign troops. US attempts to spread democracy in the Middle East and to broker peace between Palestinians and Israelis have been equally unsuccessful. Egypt's election in 2005 was a sham. The major US allies in the Middle East remain autocratic tyrannies and its closest Muslim allies, Saudi Arabia and Pakistan, are still authoritarian states. Recent American policies have reshaped Iraq along ethnic and religious lines, and have increased Islamic hatred and the possibility of terrorism against the United States.

Insecurity is thus ubiquitous. Western countries can never be wholly free from the dangers of international terrorism, and desperate efforts to insulate them by reducing freedoms are self-defeating. Any military involvement in the Third World may increase the threat of 'blowback' and should be undertaken only when it is welcomed as peacekeeping or as a last resort. Preventive war can exacerbate the dangers and corrode international law, while excessive military spending weakens the US economy without bringing greater security.

Countries are often judged by the moment when their fate was cruellest, as Belgium's was in September 1914 or Finland's in the winter of 1939–40. But, if desperation can bring out the greatest feats of courage and self-sacrifice, so power and influence can bring out some of the worst characteristics of arrogance, complacency and boastfulness. It was in the midst of Queen Victoria's epic Diamond Jubilee celebrations in 1897 that the poet of the British Empire, Rudyard Kipling, felt the need to warn his fellow countrymen against their 'frantic boasts and foolish words' and becoming 'drunk with sight of power'. However much they relied on their weapons, they too would follow in the footsteps of 'Nineveh and Tyre'.[2] Kipling was, not surprisingly, so hesitant about the way his arrogant fellow countrymen would receive his poem 'Recessional' that he threw it into the wastepaper basket from where it had to be rescued by a young American woman.[3] Yet, in October 1899 his warnings were to be vindicated when British expansionism led to the Boer War which left Britain isolated, its army humiliated by the Boer commandos[4] and its reputation sullied by the deaths from disease of Afrikaner women and children in the camps where they had been concentrated.

The Boer War foreshadowed the military history of much of the twentieth century. Everywhere imperial powers were challenged by guerrillas. Sometimes, with immense effort and patience the guerrillas were defeated, but very often the conventional armies of the colonial powers withdrew humiliated.

9/11 foreshadows the *new* security dilemma in which insurgents make insecurity ubiquitous by carrying the war to the homeland of the dominant power, further increasing the costs of counter-insurgency operations. Dealing with this new problem is going to require even more patience and political skill than dealing with traditional insurgencies, because the population of the power wounded by terrorism will demand revenge. Seeking revenge will play into the hands of the terrorists and widen the struggle. If counter-insurgency was always difficult for democratic states, this is now doubly the case.

The *new* security dilemma also has sinister parallels with one of the most unfortunate aspects of the cold war. The presence of communist moles within the West set off witch-hunts for the enemy within. The consequence was the persecution of innocents who for one reason or another were suspected of communist affiliations.[5] There is a clear danger of similar explosions of anger against the conspicuous Asian minorities living in the West. It is going to require considerable responsibility on the part of the political leadership of the majority and minority populations to minimize such dangerous tendencies, which add to the numbers of potential terrorists.

In 1988, even before the United States became the only superpower, Yale historian Paul Kennedy had pointed out to the American people that imperial overstretch had been the downfall of previous great powers.[6] Yet so quickly does the mood change in the United States that the soul-searching which Kennedy's book both reflected and gave rise to had disappeared within a decade. It was the Soviet Union which had gone the way of Tyre and the Japanese economic challenge had also weakened, while the Europeans were still so engrossed in their disputes about agricultural policy and the admission of new members that their international influence had fallen away to nothing. In January 1972, with his instinct for encapsulating the scene in a single sentence, President Nixon had declared: 'It will be a safer world and a better world if we have a strong, healthy United States, Europe, Soviet Union, China, Japan, each balancing the other, not playing one against the other, an even balance.'[7] By the millennium only the United States and China were left as serious balancers outside the economic sphere.

A superpower will be judged by the way it responds to the possession of massive military and economic strength. If it restrains itself and uses its power fairly and wisely in ways which benefit other states as well as its own people; if it employs its power to protect the global environment and in ways which do not force other states to build hostile coalitions; if it deploys its power to uphold and strengthen international institutions and thus prepare for the future; if it uses power to enhance the stability of the international economy – then it will be judged favourably by later generations. Successive German governments misused their power from 1866 to 1945, thereby plunging Europe into four devastating wars and leaving nothing behind but the memory of violent death and the repression of small states. Similarly, the Japanese abused their military power from 1932 to 1945 in a futile effort to bring China and much of the rest of East Asia under their control. The Soviet Union dominated Eastern Europe from 1945 to 1990 and bequeathed nothing but bitterness and economic backwardness.

In contrast, in the nineteenth century the United States worked with Britain to insulate Latin America from European interference through the Monroe Doctrine; in 1905 it brokered a peace treaty which ended the Russo-Japanese War; in 1918 it helped evict German invaders from France, Belgium and Russia; in 1919 it encouraged the Europeans to establish the League of Nations; its strength was decisive in turning the tide against the Axis in the Second World War and it played a central role in the subsequent establishment of the United Nations and of NATO. Of course, there was a dark side of its policies; its abolition of slavery was very late, involved a devastating civil war and was not followed by a sustained effort to alleviate discrimination against the descendants of the slaves until the 1960s; it supported corrupt and brutal dictators in Latin America and elsewhere; it withdrew into isolation rather than support the League of Nations; its demand for the repayment of the loans made to its allies in the First World War was one of the factors undermining economic stability in the 1920s and helped to lay the foundations for the Great Depression; Franklin Roosevelt proved unable to back Britain and France against the Axis until Hitler and Tojo had already conquered most of Europe and large parts of Asia.

But the United States has greater power to shape the world today than it has ever had. After 9/11 it also had more support and sympathy than it had ever accrued, but it worked to undermine rather than build international institutions and a fair and stable global economy. It blocked progress towards a comprehensive test ban treaty and a cut-off in the production of fissile material for nuclear weapons. It became associated with efforts to block agreements to protect the environment through the Kyoto Protocol without convincing other states how the protocol could be replaced by a more effective scheme. It used its power unilaterally and its leaders' 'frantic boasts and foolish words' alarmed and alienated the rest of the world. It adopted the image of a global policeman. It has continued to increase its military power even when it has no major conventional challengers.

In other words, US leaders succumbed to the temptations which we have analysed in the course of this book:

1. To act on the facile ideas about benevolent empire and spreading democracy by military force offered by the neoconservatives and their allies.

2. To build up US armed forces without giving sober thought to the fear this would create in other countries or the deterioration it would produce in the US economy.

3. To wage a war on terrorism without understanding the dynamics underlying terrorism and without any end point in sight.

4. To wage or threaten preventive wars against states on the spurious grounds that they might at some stage pose a threat to the United States and, in the case of Iraq, on the fraudulent grounds that it had been involved in 9/11.

5. To invade states, such as Afghanistan and Iraq, which it regarded as 'rogues', and to ignore the danger that it could become mired in fighting a nationalist upheaval; to remove their governments while irresponsibly failing to plan who might replace them.

6. To tell Muslim countries that the United States was not hostile to their religion and mores while consistently interfering in their polities and saying that it wanted to democratize and reform their governments.

7. To denigrate the help and legal credibility which international and multilateral institutions, such as the UN and NATO, alone could offer because their procedures were cumbersome and required consensus between the members.

8. To reduce the traditional freedoms of Americans in order to insulate continental United States from all terrorist threats while not taking on practical issues such as reducing the threat of nuclear terrorism.

9. To pursue morally ambiguous policies, such as internment without trial in Guantanamo, and the handing over of terrorist suspects to governments that practise torture.

10. To undermine international efforts to reduce the nuclear threat by dismissing negotiations towards a comprehensive test ban treaty and a fissile material cut-off, denigrating the Nuclear Non-Proliferation Treaty and enhancing US nuclear forces.

Because it succumbed to these temptations, Washington managed within a few short months to undermine all the sympathy and support which had been offered by the rest of the world after 9/11. It became identified with Russian efforts to crush the Chechen rebels; it became ever more dependent on Japan and China to buy US government bonds to offset its trade deficit. It was reduced to going cap in hand to the Ukraine, South Korea and Japan to send military forces to Iraq, even though these forces had themselves to be protected against the insurgents. It exposed Western efforts to discourage the use of torture by other governments to the charge of hypocrisy. It weakened international institutions and the rule of law. It encouraged a massive upsurge in oil prices to the detriment of the world economy, because in the face of rebel attacks it proved impossible to increase Iraqi oil output as much as had been hoped. It stretched and demoralized the US armed forces, and diverted attention from the struggle against al-Qaeda.

Even had it been possible to fight a war on terrorism, the Iraq War would have minimized the strengths and maximized the weaknesses of the United States, just as the Boer War strained and divided the British. The United States has immense economic power and conventional military strength. It is 'optimized' to fight conventional wars and there is no power, or combination of powers, which can stand up to it. But, by invading Afghanistan and Iraq, it has been compelled to fight on its enemies' terms where it is weakest. It has also been distracted from the threats by the Islamists who have infiltrated the United States and its allies and might spread terror through nuclear, chemical, biological and radiological weapons. It cannot avoid the struggle against such ubiquitous threats, but the war in Iraq was not forced upon the United States: it was chosen by the Bush administration.

Military power needs to be harboured and used as a threat or as a last resort. It should never be frittered away in poorly justified peripheral conflicts. There may be a very few cases where outside intervention to change a government is justified and possible without massive bloodshed, for example where an army has intervened to overthrow a newly elected government and install itself in power, or when the United Nations Security Council agrees that the government is responsible for genocide. But the occasions will be increasingly rare and the dangers of mass opposition will grow. Even were it to be victorious in Iraq, which seems doubtful as of the spring of 2006, it would have consumed much of its moral capital. The French and Belgians occupied the industrial Ruhr region of Germany on January 11 1923 to compel the Germans to pay reparations for the First World War. In the end, the Germans were forced to compromise, but the difficulties and international isolation that Paris and Brussels encountered meant that they never tried the process again. They had consumed their moral capital. So the occupation of Afghanistan and particularly Iraq has consumed US moral capital and made it that much more difficult to use force again, even in a good cause, without further isolation. Even Prime Minister Tony Blair might blench at taking further action on America's coat-tails.

The long-term threats to mankind are multiplying. As the only superpower, the United States had the opportunity after 1990 to focus on these problems, to persuade China, India and the other developing states, as well as its allies, to make sacrifices to protect the global environment and particularly to halt or delay global warming. Instead, one Bush aide was caught censoring and faking scientific memoranda to reduce concerns about the problem.[8] His actions symbolized the failure of the administration to give an appropriate lead. Similarly, it is plain that the United States cannot indefinitely run up international debts and that the financial panic, to which massive borrowing will eventually give rise, could throw the world economy into chaos. In the absence of a credible enemy, the extent of US defence spending has no logical justification; the administration and its supporters have criticized the Europeans for their failure to keep up and to spend more, but against whom are they supposed to be preparing? In previous centuries they would have banded together against the dominant power, but that is precisely what the Europeans have been responsible enough to avoid this time.

US policy has been reduced to a series of slogans. Among the most damaging of these is the notion that democratization is a panacea for the world's ills. The election of a government in Taiwan that is determined to press as far as possible towards independence, however much this antagonizes China, and the election of Mahmoud Ahmadi-Nejad in Iran in June 2005 with 17 million votes against 10 million for the next, only slightly less conservative candidate, should have exposed this hypothesis once and for all. Far from a panacea these and some other democratic elections may pose increasing problems for world peace. Equally pernicious, as pointed out earlier, is the American idea that the Muslim world is waiting for the United States to lead it towards democracy. The public in those countries will have to develop their own democratic institutions, if that is what they want to do. They cannot be coerced from the outside. We shall be fortunate if meddling by the United States does not lead to catastrophic state collapse in Egypt, Saudi Arabia, Syria or elsewhere.

Instead, as we have argued, the United States should increase its foreign aid to help reduce poverty and to win friends in the developing World, and it should build stronger barriers against nuclear terrorism by strengthening the IAEA and increasing funding to improve the ways in which nuclear materials in Russia and elsewhere are monitored and destroyed. It should recognize more generally that, in a globalized world, it needs international and multinational institutions to deal with problems from global warming to international terrorism, people-smuggling and drugs. This means shifting some resources from military spending but, as we have argued, military force is not the answer to many of the world's problems.

After the experience of the Boer War Kipling added to 'Recessional' a poem he called 'The Lesson'. The Boer War was 'our fault and our very great fault – and now we must turn it to use./We have forty million reasons for failure, but not a single excuse.'[9] In contrast to the message in 'Recessional', Kipling suggested this time that, if Britain learnt the military lessons involved, it could become a successful empire. But the real lesson of the Boer War was that imperialism was becoming untenable because a small group of brave nationalists could hold down 450,000 troops from the mighty British Empire. Just slightly more French failed to hold Algeria in the 1950s and half a million American troops failed to hold Vietnam in the 1960s. Those historians and other gurus who have urged the United States to become an empire are living in a nineteenth-century world when subject peoples believed that they had no chance of expelling a colonial power. Now they know better. 9/11 has also shown that weak peoples can make insecurity ubiquitous by striking at the most powerful states if they are willing to sacrifice their own lives and the lives of innocent civilians.

Washington needs to learn 'no end of a lesson'[10] from the last five disastrous years and, above all, it needs to learn restraint, not to succumb to the temptations of power.

## Notes

1 'More Say Iraq War Hurts Fight Against Terrorism', Pew Research Centre, 21 July 2005.
2 Rudyard Kipling, 'Recessional', in T.S. Eliot (ed.), *A Choice of Kipling's Verse* (London: Faber, 1953), pp. 139–40.
3 'The Story Behind a Famous Poem', *The Times*, 20 December 1937.
4 Deneys Reitz, *Commando: A Boer Journal of the Boer War* (Harmondsworth: Penguin, 1929).
5 On Western sympathizers with communism see David Caute, *The Fellow Travellers: Intellectual Friends of Communism* (New Haven, CT: Yale University Press, revised edn, 1988).
6 Paul Kennedy, *The Rise and Fall of the Great Powers* (London: Unwin Hyman, 1988), p. 369.
7 *Strategic Survey 1972*, p. 1.
8 *The Times*, 9 June 2005.
9 'The Lesson 1899–1902', in Rudyard Kipling, *The Five Nations* (Methuen, London, 1903), p. 117.
10 Ibid.

# Bibliography

## Official reports

Central Intelligence Agency, *National Strategy for Combating Terrorism*, February 2003. http://www.cia.gov/terrorism/publications/Counter_Terrorism_Strategy.pdf; internet, accessed 11 December 2004.

Council on Foreign Relations, 'Terrorism: Questions and Answers', available from http://www.cfrterrorism.org/terrorism/types.html; accessed December 2004.

National Commission on Terrorist Attacks, *The 9/11 Commission Report: Final Report of the National Commission on Terrorist Attacks Upon the United States* (New York: Norton, 2004).

National Security Council, *National Strategy for Victory in Iraq*, November 2005, www.whitehouse.gov/infocus/iraq/iraq-national_strategy_20051130.pdf; accessed December 2005.

National Security Council, *The National Security Strategy of the United States*, 2002, www.whitehouse.gov/nsc/2002; updated 2006.

Panyarachun, Anand *et al.*, *A More Secure World: Our Shared Responsibility: Report of the Secretary-General's High-Level Panel on Threats, Challenges and Change*, December 2004; http://www.un.org/secureworld/; internet, accessed December 2004.

*Review of Intelligence on Weapons of Mass Destruction: Report of a Committee of Privy Councillors under the Rt Hon. Lord Butler* (London: Stationery Office, 2004).

## Newspapers

*Friday Times* (Lahore)
*Globe and Mail* (Toronto)
*Los Angeles Times*
*New York Times*
*The Daily Telegraph* (London)
*The Economist* (London)
*The Guardian* (London)
*The Hindu* (Madras)
*The Times* (London)
*Washington Post*

## Institutes

International Institute for Strategic Studies (IISS), London.
Middle East Media Research Centre (MEMRI), Washington.
Pew Research Centre for the People and the Press, Washington.

# General

Acheson, Dean, *Present at the Creation: My Years in the State Department* (London: Hamish Hamilton, 1970).

Adelman, Jonathan R., *Revolutions, Armies and War* (Boulder, CO: Lynne Rienner, 1985).

Albright, Madeleine, *Madam Secretary: A Memoir* (London: Macmillan, 2003).

Allison, Graham, *Nuclear Terrorism: The Ultimate Preventable Catastrophe* (New York: Henry Holt, 2004).

Ambrose, Stephen, *Eisenhower The President 1952–1969* (London: George Allen & Unwin, 1984).

Ash, Timothy Garton, *Free World: America, Europe, and the Surprising Future of the West* (New York: Random House, 2004).

Bacevich, Andrew J., *American Empire: The Realities and Consequences of U.S. Diplomacy* (Cambridge, MA: Harvard University Press, 2002).

Bacevich, Andrew J., *The Imperial Tense: Prospects and Problems of American Empire* (Chicago: Ivan R. Dee, 2002).

Bacevich, Andrew J., *The New American Militarism: How Americans are Seduced by War* (Oxford University Press), 2005.

Barber, Benjamin R., *Fear's Empire: War, Terrorism and Democracy* (New York: Norton, 2004).

Barnett Correlli, *The Collapse of British Power* (Gloucester: Alan Sutton, 1987).

Beloff, Max, *The Balance of Power* (London: George Allen & Unwin, 1968).

Bell, Coral, *A World out of Balance: American Hegemony and International Politics in the Twenty-First Century* (Double Bay, NSW: Longueville Books, 2003).

Benjamin, Daniel and Steven Simon, *The Age of Sacred Terror* (New York: Random House, 2002).

Benjamin, Daniel and Steve Simon, *The Next Attack: The Failure of the War on Terror and a Strategy for Getting it Right* (New York: Henry Holt, 2005).

Bennett, Gordon A. and Montaperto, Ronald N., *Red Guard: the Political Biography of Dai Hsiao-Ali* (London: George Allen & Unwin, 1971).

Bergen, Peter L., *Holy War, Inc.: Inside the Secret World of Osama Bin Laden* (New York: Free Press, 2001).

Bland, J.O.P. (translator), *Germany's Violations of the Laws of War* (London: William Heinemann, 1915).

Blainey, Geoffrey, *The Causes of War* (Melbourne: Sun Books, 1977).

Blix, Hans, *Disarming Iraq* (New York: Pantheon, 2004).

Bloom, Mia, *Dying to Kill: The Allure of Suicide Terror* (New York: Columbia University Press, 2005).

Brooks, Stephen, *As Others See Us: The Causes and Consequences of Foreign Perceptions of America* (Peterborough: Broadview, 2006).

Brown, David J. and Robert Merrill (eds), *Violent Persuasions: The Politics and Imagery of Terrorism* (Seattle, WA: Bay Press, 1993).

Brzezinski, Zbigniew, *Power and Principle: Memoirs of the National Security Adviser 1977–81* (London: Weidenfeld & Nicolson, 1983).

Brzezinski, Zbigniew, *The Choice: Global Domination or Global Leadership* (New York: Basic Books, 2004).

Buchanan, William and Cantril Hadley, *How Nations View Each Other* (Urbana: University of Illinois Press, 1953).

Burleigh, Bennet, *Empires of the East or Japan and Russia at War* (London: Chapman and Hall, 1905).

Buruma, Ian and Avishai Margalit, *Occidentalism: The West in the Eyes of Its Enemies* (New York: Penguin, 2004).

Bush, George, *All The Best: My Letters and Other Writings* (New York: Lisa Drew, 1999).

Butler Richard, *Saddam Defiant: The Threat of Weapons of Mass Destruction and the Crisis of Global Security* (London: Weidenfeld & Nicolson, 2000).

Butterfield, Herbert, *Christianity and History* (London: George Bell, 1949).

Chang Jun and Jon Halliday, *Mao: The Untold Story* (London: Jonathan Cape, 2005).

Chaudhuri, Nirad C., *Thy Hand Great Anarch! India 1921–1952* (London: Hogarth Press, 1990).

Chomsky, Noam, *Hegemony or Survival: America's Quest for Global Dominance* (New York: Metropolitan, 2003).

Clark, Wesley K., *Winning Modern Wars: Iraq, Terrorism and the American Empire* (New York: Public Affairs, 2003).

Clarke, Richard A., *Against All Enemies: Inside America's War on Terror* (New York: Free Press, 2004).

Clifford, Clark with Richard Holbrooke, *Counsel to the President* (New York: Random House, 1991).

Close, Upton, *The Revolt of Asia: The End of the White Man's World Dominance* (New York: Putnam's, 1927).

Cole, David, *Enemy Aliens: Double Standards and Constitutional Freedoms in the War on Terrorism* (New York: New Press, 2005).

Cooper, Robert, *The Breaking of Nations: Order and Chaos in the Twenty-First Century* (New York: Atlantic Books, 2003).

Cordesman, Anthony H., *Terrorism, Asymmetric Warfare, and Weapons of Mass Destruction: Defending the U.S. Homeland* (Westport, CA: Praeger, 2001).

Daalder, Ivo H. and James M. Lindsay, *America Unbound: The Bush Revolution in Foreign Policy* (Washington, DC: Brookings Institution, 2003).

Dayan, Moshe, *Story of My Life* (London: Weidenfeld & Nicolson, 1976).

De Toqueville, Alexis, *Democracy in America*, vols 1 and 2 (New York: Mentor, 1956 [1835, 1840]).

Dillon, E.J., *Russia Today and Yesterday* (London: Dent, 1929).

Doyle, Michael, *Empires* (Ithica: Cornell University Press, 1986).

Ehrman, John, *The Rise of Neoconservatism: Intellectuals and Foreign Affairs, 1945–1994* (New Haven, CT: Yale University Press, 1995).

Falk, Richard, *The Declining World Order: America's Imperial Geopolitics* (New York: Routledge, 2004).

Feldman, Noah, *What We Owe Iraq: War and the Ethics of Nation Building* (Princeton University Press, 2004).

Ferguson, Niall, *Colossus: The Price of America's Empire* (New York: Penguin, 2004).

Ferguson, Niall, *Empire: The Rise and Demise of the British World Order and the Lessons for Global Power* (New York: Basic Books, 2003).

Freedman Lawrence, *The Evolution of Nuclear Strategy* (London: Macmillan, 1981).

Friedman, Norman, *Fifty Year War: Conflict and Strategy in the Cold War* (Annapolis, MD: Naval Institute Press, 2000).

Frum, David and Pearl Richard, *An End to Evil: How to Win the War on Terror* (New York: Random House, 2003).

Fukuyama, Francis, *The End of History and the Last Man* (London: Hamish Hamilton, 1992).

Fulbright, J. William, *The Arrogance of Power* (London: Jonathan Cape, 1967).

Gaddis, John Lewis, *Surprise, Security and the American Experience* (Cambridge, MA: Harvard University Press, 2004.

Gambetta, Diego (ed.), *Making Sense of Suicide Missions* (Oxford University Press, 2005).

Garton Ash, Timothy, *Free World: America, Europe and the Surprising Future of the West* (New York: Random House, 2004).

Gillespie, Richard, *Soldiers of Peron: Argentina's Montoneros* (Oxford: Clarendon Press, 1982).

Gordon, Philip and Jeremy Shapiro, *Allies at War: America, Europe, and the Crisis over Iraq* (New York: McGraw-Hill, 2004).

Grossman, Dave, *On Killing: The Psychological Cost of Learning to Kill in War and Society* (New York: Little, Brown, 1995).

Gunaratna, Rohan, *Inside Al Qaeda: Global Network of Terror* (New York: Columbia University Press, 2002).

Gwynn, Sir Charles, *Imperial Policing* (London: Macmillan, 1934).

Haass, Richard N., *The Opportunity: America's Moment to Alter History's Course* (New York: Public Affairs, 2005).

Haig, Alexander M., *Caveat: Realism, Reagan and Foreign Policy* (London, Weidenfeld & Nicolson, 1984).

Halberstam, David, *War in a Time of Peace: Bush, Clinton and the Generals* (London: Bloomsbury, 2002).

Halper, Stephan and Jonathan Clarke, *America Alone: The Neo-Conservatives and the Global Order* (Cambridge: Cambridge University Press, 2004).

Harvey, David, *The New Imperialism* (New York: Oxford University Press, 2003).

Hashim, Ahmed S., *Insurgency and Counter-Insurgency in Iraq* (Ithica: Cornell University Press, 2006).

Hedges, Chris, *War Is a Force that Gives Us Meaning* (New York: Anchor, 2003).

Hersh, Seymour M., *Chain of Command: The Road from 9/11 to Abu Ghraib* (New York: HarperCollins, 2004).

Herzog, Chaim, The Arab–Israeli Wars (London: Arms & Armour, 1092).

Heymann, Philip B., *Terrorism, Freedom and Security: Winning Without War* (Cambridge, MA: MIT Press, 2003).

Hoffman, Bruce, *Inside Terrorism* (New York: Columbia University Press, 1998).

Holbrooke, Richard, *To End a War* (New York: Random House, 1998).

Hooker, Virginia and Saikal Amin, *Islamic Perspectives on the Millennium* (Singapore: Institute of South East Asian Studies, 2004).

Howard, Michael and Paret Peter (eds), *Clausewitz on War* (Princeton University Press, 1984).

Howard, Russell D. and Reid L. Sawyer (eds), *Terrorism and Counter Terrorism: Understanding the New Security Environment* (Dubuque, Iowa: McGraw, 2006).

Huntington, Samuel, P., *The Clash of Civilisations and the Remaking of World Order* (London: Simon & Schuster, 1996).

Hyams, Edward, *Killing No Murder: A Study of Assassination as a Political Means* (London: Nelson, 1969).

Ignatieff, Michael, *Virtual War: Kosovo and Beyond* (London: Chatto & Windus, 2002).

Jackson, Robert and Kellen Konrad (eds), *Issues in Comparative Politics* (New York: St Martin's Press, 1971).

Jackson, Robert and Jackson, Doreen, *Politics in Canada* (Toronto: Prentice-Hall, 2005).

Jamieson, Perry, D., *Lucrative Targets: The US Air Force in the Kuwaiti Theatre of Operations* (Washington, DC: Air Force History and Museums Program, 2001).

Jenkins, Philip, *Images of Terror: What We Can and Can't Know about Terrorism* (New York: Aldine de Gruyter, 2003).

Johnson, Chalmers, *Blowback: The Costs and Consequences of American Empire* (New York: Henry Holt, 2000).

Johnson, Chalmers, *The Sorrows of Empire: Militarism, Secrecy, and the End of the Republic* (New York: Metropolitan Books, 2004).

Jonas, George, *Vengeance: The True Story of an Israeli Counter-Terrorist Mission* (London: Collins, 1984).

Kagan, Robert, *Of Paradise and Power: America and Europe in the New World Order* (New York: Knopf, 2003).

Kaplan, Robert, *Imperial Grunts: The American Military on the Ground* (New York: Random House, 205).

Keegan, John, *The Iraq War* (New York: Knopf, 2004).

Kelidar, Abbas, *The Integration of Modern Iraq* (London: Croom Helm, 1979).

Kennan, George F., *Memoirs 1925–1950* (London: Hutchinson, 1968–1973).

Kennan, George F., *The Nuclear Delusion: Soviet–American Relations in the Atomic Age* (London: Hamish Hamilton, 1984).

Kennedy Paul, *The Rise and Fall of the Great Powers: Economic Change and Military Conflict from 1500 to 2000* (London: Unwin Hyman, 1988).

Kipling, Rudyard, *The Five Nations* (London: Methuen, 1903).

Kissinger, Henry, *The White House Years* (London: Weidenfeld & Nicolson and Michael Joseph, 1979).

Krasner, Stephen D., *Sovereignty: Organized Hypocrisy* (Princeton University Press, 1999).

Kristol, William and Lawrence Kaplan, *The War over Iraq: Saddam's Tyranny and America's Mission* (New York: Encounter Books, 2003).

Kupchan, Charles A., *The End of the American Era: U.S. Foreign Policy and the Geopolitics of the Twenty-first Century* (New York: Knopf, 2002).

Laqueur, Walter, *No End to War: Terrorism in the Twenty-First Century* (New York: Continuum, 2003).

Lea, Homer, *Valor of Ignorance* (New York: Harper, 1909).

Leone, Richard C. and Greg Anrig Jr (eds), *The War on Our Freedoms: Civil Liberties in an Age of Terrorism* (New York: Public Affairs, 2003).

LeVine, Mark, *Why They Don't Hate Us: Lifting the Veil on the Axis of Evil* (Oxford: Oneworld Publications, 2005).

Lewis, Bernard, *The Crisis of Modern Islam: Holy War and Unholy Terror* (London: Weidenfeld & Nicolson, 2003).

Lippmann, Walter, *Public Opinion* (New York: Free Press, 1997 [1922]).

Lippmann, Walter, *The Cold War: A Study of US Foreign Policy* (New York: Harper & Row, 1972).

Lodge, Juliet (ed.), *Terrorism: A Challenge to the State* (New York: St Martin's Press, 1981).

Lodge, Juliet, *The Threat of Terrorism* (Brighton: Wheatsheaf, 1988).

Makiya, Karan, *Cruelty and Silence* (London: Jonathan Cape, 2003).

Mandelbaum, Michael, *The Case for Goliath: How America Acts as the World's Government in the 21st Century* (New York: Public Affairs, 205).

Mandelbaum, Michael, *The Ideas That Conquered the World: Peace, Democracy and Free-Markets in the Twenty-First Century* (New York: Public Affairs, 2002).

Mann, Michael, *Incoherent Empire* (New York: Verso, 2003).

Marder, Arthur J., *Fear God and Dread Nought: The Correspondence of Admiral of the Fleet Lord Fisher* (London: Jonathan Cape, 1956).

McNamara, Robert, *In Retrospect: The Tragedy and Lessons of Vietnam* (New York: Times Books, 1995).

Mead, Walter Russell, *Power, Terror, Peace, and War: America's Grand Strategy in a World at Risk* (New York: Knopf, 2004).

Meernick, James David, *The Political Use of Military Force in US Foreign Policy* (London: Ashgate, 2004).

Moens, Alexander, *The Foreign Policy of George W. Bush, Values, Strategy, Loyalty* (Aldershot: Ashgate, 2004).

Mommsen, Wolfgang J. and Gerhard Hirschfield (eds), *Social Protest, Violence and Terror in Nineteenth- and Twentieth-Century Europe* (London: Macmillan, 1982).

Naipaul, V.S., *Among the Believers: An Islamic Journey* (London: André Deutsch, 1981).

Newhouse, John, *Imperial America: The Bush Assault on the World Order* (New York: Knopf, 2003).

Nixon Richard, *The Memoirs of Richard Nixon* (London: Sidgwick & Jackson, 1978).

Nixon Richard, *1999: Victory without War* (London: Sidgwick & Jackson, 1988).

O'Brien, Patrick Karl and Clesse Almand (eds), *Two Hegemonies: Britain 1846–1914 and the United States 1941–2001* (Aldershot: Ashgate, 2002).

Odom, William E. and Robert Dujarric, *America's Inadvertent Empire* (New Haven, CT: Yale University Press, 2004).

Packer, George, *The Assassin's Gate: America in Iraq* (New York: Farrar, Strauss & Giroux, 2005).

Perlmutter, Amos, Michael Handel, and Uri Bar-Joseph, *Two Minutes over Baghdad* (London: Frank Cass, 2003).

Pillar, Paul R., *Terrorism and U.S. Foreign Policy* (Washington, DC: Brookings Institution, 2001).

Pipes, Daniel, *Conspiracy: How the Paranoid Style Flourishes and Where it Comes From* (New York: Free Press, 1999).

Pollack, Kenneth M., *The Threatening Storm: the Case for Invading Iraq* (New York: Random House, 2002).

Posner, Gerald L., *Why America Slept: The Failure to Prevent 9/11* (New York: Random House, 2003).

Posner, Richard A., *Preventing Surprise Attacks: Intelligence Reform in the Wake of 9/11* (Lanham, MD: Rowman & Littlefield, 2005).

Powell, Colin with Joseph Persico, *My American Journey* (New York: Ballantine, 1995).

Prestowitz, Clyde, *Rogue Nation: American Unilateralism and the Failure of Good Intentions* (New York: Basic Books, 2003).

Priest, Dana, *The Mission: Waging War and Keeping Peace with America's Military* (New York: Norton, 2003).

Ranelagh, John, *Agency: The Rise and Decline of the CIA* (London: Weidenfeld & Nicolson, 1986).

Rashid, Ahmed, *Militant Islam: Oil and Fundamentalism in Central Asia* (New Haven, CT: Yale University Press).

Reich, Walter (ed.), *Origins of Terrorism: Psychologies, Ideologies, Theologies, States of Mind* (New York: Woodrow Wilson International Centre for Scholars, 1990).

Reitz, Denys, *Commando: A Boer Journal of the Boer War* (Harmondsworth: Penguin, 1929).

Risen, James, *State of War: The Secret History of the CIA and the Bush Administration* (New York: Free Press, 2006).

Rogers, Paul, *A War on Terror: Afghanistan and After* (London: Pluto Press, 2004).

Roosevelt, Archie, *For Lust of Knowing: Memoirs of an Intelligence Officer* (London: Weidenfeld & Nicolson, 1988).

Rosen, Jeffrey, *The Naked Crowd: Reclaiming Security and Freedom in an Anxious Age* (New York: Random House, 2004).

Rubinstein, Richard, *Alchemists of Revolution* (New York: Basic Books, 1989).

Sanders, Christopher, *America's Overseas Garrisons: The Leasehold Empire* (Oxford University Press, 2000).

Schultz, George, *Turmoil and Triumph: Diplomacy, Power and the Victory of the American Ideal* (New York: Scribner's, 1993).

Sederberg, Peter C., *Terrorist Myths* (Englewood Cliffs, NJ: Prentice-Hall, 1989).

Shadid, Anthony, *Night Draws Near: Iraq's People in the Shadow of America's War* (London: Henry Holt, 2005).

Shawcross, William, *Allies: The U.S., Britain, and Europe, and the War in Iraq* (New York: Public Affairs, 2004).

Sherry, Michael, *In the Shadow of War* (New Haven: Yale University Press, 1997).

Sifry, Micah and Cerf, Christopher, *The Iraq War Reader: History, Documents, Opinions* (New York: Touchstone Books, 2003).

Sick, Gary, *All Fall Down: America's Fateful Encounter with Iran* (London: Tauris, 1985).

Silberstein, Sandra, *War of Words: Language, Politics and 9/11* (London: Routledge, 2002).

Slugett, Peter, *Britain in Iraq 1914–1932* (London: Ithaca Press, 1976).

Snyder, Jack, *From Voting to Violence: Democratization and Nationalist Conflict* (New York: Norton, 2000).

Soros, George, *The Bubble of American Supremacy: Correcting the Misuse of American Power* (New York: Public Affairs, 2003).

Snepp, Frank, *Decent Interval: The American Debacle in Vietnam and the Fall of Saigon* (Harmondsworth: Penguin, 1980).

Stern, Jessica, *Terror in the Name of God* (New York: HarperCollins, 2003).

Stohl, Michael (ed.), *The Politics of Terrorism* (New York: Marcel Dekker, 1988).

Talbott, Strobe and Nayan Chanda (eds), *The Age of Terror: America and the World After September 11* (New York: Basic Books, 2001).

Tawney, R.H., *Religion and the Rise of Capitalism* (Harmondsworth: Penguin, 1961).

Terraine, John, *A Time for Courage: The Royal Air Force in the European War* (New York: Macmillan, 1985).

Thackrah, John Richard, *Encyclopedia of Terrorism and Political Violence* (New York: Routledge, 1987).

Thompson, Edward, *The Making of the Indian Princes* (London: Curzon Press, 1978).

Thompson, Robert, *Defeating Communist Insurgency: Experiences from Malaya and Vietnam* (London: Chatto & Windus, 1974).

Todd, Emmanuel, *After the Empire: The Breakdown of the American Order* (New York: Columbia University Press, 2003).

Towle, Philip, *Pilots and Rebels: The Use of Aircraft in Unconventional Warfare* (London: Brasseys, 1989).

Towle, Philip, *Enforced Disarmament from the Napoleonic Campaigns to the Gulf War* (Oxford: Clarendon, 1997).

Townshend, Charles, *Terrorism: A Very Short Introduction* (Oxford University Press, 2002).

Truman, Harry, S., *The Truman memoirs: Years of Trial and Hope* (London: Hodder & Stoughton, 1956).

Tucker, H.H. (ed.), *Combating the Terrorists: Democratic Responses to Political Violence* (New York: Facts on File, 1988).

Vespa, Amleto, *Secret Agent of Japan* (London: Victor Gollancz, 1938).

Waller, Maureen, *London 1945* (London: John Murray, 2005).

Walt, Stephen M., *Taming American Power: The Global Response to US Privacy* (London: Norton, 2005).

Walzer, Michael, *Arguing about War* (New Haven, CT: Yale University Press).

Wardlaw, Grant, *Political Terrorism* (Cambridge: Cambridge University Press, 1989).

Weissman, Steve and Herbert Krosney, *The Islamic Bomb: The Nuclear Threat to Israel and the Middle East* (New York: Times Books, 1981).

Whittaker, David J. (ed.), *The Terrorism Reader* (New York: Routledge, 2001).

Wilkinson, Paul, *Terrorism and the Liberal State* (New York: New York University Press, 1986).

Willoughby, John, *Remaking the Conquering Heroes: The Postwar American Occupation of Germany* (New York: Palgrave, 2001).

Woodward, Bob, *The Commanders* (New York: Simon & Schuster, 1991).

Woodward, Bob, *Bush at War* (New York: Simon & Schuster, 2002).

Woodward, Bob, *Plan of Attack* (New York: Simon & Schuster, 2004).

Woodward, David, *Sunk! How the Great Battleships Were Lost* (London: George Allen & Unwin, 1982).

Woolf, Franklin R., *Of Carrots and Sticks or Air Power as a Nonproliferation Tool* (Maxwell, AL: Air University Press, 1994).

Zakaria, Fareed, *The Future of Freedom: Illiberal Democracy At Home and Abroad* (New York: Norton, 2003).

## Selected journal articles

Albright, David and Kimberly Kramer, 'Fissile Material: Stockpiles Still Growing', *Bulletin of the Atomic Scientists* (November/December 2004).

Friedberg, Aaron L., 'Britain and the Experience of Relative Decline', *Journal of Strategic Studies* (September 1987).

Gause, F. Gregory, 'Can Democracy Stop Terrorism?', *Foreign Affairs* (September/October 2005).

Huntington, Samuel P., 'The Clash of Civilizations', *Foreign Affairs* (Summer 1993).

McNeill, William H., 'Decline of the West?', *New York Review of Books* (9 January 1997).

Kagan, Robert, 'America's Crisis of Legitimacy', *Foreign Affairs* (March/April 2004).

Laqueur, Walter, 'World of Terror', *National Geographic* (November 2004).

Long, Michael, 'Half-life: The Lethal Legacy of America's Nuclear Waste', *National Geographic* (July 2002).

Snyder, Jack, 'One World, Rival Theories', *Foreign Policy* (November/December 2004).

# Index

Abu Ghraib prison   148
  abuses   151–2, 187
Ackroyd, Peter   142
administrative review boards
    150
Afghanistan   11, 97
  1998 missile strikes against
    109
  Bagram Airbase   148
  context and war   169–71
  post-war   177–8
  as quagmire   188
  resistance to occupation   87
  Soviet intervention   169–70
  war   169; moral
    justification   55; and
    neoconservatives   17; and
    Northern Alliance   171; start
    of   171; stated US goals
    176; support for   45, 94, 110
Africa   32
  interference debate   21
Ahmadi-Nejad, Mahmoud   202
Air Force, US   97–8
'Air Power as a Non-Proliferation
    Tool'   109
aircraft strikes, European
    memories of   114
airline security   154
Al Tawita reactor   107
Al-Aziz, Zaynab Abd   75
Al-Bahr, Nasser   115
al-Haideri, Adnan Saeed   111
al-Ilah, Abd   172
al-Qaeda   19, 45, 110
  attacks by   124
  Bush on   135
  CW facility links   112
  establishment of   170
  on Iraq constitution   182
  linked to Iraq   173
  numbers trained   130
  organization   134

religious beliefs   131, 134
  US aim to close down   125,
    176
Al-Qimni, Sayyid   72–3
al-Zarqawi, Abu Musab   130, 190
Albania   13
Albright, Madeleine   69, 92
allies, US need for   61, 96
Allison, Graham   159, 163
American Container Security
    Initiative   156
Amnesty International   151
anthrax attacks   140
anti-Americanism   3, 17
anti-Iraq coalition (2003)   49–51
Anti-Land Mines Agreement
    140
anti-terrorist strategies   134–5
Arar, Maher   148
arms races   119
  Bush on   54
Army, US
  distaste for guerrilla warfare
    97–8
  reflecting US culture   98
ASEAN   7
Asian peoples' wars   5–6
assassination
  reputation for   116, 117
  and terrorism   116
asymmetrical warfare   123, 125,
    126
Australia   173
authoritarian governments,
    release from   86–7, 90
'axis of evil'   35, 47, 169, 186
  harm of rhetoric   1
  and loss of support   94
  and preventive war   117–19

Baader-Meinhof Gang   131
Baath Party   172, 178, 190
  post-war role   183

Bacevich, Andrew J.   25
Bagram Airbase   148
balance of power   7, 55–7, 198
  absence of   5; danger of
    absence   118, 120; and US
    actions   118
  China, India and US   98–9
Bali bombings   176
Barber, Benjamin   25
Barder, Brian   51
Barrington, Nicholas   51
Belmarsh Prison   148
Beloff, Max   55
Berlin crisis (1948–9)   85
bin Laden, Osama   46, 72, 119,
    141, 157
  Afghan refusal to hand to US
    124
  asylum application (1975)   75
  attempted capture of   124, 125
  capture as US goal   176
  citing US failures   187
  declaring jihad   41, 171
  finances   130
  grievances   133–4
  ideological message   128
  and Khartoum CW plant   109
  post-9/11   45
  and re-election of Bush   89
  recruitment by CIA   170
Biological Weapons Agreement
    140
Bismarck, Otto von   97, 192
Blair, Tony   95, 201
  on radicalized Muslim
    youth   133
  support for US   49–50, 51
  WMD 45 mins dossier   112
Blix, Hans   48–9, 174
Bodin, Jean   6
Boer War   197, 201, 202–3
Bolton, John R.   29
Bonn Agreement   177
border controls   155–7, 164
Border and Protection
    Agency   155
Bosnia   11, 13, 32, 88, 97
  interference debate   21
Boutros-Ghali, Boutros   14

Brazil   98
Bremer, Paul   180, 184
Brezhnev, Leonid   102
Brighton bombings   127
British Joint Terrorism Analysis
    Centre   132
Brzezinski, Zbigniew   92
Buchanan, Patrick   28
budget deficit, US   27, 34, 59,
    64, 99, 163–4
Bush, George H.W.   70, 92, 160
  experience of international
    relations   2–3
  foreign policy approach   2–3
  on occupation of Iraq   2, 32
Bush, George W.   1
  on al-Qaeda   173
  character   18, 36–7
  defining enemy   134–5
  denial of empire   23
  errors of   96–7
  on evil   135
  lack of apologies   57–8
  linking 9/11 to Iraq   32
  on military strength   53–4
  neoconservative rhetoric   41
  Pakistani response to
    re-election   89
  on preventive war   105
  religious beliefs   2–3
  spreading democracy   23–4
  on surveillance of citizens   146
  as 'uniter'   17
  warning received of 9/11   124
  words and ideas   40–1
Butler, Lord/Report   51
Butler, Richard   172
Butterfield, Herbert   55
Byrd, Robert   110

Calipari, Nicola   113
Camp X-Ray   148
Canada
  coordination policies   142
  opposition to war   49
Carter, Jimmy   39, 60, 68, 97,
    144
cause of war   174, 175
Charles, Prince   116

chemical weapons    46, 109, 201
  defence against    154
  facilities in Iraq    112
  as justification for war    173
  Khartoum    112
Chen Shui-bian    68
Cheney, Richard    40, 60,
  117, 160
Chertoff, Michael    154
Chile: opposition to war    56
China    77, 98
  challenge from    65–71, 80
  defence budget    54
  disapproval of US policy    47–8
  economic growth    59, 69
  Nixon's visit to    66–7
  rising power    15, 97
  and US dominance    58
  US indebtedness to    69, 99,
    200
  US relations with    69–70;
    history of    65–8; and
    Korea    66
Christians/Christianity    21–2,
  27
  denouncing Iraq war    174
  Iraq as just war    38
  versus evil    38
Churchill, Winston    66, 126
CIA
  criticisms of    157
  limitations of    158
  and Soviet–Afghan war    170
citizens as enemy combatants
  149
civil liberties    143–4
  abuses of US    164
  curtailment of US    130, 159,
    200
  and Patriot Act    144–5
civil war in Iraq, possible    191,
  192
civilizations
  accommodating differences
    19
  clash of    16, 18–22, 36, 41
  concept of    28
  conflicts between    18–19;
    avoidance of    20, 21

existing    18
gap between Arab and
  West    76
non-interference in    20–1
and political alignments    18
Clark, Wesley    87
clash of civilizations    16, 18–22,
  36, 41
Clinton, Bill    8, 57, 60, 109, 124,
  150
Close, Upton    xi, xiv, 64
coalition of the willing    173
coalition-building    93–6
  and axis of evil speech    94
Coast Guard, US    155
cold war    77, 80
  concepts    6
  and international relations    5
  and nuclear deterrent    5
  security dilemma    14
  and United Nations    11–12
collective action    15
collective security    7
colour-coded threat system    141,
  155
Combatant Status Review
  Tribunals    149
  panels    150
communism    64–5
  containment of    85
  demise of    80
Comprehensive Test Ban Treaty
  140, 199, 200
compromise, value of    35
conduct of war    174
conflict
  after independence    90–1
  along cultural lines    20, 21
  avoiding    20, 21
  increase in    10
  post-Cold War    14
  sectarian    90
  within Western societies    78,
    79
  *see also* Afghanistan; Iraq
Congo    32
Congress    18
  approving preventive strategy
    110–11

Congress – *continued*
  failure to prevent mistakes 92, 96
  and illegal combatants 147
  and war crimes trials 149
consequences of war 174
conspiracy theories 75
constitution, Iraqi 182–3, 184
  unresolved issues 182–3
container security 155–6
Cooper, Robert 34
copycat terrorist acts 133
costs of warfare , economic 97
  *see also* economy
counter-insurgency 188
  failures 185
  US weakness 64
  Western experiences of 2, 185
  *see also* insurgencies; terrorism
Counterterrorism Center, National 158
criminal justice system, parallel 144
  unnecessary 141
cruise missiles 115
Cuba 92
  missile crisis (1962) 85
culture
  Muslims dislike of US 3
  and political realignments 18–19
  universalism 19
  Western 21, 34
Cyprus 90, 185

Danner, Mark 141
Dayan, Moshe 107
Dayton peace conference 58
de Tocqueville, Alexis 16, 91
de Villepin, Dominique 48
defectors, Iraqi 111
defence spending
  Europe 30, 61
  US 22, 26, 30, 54, 99, 136–7, 163, 164, 197, 202
democracy 141
  failings in US 91–3
  and military power 89–93

and popular control in US 91–2
possibility in Iraq 91
preconditions for 90
US view as ideal 90, 202
democracy, spreading 23–4
  by force 17, 53, 199
  and discredit of US democracy 153
  as duty 52
  and economic resources 26–7
  to Arab world 38–9, 41, 196, 200, 202
  unwilling recipients 71, 84, 202
Deng Xiaoping 68, 70
detentions 152
  of 'enemy combatants' 149, 150
  fuelling terrorism 153
  of non-citizens 146, 147
  secrecy surrounding 153
discrimination against Muslims 79
diversity within and across states 10
Doonesbury cartoon 40
Dubcek, Alexander 116

Eastern Europe
  nuclear materials 160, 161, 163, 202
  support for US 49
economic deprivation and violence 127, 129
economy of US 26–7, 99, 163–4
  increasing problems 97, 200
  overreach 26–7
Egypt 197
  attacks by Israel 106–7
  disapproval of US policy 47
  renditions 148
Eisenhower, Dwight 60, 61, 66, 92
elections in Iraq 86, 181–2
  constitution 183
  new assembly 183–4
Elgar, Bob 174

empire
America as   16, 22–7, 41;
   critics of   25–7; denial of
   23, 24; military   26;
   overreach   24
liberal form of   23
enemy combatants   147–51
*see also* illegal combatants
enriched uranium-235   160–1
ethnic minorities   10
Europe/Europeans
awareness of costs of wars
   114
colonial experience   32, 52
defence spending   30, 61
disapproval of US policy   48,
   51–3
doubts on Iraq war   33
experience of terrorism   60
historically based attitudes
   1–2
memories of air strikes   114
neoconservative view of   31
opposition to US policy   51; as
   threat to security   51
support for Afghanistan
   conflict   94
and US dominance   58
US need for future support   61
view of war   113, 114–15;
   preventive   119
EUROPOL agreements   142
evil
Blair's beliefs   50
Bush on   135
US perception of   35, 141
versus Christianity   38
'war' on   125
exceptionalism, American   1, 3,
   17, 34
exit strategy   176
George H.W. Bush on   2

FAA (Federal Aviation Agency)
   157
Faisal I, King   171
Faisal II, King   172
Falwell, Jerry   38
FBI   157

fear   134
and curtailment of civil liberties
   130
as weapon   128
FEMA (Federal Emergency
   Management Agency)   155
Ferguson, Niall   23–4
financial costs of Iraq war   163–4
*see also* defence spending
fire discipline of US military
   113–15
First World War: European
   experience   114
Foreign Intelligence Surveillance
   Act   144, 145
foreign policy of US
and American democracy   91–2
basis of   36
Eastern European support   49
formation of   16–41
and hegemony   16–17
homeland support   47
influencing factors   17–18
mistakes   123, 136
Muslim hostility   47, 88
support from Blair   49–51
*see also* Afghanistan; Iraq
France   30
failed counter-insurgency   185
and Iraq invasion   34, 173
opposition to US policy   48, 49
US hostility towards   57–8
war in Indochina   5, 6, 66
Friedman, Thomas L.   34
Frum, David   29, 35, 36
fuel-cycling radioactive material
   163
Fukuyama, Francis   29
Fulbright, William   91, 92
fundamentalism *see* Christian;
   Muslim; religious terrorists
future challenges for US   61

Gandhi   77
Geneva Conventions   147, 149,
   150, 153
Gephardt, Richard   110
Germany   198, 201
experience of terrorism   60

Germany – *continued*
  opposition to US policy
    48, 49
  peaceful solution to Iraq    30
  post world war II    86
Giap, General    87
global warming    202
globalization    133, 165
  and diversity    10
  and erosion of sovereignty    13
  and increased insecurity    9
Goldsmith, Lord    50
Goliath, US as    24–5
Gonzales, Alberto R.    145, 148
Gorbachev, Mikhail    70, 93,
    160
Goss, Porter J.    158, 159
Graham, Franklin    22, 38
Green Zone    179, 186
Guantanamo Bay prison    140,
    148, 149, 200
  abuses    151
guerrilla warfare    196
  British success    185–6
  US distaste for    97–8
  and US weaponry    33
  and Western interventionism
    87
  *see also* insurgencies; terrorism
Gurr, Ted    128
Gwynn, Charles    98, 185–6,
    187–8

Haig, Alexander    68
Haiti    11, 13
Hamas    19, 184
Hamdan, Salim Ahmed    149,
    150
Hammarskjöld, Dag    116
Hay, John    91
hearts and minds    168, 189
hegemony of US    4, 5, 13, 22
Herz, John    14
HEU (highly enriched uranium)
    162–3
Heyman, Philip B.    141
Hezbollah    19
Ho Chi Minh    67
Hoffman, Bruce    98, 188

homeland security    139–65
  and civil rights abuses    164
  defence measures    154–5
  illusions of    165
  insecurities    164, 165, 197
  and loss of privacy    165
  unnecessary actions    141
Homeland Security, Department
    of    140, 154–5
hostility
  and military power    89
  Muslim    47, 88
hubris, US    25
human rights
  in China    70
  of illegal combatants    147
  Sino–US disagreements    65
  violations; Abu Ghraib prison
    150; Guantanamo Bay    150;
    in times of war    140–1; US
    hypocrisy    187
  *see also* civil liberties; prisons
humanitarian crises    10, 12, 13
humanitarian interventions    6
  justification for    88
Huntington, Samuel    18–20,
    21
hurricanes
  economic cost of    196
  Katrina    60, 155
  responses to    155
Hussein, Saddam    75, 107, 116,
    158, 179
  Bush on    135
  driven from Kuwait    20–1
  G.H.W. Bush on    2
  and Israeli actions    107
  as justification for war    95,
    102, 173, 174
  linked to    9/11 38
  NBC weapons    104, 111
  and oil supplies    40
  overthrow of    86, 120, 181
  pressure to remove    37
  previous US support for    34
  regime    46–7, 175, 176, 178,
    190; start of    172
  support from US    47
  as target    46, 184, 186

temptation to depose 46
threat from 118

IAEA (International Atomic
    Energy Agency) 47, 120,
    162, 202
identification, terrorist group 128
ideology 127–8, 134
    of US policy 17
illegal combatants 147–51
    justification for 152–3
    renditions 148
    trials of 148
image of America 38–9, 60, 89–90
    damage by Iraq war 175
    and prisoner abuse 150–1
    unfavourable 88
image of Israel 108
immigration and border controls
    156
imperial overstretch 33, 58–9, 198
imperialism 58–9
India 48, 98, 99
    defence budget 54
    independence 90
    and Pakistan; interference
        issues 21; US policies on
        dispute 98
    resistance to Westernization 77
Indonesia 88, 130
insecurity 197
    and military strength 15
    *see also* homeland security;
        security
insurgencies
    Afghanistan 177
    British success 185
    destroying US empire 22
    ending 185–8
    in Iraq 86–7, 173, 178, 181,
        189, 190; reasons for 87;
        US strategic error 192
    and political subversion 187
    as preventing US domination
        86
    success of 87
intelligence
    failures 119–20, 157, 189
    misinformation 158

new director of 157–8
for preventive war 110
reorganization 154
and response to terrorism 117
intelligence agencies 157–9
    during cold war 158
    lacking accountability 159
    limitations of 158–9, 164
Intelligence Capabilities of the
    United States, Commission
    on 157
interests, US
    oil 39–40
    and preventive war 13
internal colonies 133
International Criminal Court 7,
    57, 140
international institutions 7, 202
    US encouragement for 53
    US weakening of 200–1
international law 34
    and intervention 8–9
international relations
    concepts 6–9; cold war 4
    dominant issues 16
    new world order 4–5, 9
    realities 9–10
internet surveillance 145
interrogation policy 151
intervention
    financial burdens of 28
    future limits to 85
    international 13–14
    and military power 27
    and sovereignty 8–9, 12;
        limited 12–13
    terrorism as consequence 26,
        132, 133
    UN grounds for 12
    UN selective sanctioning 13–14
IRA 60, 189
    Brighton bombings 116, 127
    US funding of 115
Iran 95, 103, 202
    attack by Iraq 172
    and axis of evil 37, 47, 169
    consequences of use of WMD
        118–19
    Embassy hostages 71, 113

Iran – *continued*
  HEU   162–3
  nuclear weapons   71, 103, 104
  post-9/11   45
Iraq   11
  attack on Iran   172
  and axis of evil   37, 47
  context and war   171–3
  CW facilities   112
  future scenarios   191
  history   171
  invasion of Kuwait   172
  lack of WMD   157
  linked with 9/11   111, 119,
    126, 173
  post-war   178–81;
    constitutional developments
    181–4; violence   179, 190
  similarities with Vietnam   189
Iraq war (1990–1)   20, 172
  economic costs of   34, 97,
    196
Iraq war (2003)
  casualties   175, 180
  economic cost of   59
  increased terrorism   125, 126,
    136, 196, 197
  irresponsibility of   200
  as 'just war'   126, 173–4
  justifications for   135, 173–6
  legitimacy concerns   95, 176
  and neoconservatives   17
  pressure post-9/11   46, 47
  as preventive strategy   110–11,
    112–13
  as quagmire   87, 188
  resulting Muslim radicalization
    132, 133, 134
  underestimated nationalism
    85, 86, 192
Islamic Conference, Organization
    of   72
Islamic Front for Holy War,
    International   109
Islamist movement: challenge
    of   65
  *see also* Muslim
Islamophobia   78
isolationism   139–40

Israel   3, 90, 185
  attack on Al Tawita reactor   107
  attacks on Egypt   106–7
  HEU   162–3
  image as aggressors   108
  Munich Olympics   115
  Palestine conflict   33, 184,
    196–7
  pre-emptive and preventive
    strategy   106–8; criticisms
    of   113
Italy: experience of terrorism   60

Japan   77, 86, 98, 99, 198–9
  troops in Iraq   95
jihad   19
  declared by bin Laden   171
  justification for   129
Johnson, Chalmers   26
Johnson, Lyndon   46, 60, 85
Johnson, Samuel   143
just war theory   126, 173–4
Justice, Department of   153–4

Kagan, Donald   29
Kagan, Robert   29, 30–1, 32–4,
    35, 37, 51
Kaplan, Robert D.   24
Karpinski, Jane   152
Karzai, Hamid   171, 177
Kashmir   116
Kennan, George   77, 80, 85, 92
Kennedy, John   60, 85, 93
Kennedy, Paul   58–9, 99, 198
Kenya   124
Khalilzad, Zalmay   190
Khan, A.Q.   103
Khartoum CW factory   109, 112
Khomeini, Ayatollah   76, 172
Khrushchev, Nikita   93, 102, 103
Kim dae Jung   93
Kim Il Sung   50
Kim Jong Il   95, 102, 103
Kipling, Rudyard   197, 202–3
Kissinger, Henry   66, 67, 70, 92
Korea, North and South   95, 96,
    99, 102, 103
  post-Japanese occupation   87
Kosovo   11, 32, 55, 88, 97

Krasner, Stephen  7
Krauthammer, Charles  29, 35
Kristol, Irving  29
Kristol, William  29, 30, 35, 37
Kurdistan  179
Kurds in Iraq  172, 181, 182,
    183, 184, 190
Kuwait  130
  invasion by Iraq  172
Kyoto Protocol  57, 140, 199

Lagos, President Ricardo  56
Lansdale, Edward  98
Latin America  53, 199
  disapproval of US policy  47–8
Lea, Homer  91
League of Nations  7, 53, 199
  and Iraq  171
  and preventive war  105–6
  US support for  57
Lebanon  19, 185, 187
Lebed, Alexander  160
Leclerc, General  6
legitimacy of invasion  35, 95,
    176
Levin, Carl  118
Lewis, Bernard  71
Li Peng, Prime Minister  70
Liberia  13
library records  145
Libya  119
  nuclear weapons  103
  US air strikes against  108–9
Lippmann, Walter  77
London bombings  19, 65, 126,
    176
  British-born terrorists  78, 116
  previous threat level  132
Los Alamos National Laboratory
    breach  161
losing the peace  168
Luck, Edward  11

Machiavelli, 192
Madrid attacks  19, 65, 132, 176
  and election result  31
  and Iraq involvement  96, 126
*Maine*  112
Malaysia  90

Mandelbaum, Michael  24–5
Manhattan Project  5
Mann, Michael  25
Mao Zedong  66, 67, 68, 102, 103
  Maoists, French  131
Marshall, George/Plan  180–1
martyrdom  131, 135
McCarthy era  143
McNamara, Robert  168
Mearsheimer, John J.  17
media
  dominance of Western  75
  downplaying casualties  180
  and humanitarian crises  12
  lack of criticism in US  97, 180
  in post-war Iraq  179–80
messianism  129–30, 131
Middle East  196–7
  road map  33, 184
military bases, global span of US
    22, 25
military commissions  148–9
military expenditure  *see* defence
    spending
military force protection and
    insurgents  186
military forces, US
  fire discipline  113–15
  mistakes by  113–14
  overstretched  27–8
military intervention
  as cause of terrorism  123, 136
  European view of  114–15
  fears of increasing US  95
  increasing terrorism  165
  as norm  55, 107–8
  policy of Europe and US  32–3
  and political processes  98
  within other territories
    115–16, 117
  *see also* intervention
military power
  and democracy  89–93
  Europe and US difference
    51–2
  growth of US  53–5, 200
  increasing hostility  89
  and insecurity  15
  overrated  89

military power – *continued*
  response to demonstrations of 87–8
  temptation of 18, 55, 56, 84, 196
  US as problem 54
  used defensively 88
  uses and abuses of 85–9
military tribunals 144
  unnecessary 141
Milosevic, Slobodan 50
Mogadishu 113
Mohamed, Mahathir 73, 76
Monroe Doctrine 140, 199
moralism 29
morality
  and force 28
  and foreign policy 35
Morocco 130
Mossad 116
Mubarak, President 47
mujahidin 170, 171
multilateral institutions 202
  distrust of 37
multilateralism, need for 15
Munich Olympics 115
Munro, Alan 51
Musharraf, General Pervez 72, 177
Muslim diaspora 131, 132
Muslim world
  alienation of 4; by modernity 71–2, 74
  anger at Iraq war 176, 178
  challenge from 71–80
  conspiracy theories 75
  growing gap between the West 76
  hostility to US 3, 88
  identity across borders 88
  minority militants 71
  modernity and conservatism 74, 75
  responsibility for terrorism 72–3
  US relations with 70–1

NAFTA 7
Naipaul, V.S. 75, 76

Nasser, President 107
nation-building 11
National Counterterrorism Centre 154
*National Security Strategy* 31, 134, 135
*National Strategy for Combating Terrorism* 134–5
*National Strategy to Combat WMD* 104, 134
*National Strategy for Victory in Iraq* 191
nationalism
  Iraqi 85, 86, 192
  US 28
NATO 7, 60, 61, 199
  on 9/11 attacks 44
  Clinton's support for 57
  defence budgets 54
  post 9/11 45, 46
  Rumsfeld on 9/11 and Iraq 111
NBC weapons 104, 111, 173, 201
  defence against terrorist use 154
  *see also* nuclear weapons
Negroponte, John D. 157
neoconservatives 22, 28–36, 173
  categories 28
  and destruction of empire 27
  empowered by 9/11 37
  focus and leadership 30
  ideals of 29–30
  impact on policy 30
  and military action 17, 199
  mistaken beliefs 35
  providing leadership 17
  state power and global politics 29
new security order 4–5
new world order 16
  avoiding conflicts 20
New Zealand: opposition to war 56
Nixon, Richard 60, 66, 67–8, 85
  on balance of power 198
non-citizens: detention of 147

North Korea   95, 96, 119
  and axis of evil   37, 47, 169
  consequences of use of WMD
    118–19
  interference issues   21
  and nuclear weapons   103, 104
Northern Alliance   45, 171, 177
Northern Ireland   189
NSA (National Security Agency)
  145, 146
nuclear facilities   33
  insecurity of US   161–2
  justification for destroying
    102
Nuclear Non-Proliferation Treaty
  104, 200
nuclear programmes
  and compromise   33
  Iraq   47
nuclear terrorism   107–8,
  159–63, 164, 201, 202
  steps to curtail   162–3
nuclear waste   162, 163
nuclear weapons
  as cold war deterrent   5, 106
  ease of producing   159
  ex-Soviet material   160, 161
  missing material   160
  potential impact in Manhattan
    162
  proliferation dangers   102–4;
    preventing   162
  radiological weapons   160,
    161, 201
  removing HEU and plutonium
    162–3
  sales of   161
  *see also* weapons of mass
    destruction
Nunn–Lugar Soviet Nuclear
  Threat Reduction Act (1991)
  160, 162, 163

occupation of Iraq   87, 176, 177
  consuming moral capital   201
  lack of preparation   192
  Marshall Plan ideas   180
  Muslim anger   178
  popular support in US   185

US staying power   185
  violence   179, 190
oil   201
  importance of   39–40
  West as plundering   76
  Western dependence on Arab
    76
oil for food programme   47
Oklahoma City   127
Omar, Mullah   125, 176
Operation Enduring Freedom
  168
Operation Iraqi Freedom   168
overreach   24, 33, 58–9

Padilla, Jose   149
Pakistan   48, 98, 99, 130, 177
  HEU   163
  and India   21
  public opinion of US   88
  selling nuclear equipment
    103
  support for Afghanistan action
    94
Palestine   33
  Hamas   184
Pan Am Flight   103 127
Papas, Thomas M.   152
Patriot Act   144–7, 159
  and Fourth and Fifth
    Amendments   144
  surveillance of citizens   145–6
  and terrorist funding   155
patriotism and civil liberties   143
peacekeeping   12, 89
  European experience   2
  interference issues   21
  and sovereignty   8
  use of military power   88
peoples' wars   5–6
Perle, Richard   29, 35, 36
Philippines   52
Podhoretz, Norman   29, 30
Police Service, Iraqi   190
political dissent and Patriot Act
  145
popular control and government
  decisions   91–2
Powell, Colin   37, 49, 111, 176

power
    burden of   196–203
    temptations of   199–200
pre-emptive strategy   104, 105
    legitimacy of   104
    US move towards   108–10
    *see also* preventive war
precision attacks   115–17
precision guided munitions
    (PGMs)   53
presidents of America   92–3
    *see also individual presidents*
preventive war   1, 197, 200
    advantages   119
    as counter-productive
        99–100
    dangers of   105
    disadvantages   119–20
    European views on   113
    Germany 1860s   55
    and inaccurate intelligence
        110
    and increased terrorism   119
    Iraq (2003)   112–13
    justification for   13, 102, 135,
        140, 174
    legitimacy of   104–5, 108
    precedents for   105–8
    pressure for   109–10
    temptation of   102–20
    US decision to launch   37,
        110–13
    and US interests   13
    US move towards   108–10
    *see also* pre-emptive strategy
prisons   148, 150
    abuse   150, 151–2, 153; and
        increased terrorism   151
    legitimacy of   149
Project North Star   142
'Project for the New American
    Century'   111
*Pueblo*   54
Putin, Vladimir   44

quagmires   87, 188–92

radical Islam   131–2
    *see also* al-Qaeda; Muslim

radiological weapons   160,
    161, 201
Ramsay of Cartvale, Baroness   50
Rashid, Ahmad   170
Reagan, Ronald   35, 60, 68, 93,
    108
realism   28, 29, 39
reconstruction of Iraq   180–1, 189
Red Brigades   131
Red Cross   151
regional organizations   7
religion
    bin Laden   128
    Bush and   2–3, 38
    group identification   88
    leading to wars and terrorism
        18–19
    and US values   21–2
religious terrorists   128, 129–30,
    131
renditions   148, 200
reprisal, terrorism as   127, 128
Resolution 1441   48, 172
resources for terrorism   127, 128
restraint
    factors compelling   97–9
    importance of   96–9
    need for Western   77–8, 80, 203
    US economy as   99
revolution in military affairs   38
Rice, Condoleezza   49, 60
Rickover, Hyman   112
Ridge, Tom   154
Robb, Charles S.   157
Robertson, Pat   38
Robespierre, M.   126
rogue states   120, 135, 200
    acquisition of WMD   102;
        inability to control   103;
        spreading to terrorists   102,
        103; use of   103
    irrational leaders   102–3, 120
Roh Moo-Hyun, President   96
Roosevelt, Franklin   60, 61,
    199
Rumsfeld, Donald   38, 46, 47,
    58, 111
    on 'old Europe'   49
Rushdie, Salman   65, 76

Russia
on 9/11 attacks   44–5
defence budget   54
intervention by   13
opposition to war   49
and US dominance   58
Rwanda   13

Samarra, Golden Mosque   192
Santo Domingo   92
Saudi Arabia   130
disapproval of US policy   47
post 9/11   45
Schlesinger, James R.   152
Schlesinger Jr, Arthur   25
Schroeder, Chancellor   48
Schultz, George   68
secession, allowing   68–9
Second World War   86
European experience of   114
pre-emptive strikes   105–6
security
changing nature of   15
collective   7
debate   10–12
definitions   11
and freedom   142, 143, 144
or justice   152–4
old and new dilemmas   14–15,
197–8
and open borders   142
*see also* homeland security
Security Council   11, 12, 13, 98
and Iraq war (2003)   32, 111,
136, 173
on occupation of Iraq   188–9
Resolution 1441   48, 172
sanctioning intervention   13–14
security forces, Iraqi   190, 191
Sederberg, Peter C.   128
Sen, Amartya   19
September 11 Commission report
157
September 11 attacks
empowering neoconservatives
37
good and evil world   141
and homeland insecurity   140
ideal response   124

inadequacy of response   1, 136
initial sympathy for   44–5, 51,
59
and Iraqi involvement   111
and neoconservative agenda
28–9
possible responses   125
support for retaliation   45, 94;
UN sanction   13–14
temptation of Iraq   45–9
and US military expansionism
26
US response   2–3, 4, 9, 17,
104, 123–4, 125
warning received   124–5
Serbia   54–5
Shah of Iran   71, 76
Shawcross, William   35
Shiities in Iraq   181, 182, 183,
184, 190
'shock and awe'   6, 98
Sierra Leone   32, 88
Silberman, Lawrence H.   157
Singapore   90
Singh, Uddham   64
sneak and peek searches   145
Snyder, Jack   91
Somalia   13, 185, 187
South Africa, HEU   163
South Korea   99
troops in Iraq   95, 96
sovereignty
conceptions of   6–8
conditional on US approval   118
erosion of   13
and intervention   8–9, 12
limited   12–13
new vocabularies of   8
and reality   7
seen as expendable   5
UN on   14
Soviet Union   199
Afghan war (1979–89)   20, 170
collapse of   54, 56, 84, 85;
effect of   16; reconfiguration
of global politics   18; and US
hegemony   22; and US as
superpower   108; violence
90–1

Soviet Union – *continued*
  nuclear stockpile   160, 161
Spain   130
  1898 US war with   112
  ETA terrorism   60
  Madrid attacks   176;
    individuals involved   132;
    and Iraq involvement   96
  post-Madrid attacks   31
Sri Lanka   19
Stalin, Joseph   46, 93, 102, 103
states, fragility of   15
Stern, Jessica   129
suicide bombing   19, 130
Sunnis in Iraq   178, 181, 182,
    183, 184, 190
Supreme Court ruling on
    detainees   150
Syria   95, 119

Taiwan   58, 65, 69, 99, 202
  1958 crisis   66
  GDP   68
  interference issues   21
  Nixon's concessions   67
  Sino–US negotiations   68,
    69–70
Taliban   45, 177
  British citizens   116
  destruction of   119
  establishment of government
    170–1
  *see also* Afghanistan
Tamil Tiger nationalists   19
Tanzania   124
Tawney, R.H.   74
terrorism   8
  attacks in 1990s   124
  causes of   127–8, 132, 133, 136;
    detentions   153; military
    intervention   123, 125, 126,
    185–6; treatment of prisoners
    151
  containment policy   136
  countering   2, 134–5, 185,
    198; ideal strategies   4,
    136–7, 188; successes   135;
    US strategies   134–5
  and culture   19

definitions   126–7, 134–5
'home-grown'   116, 132
impossibility of eradicating
    118
increase in   9–10, 176, 198
Islamic   78–9, 80, 124; as
    resistance to Westernization
    77
Libyan supported   108–9
likelihood of   77–8, 79
living with risks   165
misunderstanding   123–37
new and old   127–30, 197–8
nuclear   107–8, 159–63, 164,
    201, 202
as reprisal   127, 128
response to; effective   117,
    123; in Third World states
    116–17; US   134–5
right way to counter   165
risks of inaction   117
violence-prone groups   127–8,
    129–30
Western mistakes   6
and Western power   5
*see also* counter-insurgency
terrorist organizations
  fanaticism   130
  impromptu groups   132
  power structure   130
  rise of   4–5
  *see also* al-Qaeda
Terrorist Screening Centre   154
terrorists
  assets of   155
  construction of reality   129
  grievances   132, 133–4
  home-grown   156
  recruitment of   133
  religious   4, 128, 129–30, 131
  UK as source of   116
Thatcher, Margaret   93
  Brighton bombing   116
Thompson, Robert   98, 186–8
threats from Muslim world   15
Tiananmen Square   70
Tibet   69
Todd, Emmanuel   26–7
Tokyo subway attack   127

torture 147, 148, 200
  at Guantanamo Bay 150
  limited definition of 152
  of prisoners 141, 151,
    187
trade: China–US disagreements
  65
transportation system security
  154–5
Treaty of Saadabad (1937) 171
tribunals, types of 150
Truman, Harry 60, 61, 93
Tunisia 130
Turkey 56, 130

Ukraine 95–6
unilateralism of US 29, 56–7,
    93, 94, 115
  alienating potential support
    89–90
  bandwagon effect 93–4, 95
  foreign concerns with 96
United Kingdom 130
  19th-century imperialism 58
  Boer War 197, 201, 202–3
  IRA terrorism 60
  and Iraq invasion 173
  legal debate 50–1
  Muslim population 133
  public opposition to war
    50–1
  Security Council 48, 49
  as source of terrorists 116
  support for US 49–51
United Nations 7, 37, 53, 105,
    199
  on 9/11 attacks 44
  anti-terrorism guidelines 157
  Bush and 38
  and cold war 11–12
  definition of terrorism 126
  on Guantanamo Bay 150
  guidelines for acceptable war
    175, 176
  and sovereignty 6
  Soviet–Afghan war 170
  US disparagement of 56
  on use of force 11
  *see also* Security Council

United States
  balance of payments deficit
    59, 64
  budget deficit 34, 59, 64, 99
  character reflected in Army 98
  dependence on foreign
    investment 64, 99, 200
  economy 99; weakness 26–7
  good and evil 141
  image of 38–9, 60, 88, 89–90,
    150–1, 175
  and Native Americans 23, 24
  protection of values 21–2
  *see also* Congress; foreign policy
universities, Muslim 72–3
*USS Cole* 115, 116, 124
*USS Vincennes* 113

values, American 34
Vietnam Syndrome 32, 196
Vietnam War 52, 85, 87, 94,
    185, 187, 203
  fire discipline 113
  hearts and minds 168, 189
  lack of support for US 94
  mistakes 92, 189
  US as liberators 85–6
  US strength 54
violence-prone groups 127–8,
    129–30
von Balestrem, Count 54
von Clausewitz, Karl 113

Walker, Harold 50
Walt, Stephen M. 17
Walzer, Michael 173
War Crimes Tribunal Courts 7
war crimes tribunals 53
  Guantanamo suspects 149
'war on terror' 118, 143
  Bush's goals 125
  confused political aims 186
  and disarming Iraq 173
  error of 135, 136, 168
  futility of 165
  hindered by Iraq war 184–5
  misunderstanding terrorism
    200
  objectives for success 125

warfare
  economic costs of   97
  high-tech   53, 180
weapons inspections in Iraq
      48–9, 172, 174, 175
  March 2003 curtailment
      112–13
  need for more time   174
weapons of mass destruction
  45-minutes dossier   112
  as equalizing power   118
  lack of control of   103
  lack of Iraqi   32, 51, 111, 119,
      126, 173
  passing on to terrorists   102
  and rogue states   102
  *see also* nuclear weapons
weapons of terrorism   9
Western world
  Muslim criticism of   75–6, 131
  need for restraint   77–8, 80
  threats faced by   134
  values   20, 34

Wilhelm II, Kaiser   55
Wilson, Woodrow   57
wiretaps   144, 145–6
withdrawal from Iraq   191–2
WMD   *see* weapons of mass
      destruction
Wolf, Franklin   109
Wolfowitz, Paul   29, 37, 38, 46,
      47, 173
women, Muslim   73, 171
  in post-war Iraq   179, 183
Woodward, Bob   57, 93, 94, 95
Wright, Patrick   50

Yeltsin, Boris   160
Yemen   115, 130
Yousef, Ramzi   124
Yugoslavia   91